UTAH

UTAH
SECOND EDITION

MAUREEN KEILTY
Photography by Dan Peha

THE
MOUNTAINEERS
BOOKS

 Published by
The Mountaineers Books
1001 SW Klickitat Way, Suite 201
Seattle, WA 98134

First edition, 1993. Second edition: first printing 2000, second printing 2004.

Published simultaneously in Great Britain by Cordee, 3a DeMontfort Street, Leicester, England, LE1 7HD

Manufactured in the United States of America

Project Editor: Dottie Martin
Editor: Doris Cadd
Series Design: The Mountaineers Books
Layout: Gray Mouse Graphics
Mapmaker: Ben Pease
Photographs: © Dan Peha, Sun Dagger, Inc.

Cover photograph: *Wilson Arch near Moab draws hikers of all sizes and stamina.*
© Dan Peha, Sun Dagger, Inc.
Frontispiece: *Rock-climbing hikers check out the views at Cleveland–Lloyd Dinosaur Quarry.*
© Dan Peha, Sun Dagger, Inc.

Library of Congress Cataloging-in-Publication Data

Keilty, Maureen, 1952-
  Best hikes with children in Utah / Maureen Keilty.— 2nd ed.
     p. cm.
Includes index.
  ISBN 0-89886-709-6
  1. Hiking—Utah—Guidebooks. 2. Family recreation—Utah—Guidebooks.
3. Utah—Guidebooks. I. Title.
  GV199.42.U8 K43 2000
  917.9204'34—dc21
                                                              00-009644
                                                                  CIP

For all those dedicated
to preserving Utah's wild places,
and for Niko,
whose small footprints lead us there

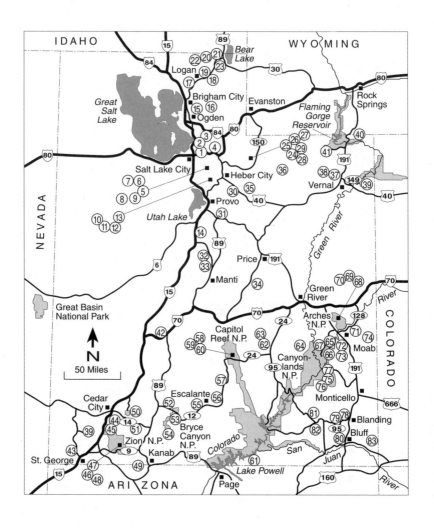

CONTENTS

Legend

—(80)—	Interstate Highway	🖎	Rock Art
—(191)—	US Highway	◤.	Ruins
—(12)—	State Highway	■	Building/Point of Interest
—[279]—	County/Forest Service Road	▲	Mountain Peak
━━━━••••	Paved Road and Tunnel	) (	Pass
═══ = = =:	Unpaved and Jeep Roads	(P)(S)	Parking/Start Trail
- - - -------	Subject Trail/Other Trail	(A)	Suggested Turnaround
▲	Campground		River/Creek with waterfall and Rapids
𝍢	Picnic Area		Lake or Pond
◼	Overlook/Photo Opportunity	♀	Spring
♿	Handicapped Accessible		Marsh
— - — - —	Boundary		Cliff

ACKNOWLEDGMENTS

Just as "it takes a village to raise a child," it required the help of many to prepare the second edition of *Best Hikes with Children in Utah*™. "Thank yous" go to the many rangers, recreation officers, and office receptionists employed by Utah's five national parks, its state parks, and the U.S. Forest Service. Their input kept me on track in providing accurate, safe, and well-interpreted trails for children. The staff at Red Butte Garden, Ogden Nature Center, the Scott M. Matheson Wetland Preserve, the Cleveland-Lloyd Dinosaur Quarry, and many other "child-friendly" sites also provided essential feedback on trail descriptions. Special thanks to the Tierneys, Catherine, Lennox, and Stephen, for their caring hospitality and tips on Salt Lake City's trails and tales. Mark Grosser and daughter Sahra added both companionship and trail feedback to our research trip in Central Utah. Hugs go to my son Niko who began "child testing" trails with me even before he was born! And for my husband Dan, my partner since the day we met in a Utah canyon, thank you for all the steps behind us and those yet to come. Your support, endurance, and eye for accuracy keep us on the most fascinating trails.

Opposite: *Ancient handprints mirror the prehistoric cultures of Utah's canyon country.*

INTRODUCTION

Youth, with swift feet, walks onward in the way;
as the land of joy lies before his eyes.

—Bulwer

Utah is a hiking paradise for families. Trails thread from the red-rock canyons of the south to the mountain slopes of the north, offering myriad choices suited for all family members. Every trail selected for this book has the capacity to enthrall your toddler, enthuse your teenager, and allow grandparents to join in the family fun. However, keeping the hikes fun for everyone requires some preparation.

ON YOUR MARK...

Choose a child-friendly trail. (All the hikes in this book qualify.) The trail should be a short distance from, or en route to, another destination. Walks in city parks can be naturally fun for youngsters who stop to examine life under a rock or listen for birds that sing to each other. A planned "hike break" on a long drive from, say, Salt Lake City to Bear Lake can make the trip bearable for the whole family.

Consider the trail's name or destination as a possible influence on your child's enthusiasm for the trek. Parents of a 5-year-old we met on a trail told us they'd planned their family's 6-mile hike to Lake Alice (located in Wyoming) to be a 2-day event. Instead, their daughter, so eager to see the lake named for her friend and a storybook character, said she was "determined to make it in 1 day," and she did! Names like "Emerald Pools," "Little Wild Horse Canyon," "Wind Cave," even "Mount Baldy" appeal to youngsters and motivate them to complete the trek.

Listen to what other parents say about their children's hiking experience. Their tips can serve as guidelines for your trail selection.

Evaluate the hike's safety for your youngsters. A well-marked path that covers level terrain and has fenced overlooks is ideal for small children. On the other hand, experienced and prepared young hikers like the challenge of following cairns or tree blazes to reach an awesome

Opposite: *A toddler begins his first hike to an aspen meadow.*

vista or a distant archaeological site. Both types of trails are safely hiked when the proper types of food, water, and clothing are carried (see the "What to Take" section).

Select a length of the trail that allows your youngest to proudly announce, "I hiked the whole way," and your oldest to admit, "Yeah, it was fun." Most of the trails in this book show turnaround points for ready-to-head-back hikers.

Talk enthusiastically to your crew about the hike. Use words like "explore," "walk," or "along the way we'll see . . . " Avoid saying "steep," "easy," or "difficult." Describe the destination and, just as importantly, the creek they'll dip their feet in, the ancient rock art they'll see, or the animal tracks they'll spot along the way. Let kids know you're confident and excited about exploring nature; they'll be eager to join you.

GET SET . . .

For children, packing for the trip can be as much fun as the hike itself. At the grocery store have youngsters select their trail treats. They'll enjoy picking out the nuts and dried fruit for their own "gorp," then bagging it at home. Assign someone to be the group's water-bottle filler or the day pack packer; let trip preparation become an event they eagerly anticipate.

Involve hikers in gathering their hiking gear. A map and a guidebook, a first-aid kit, a compass, and a whistle are among the necessary items they can put in the day pack. If old or new hiking boots are to be worn, go for a prehike walk with children to make sure the shoes fit properly.

Plan to arrive at the trailhead early in the day. An afternoon thundershower may do little more than muddy a trail, but it can also dampen a youngster's interest in hiking for a long time. Allow enough time to play a balancing game while crossing a creek or to watch a beaver reappear from its den. Stop to savor the serene symmetry of an aspen grove or the busy world of an anthill.

Before setting foot on the trail, have children use the nearest toilet facility. (Information on the availability of toilet and drinking water facilities is included at the end of each trail description in this book.) Make sure everyone has his or her own water bottle and/or day pack. Remind kids about staying on the trail and with the group.

Have your kids wear bright clothing. It's much easier to keep track of an orange baseball cap or a red jacket bopping ahead of you than it is to watch for a brunette in blue jeans in the forest's shadow. And brimmed hats are a hedge against sunburn and eyestrain.

Assign a hike leader. Somehow this revered status gives kids an energy boost and encourages them to pay closer attention to the map and watch for landmarks. Switching the title to a child whose energy is waning keeps the group moving at a steady pace. It's a good idea to let your young leaders know in advance where this "change of command" is to take place.

Invite your child's friend to join the hike. Complaints, aches, and pains are lessened considerably when a close companion comes along. Neither will want to appear slow in front of the other, and the two will concoct unheard-of games.

For trips to national or state parks, or to popular campgrounds, call the park or national forest office to inquire about children's programs offered. Young visitors to national parks in Utah are invited to become Junior Rangers via specially scheduled programs throughout the summer months. State parks and popular campgrounds also host an interpreter who presents fun campfire talks the whole family will enjoy.

START HIKING!

Once the hike begins there are many ways to keep little ones' interest and energy vibrant. Explore the sights, sounds, and textures along the way. Stir up inquisitiveness by announcing, "Touch a rock as tall as your knee," or "Feel something fuzzy," or "Smell the next flower." Take time to marvel at the "sparkly" rock your daughter just found, or to watch a spider negotiate the strands of its web. Remember, your child's awe at an anthill is just as valid as your inspiration at a mountaintop.

Allow spontaneity to redirect your trip or simply season it with a variety of interests. While researching the trails of southern Utah, we arrived too late to hike an intended canyon by nightfall. Instead of waiting for morning light, we ate a small dinner, took a short nap on a slickrock bed, then walked the trail under the light of the full moon. For months our toddler asked for "moon walks," and now we plan many of our hiking trips to happen during the full moon.

Your child's natural curiosity can lead to a world of tiny white insects under a rock, or a bird's nest strung with tinsel from a discarded Christmas tree. Let children's imaginations find the forest to be filled with rock gnomes and flower fairies. No doubt your child will discover something you simply know nothing about. When your son discovers a snail, enhance his interest by asking, "Can you find a snail's mouth? How does it see? Can you find its foot? Do you think it can hear us talk?" For lingering questions that must be answered, have your child talk to the park's interpreter or the forest's ranger, both of whom are trained to clearly explain the area's natural and cultural history.

Praise, Patience, and Playfulness

Frequent fuel stops, announced with "We'll have a drink of water and some gorp when we reach the top of this hill," help keep the hike moving. But keep the rest stops brief, no more than 90 seconds long. Breaks in hiking that last longer than 5 minutes can defeat the purpose of stopping. Not only do they increase the hiking time considerably, they also cause children and adults to lose their motivation. The drive to get going again diminishes as the cardiovascular system slows down. You have to start all over to attain the efficiency your climbing muscles had before stopping. A group that stands during rest stops will want to keep moving.

As most parents know, children thrive on praise and patience. Be liberal with both on a hike. Compliments given early in the trip are more effective than those used later to encourage tired hikers. Your interest in your children's discoveries will fuel their drive. Let your crew know how proud you are of their hiking strength and that they have picked up trash along the trail. Praise given in the presence of other children and adults has a lasting influence.

When kids lose interest during a hike, turn the trip into a fun stroll. Try skipping or walking backward. Walk in bare feet. (Be sure the trail surface is free of sharp objects.) Sing a song the kids know and can join in on. Encourage the hike leader to make up his or her own way of walking that others could copy.

A toddler riding in a backpack is easily entertained (as was ours for the 300-plus miles he hiked with us) by a pine cone you ask him to hold, or a pretty rock he finds at a rest stop. Our Niko had great fun teasing Mommy or Daddy with his "tickle wand," a long grass stem with a tassel top. We chanted many a Mother

Mormon crickets

Willow or cottonwood "down" adds fun to any hike.

Goose rhyme, and he became quite a poet during our research trips.

The following techniques, adaptable to many hikers of many ages, are sure to eliminate trek tedium:

Magical Mystery Tour. Let the hike's destination be a mystery your sleuths unravel as they walk the trail.

Color Match. While walking, children look for colors in nature that match the colors of the clothing they are wearing.

Silent Fox Walk. Instruct children to place each step with their weight coming down on the outside of the foot and rolling to the inside. With practice they'll move with fluidity and silence.

Fantasy Fun. Mark Twain once said, "You can't depend on your eyes when your imagination is out of focus." During a long hike, you can lift tired spirits by skipping along the trail, pretending it's the "yellow brick road." Salute the rocks guarding the entrance to the canyon. Compliment the creek for its song. Shake hands with the trees; sing to the sagebrush. Keep your imagination in focus—it can be contagious.

Open House. Make a game of naming and counting the homes of insects and other animals. Have children watch for bird nests, spider webs, entrances to ground squirrels' homes in the forest duff, insect galls (swellings holding insect larvae found on plant stems), rotting logs, and other examples of wildlife homesites.

Feeding Free. Living creatures find their food in their habitat. A squirrel scampering through the woods with a pine cone in its mouth, a woodpecker drilling a tree trunk in search of insects, and a moose browsing in a willow thicket are all examples of one species feeding on another. Show children such pairings of an animal with its food, and ask them to point out others as they walk.

Little, Round, Red House. Share this story while waiting for a storm to subside or taking an extended break. You'll need a pocketknife and an extra apple, which you will keep hidden until the story's end. As you tell the story, describe environments similar to the ones you've just hiked. "One day a little boy (or girl; personalize your story to best captivate your audience) had nothing to do, so he asked his mother for a game to play. She told him to go outside and look for a 'little, round, red house without windows or doors, but with a star inside'." Be descriptive about the places in the forest or canyon the boy visited in his search. Have him ask the trees, rocks, and animals you may have passed during your hike where he might find the little, round, red house without windows or doors, but with a star inside. The answer he gets to each question is go and ask the "ground squirrel living under the giant fir tree," or "the quiet brook crossing the forest," or "the canyon wren singing from a cliff top." The boy in your story may ask as many "Where is . . . " questions as will hold your audience's interest. "When the boy returned home, he stopped in an orchard and asked the wind to help him find the little red house. Just then, the wind shook an apple from the tree. The boy picked it up and realized the apple was little, red, round, and it had no windows or doors." (Present your apple.) To find the star inside, he cut the apple in half (be sure to cut it horizontally), and sure enough— there was a star (formed by the seed/core arrangement)! Children enjoy eating segments of the little red house as much as they like listening to the story.

Above all, show respect for the natural world you have entered. Let youngsters know you care that the group walks only on the trail to avoid injuring plant life—even a dandelion.

ENVIRONMENTAL ETIQUETTE

Hiking in Utah's canyons and mountains brings a great sense of freedom, but with that comes the responsibility to leave the land in its pristine state. The following reminders are in no way all-inclusive.

Stay on the Trail
Walking alongside the trail tramples vegetation. Do not allow youngsters to cut across switchbacks to go downhill faster; water will follow their path and erode the trail.

The stay-on-the-trail habit is especially necessary in desert areas. Here cryptobiotic crust, previously called cryptogamic soil, blankets sandy surfaces with its dark, lumpy form. Consisting of microorganisms, lichens, mosses, algae, and fungi, the layer forms a web that holds the sand and soil particles in place. Stepping on cryptobiotic crust destroys a vital link for life in the desert.

Pack It Out
Trash of any kind must be packed out. After a fuel stop, check for discarded nut shells, orange peels, or cellophane wrappings. A potato chip, though it may decompose, disrupts the necessary gathering instinct of whatever animal may find it. The salts, sugars, and oils of most human snack food can kill wildlife. **In state and national parks it is against the law to feed wild animals.**

How and Where To "Go"
While on the trail, teach your children to urinate at least 200 feet from a water source or campground. Show them the safe length by measuring the distance in steps—about 100 kid strides. It is no longer acceptable to bury toilet paper because animals will dig it up. Carry it out in a plastic bag. Human waste should be deposited at least 200 feet from a stream or lake, in a hole 6 inches deep, capped by sod or soil taken from the same spot.

Don't Pick the Flowers
Little hands are prone to picking wildflowers. To prevent this innocent destruction of trailside beauty, I explain to young hikers that flowers are like you and me; they cannot live without their bottom half, the stem. I tell them it makes me sad to see flowers taken from their home. (It's also illegal in many areas.) When your child finds other equally alluring items such as "sparkly" rocks or deer antlers, say, "I wonder if the next hiker will have eyes as sharp as yours and see this pretty . . . . "

Tread Carefully in Ancient Homes
Innocent destruction also occurs when little or big hands touch rock art. Natural oils of the human skin deteriorate the rock, causing

Newspaper Rock, Canyonlands

images that have withstood 1000 years or more to begin breaking down. Equally fragile are the walls surrounding an ancient site. Remind your companions that you are visiting another person's home or treasured work of art, and to treat it as if he or she were watching your visit.

Walk and Speak Softly

The trails take you into the homes of deer and moose, marmots and pikas, lizards and jackrabbits, hawks and hummingbirds, even mountain lions and rattlesnakes. Noise destroys the tranquillity needed to spot wild animals. Speaking in a quiet tone will remind children they are visiting a place where peace prevails. Perhaps the sighting of a ferret or owl will reward their hushed behavior.

Selecting a Rest Stop or Campsite

It's best to remain on the trail during a treat stop to avoid impacting the surrounding terrain. Choose a wide area where foot traffic can pass unimpeded. In popular areas, especially in state and national parks, plan rests at turnaround points or viewpoints.

Campsites should be selected far from the trail at an established site or on a nonvegetated patch (avoid cryptobiotic crust!). Use a gas stove for cooking. If your campers want a campfire and fires are allowed, keep it small and in a pit, preferably in an established camp-fire site. Drown it with water. (A good way to make sure the fire is completely out: Have an adult run his or her fingers through the soaked ashes.) Scatter the ashes and leftover wood. Dishwashing should take place away from the water source. The best pot scrubber I know of is a smidgen of wet sand or gravel applied with a bit of elbow grease. Avoid using soap, regardless of whether it's biodegrad-able. Leftover food should be packed out.

Careless campers leave a "hurtful sight," as one young hiker told me. Your group will feel better if they contribute to cleaning up the natural environment. I've seen many children at the end of a hike proudly empty their pockets of candy wrappers and orange peels found along the trail. Report any serious violation at the nearest for-est ranger office.

HIKING SAFETY

Just as walking to school entails a certain amount of risk, so does hiking any of the trails described in this book. Safety is not a matter of how easy or challenging the trail is. It's a product of common sense, coupled with preparation and a positive attitude.

Every effort has been made to describe these trails as accurately as possible. Weather and trail use, however, can alter the trail condi-tions from day to day. Trail maintenance, or lack thereof, can also influence the trip considerably. Your physical condition has as much bearing on the hike as the weather or the route does. If a youngster is showing signs that the hike is doing more harm than good, be pre-pared to turn around. Before leaving, give the child the sense that a destination has been reached so that the trip feels like a success.

Drinking Water

No matter how pure the pothole pool or mountain stream ap-pears, the water in it should be considered unsafe for drinking until properly treated. And please, never put your hands or feet in a filled pothole. Life there is short, and human hands add oils that pollute these miniature habitats.

The most common threat to backcountry water is the presence of microscopic *Giardia* cysts, which are transmitted primarily by ani-mals (and some humans). Flulike symptoms of giardiasis, from stom-ach cramps to severe diarrhea, appear in 5 to 14 days and can last as long as 6 weeks if untreated. Taking prescription medication is the only cure for this potentially serious disease.

Day hikers should be able to carry all the water they require: 2 quarts to a gallon a day for strenuous or desert hikes. One quart per person is sufficient for most day hikes less than 4 hours long.

Avoid bringing boxed or bottled drinks, as they not only add to the trash to be carried back, but also exacerbate the body's need for water in order to digest the sugars and fruit flavors in the drinks.

Don't encourage water-bottle sharing. Kids spread their infections by sharing others' bottles, and the habit prevents parents from determining if their hikers are drinking enough. Headaches are the first symptom of dehydration. Another sign is dark yellow urine. Remember, stamina is diminished as much as 25 percent when an adult loses 1.5 quarts of water. Kids may not show their water loss by sweating, and will need reminders to drink, especially during cool hikes. Before starting any hike encourage everyone to drink up!

Hypothermia

Hypothermia, the lowering of internal body temperature, is a serious threat to hikers in cool temperatures. Wind, exhaustion, and wetness aggravate this number-one killer of outdoor recreationists. Most cases of hypothermia develop in air temperatures of 30 to 50 degrees Fahrenheit.

Because of their relatively small body sizes, children show signs of hypothermia sooner than adults exposed to the same conditions. Whiny, uncooperative, or listless kids may be exhibiting the first signs of hypothermia. More advanced symptoms include uncontrollable fits of shivering, slurred speech, frequent stumbling, memory lapses, and apparent exhaustion even after a rest. Many hypothermia victims, children particularly, deny feeling cold, so watch for other signs.

Staying dry is probably the best way to prevent hypothermia. Wet clothing loses about 90 percent of its insulating value. Wool loses less heat than cotton and some synthetic fabrics. Prevent getting wet when the rain starts because it's next to impossible to dry the clothes during a rainstorm. Sufficient fluid intake also helps prevent hypothermia from developing.

Treatment for hypothermia begins with getting the victim out of the rain and wind. Remove all wet clothes and replace them with warm, dry ones. A prewarmed sleeping bag may be needed.

Lost-Proofing Kids

Ardent butterfly chasers are apt to lose their way. All children, be they adventurous or stay-on-the-trail types, should know what to do when they discover they are no longer with the group. Tell them to pick a tree as a companion and stay in one place. Teach them not to go in search of the trail or a hiking partner. Encourage them to use the whistle; three blasts is an international distress call. Make sure they know that waiting is the best thing for them to do because help is on the way.

Kids might accept these reminders if told in a story format. While driving to the trail make up a tale about a child who discovered she was lost in the woods. Colorfully describe where she sat and waited on a seat of pine boughs she collected, how she called out "Momma" a few times, then blew her whistle three times. End your story with the parents showing their happiness when they found her waiting for them.

Prevent lost hikers by assigning trail partners. Remind children they are to stay on the trail at all times. When they meet another trail, they should wait for the rest of the group. Let the hike leader know he or she should stop at various intervals to make certain everyone is keeping up. At camp, show children the boundaries within which they can explore on their own. Walk to the water pump and toilet with children so they know the path.

WHAT TO TAKE

Starting from the feet up, hiking shoes or boots, properly fitted and broken in, are a prerequisite for enjoyable hiking. Sneakers or running shoes work well for the short paved trails in this book, and may be adequate for long treks where the trail is relatively free of rock and tree roots. However, boots are a necessity for full day hikes and backpack trips. For children, wearing hiking boots gives the outing special importance.

Unfortunately, hiking boots for children are expensive, especially considering that they're often outgrown in one season. Other than boots found at yard sales and used clothing stores, the least costly hiking shoes are high-top sneakers. Those made with leather or a similar stiff material provide needed ankle support. Lugged soles help grip slippery rock surfaces and provide traction on muddy terrain.

For those buying boots, timing is the first consideration. Plan to shop well in advance of the hiking trip. Time spent wearing the boots around the house is a necessity for breaking them in. When they try on the boots, children should wear heavy socks. Make sure the boot is snug enough to prevent rubbing, but not so tight it pinches. Boots improperly fitted or not broken in can diminish the joy of reaching a spectacular viewpoint. I still remember, at the top of the first 14,000-foot mountain I climbed, the miserable, teary-eyed face of a young hiker who described her boots as "torture chambers." Children forced to hike under such conditions won't relish doing it again, regardless of your enthusiasm.

Packs

Another hiking requirement for children is a pack. Even beginning hikers like shouldering at least some of the "essentials" (see next section), as well as their "very own" water bottle or sweater. For longer treks, those that involve an overnight camp, larger day packs or backpacks are needed.

Make the packing process a group project, giving each hiker an opportunity to select what he or she carries. Take time to show children how to load the pack evenly and how to attach the sleeping bag or tent securely. Tell children it's important they remember what's in their packs. This prevents the repeated "Where's the gorp?" and "Who's got the map?" questions that whittle away rest stops. Remind children that once the pack is loaded, they are not to sit on it unless, of course, they like eating cracker crumbs and squashed apple for lunch.

Let each child know that he or she is carrying something the entire group needs. Whether it's a bag of quick-energy chocolates, or the map and first-aid kit, if the young hiker believes the items in his or her pack are important, the child will feel like an important member of the group.

For parents carrying their toddler in a backpack, a fanny pack worn with the zipper-bag in the front proves a useful storage spot for little goodies. I rarely left on a hike with our child without carrying a collection of goldfish crackers, a slice of fruit leather, and a little bag of animal-shaped fruit jellies. It was easy to hand those items to him over my shoulder while maintaining the hike's pace.

The Ten Essentials

The Mountaineers, over years of teaching mountaineering, have developed a list of ten items that should be carried on every hike. The Ten Essentials provide the necessities for coping with emergencies caused by foul weather, an injury, or unexpected incidents.

1. **Extra clothing.** Another layer of warm clothing is a hedge against wet or torn pants or sudden weather changes. Include a knit hat in the pack. A rain poncho can also be quite valuable.
2. **Extra food.** An extra high-energy bar per person (preferably hid-

den in your pack) is a reliable cure for hungry, irritable hikers should the trip take longer than expected.

3. **Sunglasses and/or sun hat.** Bright, high-altitude sunshine can tire little eyes. Little ones unaccustomed to sunglasses are best protected by a wide-brimmed hat, but do keep the hike short. I learned this lesson well when my toddler, who had worn a protective sun hat throughout our sunny several-mile hike in Capitol Reef, cried, "Eyes hurty" at the day's end.

4. **Pocketknife.** One of the most useful items, especially if one of its attachments is a tweezer, an irreplaceable tool for hikers in canyon country who invariably have cactus barbs to remove from tender skin.

5. **Firestarter candle or chemical fuel.** During an unforeseen overnight camp, a campfire can be a lifesaver.

6. **Matches in a waterproof container.** A fire is not possible without reliable matches, which are available at sporting goods stores.

7. **Flashlight.** Keep fresh batteries in it and hope it's not needed to guide your crew down a trail at night.

8. **First-aid kit.** Check to make sure it's complete, but hope it's not needed.

9. **Map.** Always carry a map of the overall area you are hiking in.

10. **Compass.** Orient yourself with the compass and the map before setting foot on the trail.

To make the getting-ready process quicker, keep as many of these essentials as possible gathered together in one location. *In addition, be sure to tell someone your hiking plans and when you can be expected back.*

Children require other items or niceties, as follows. Sunscreen is essential for all skin, young or old, tanned or lily white. Even overcast days can result in serious burns for unprotected skin. Select a sunscreen that is formulated for children and test it before leaving home. A lip balm with sun protection could be carried in every hiker's pocket.

Insect repellent is worth a hundred pounds of protection. (The tiny 1-ounce squeeze bottles are great.) No-see-ums, common in sagebrush country, prowl invisibly around the ear. Protect this delicate area by dabbing a few drops of the repellent on the neck. Those opposed to using harsh chemicals on their own or their little one's skin recommend eating garlic, or rubbing vanilla extract in the area. Avon's Skin-So-Soft lotion also works well to repel the insects.

A whistle, carried by each child who understands that it is only to be used in an emergency, can help locate a lost hiker.

Additional medicine or supplies your child needs should also be packed. Extra toilet paper and plastic bags in which to carry used "T.P." are suggested. A change of underwear and socks can erase the memory of an embarrassing accident and allow the trip to continue. A shovel or trowel for personal sanitation use is also recommended. A pair of pliers and an extra rain poncho are useful items.

String or shoelace, a bandanna, magnifying lens, paper and pencil, a flower or tree guidebook, even a tiny book of stories are useful for examining the environment or passing time during a thunderstorm. A white handkerchief draped across the water's surface can be used to show what fish eat.

Trail Treats

For some little hikers, special trail food is their favorite part of the sport. Children like selecting the gorp and pouring it into individual bags. They can be useful in preparing other items, too, like carrot sticks, little containers of peanut butter (with screw-type lid only), or packages of crackers. Encourage kids to suggest finger foods (string cheese is popular) and a one-pot meal, such as macaroni and cheese, tuna and noodles, or chili.

For the most part, freeze-dried dinners, despite their gourmet-sounding names, do not fare well with children. Stay with their favorite or try new concoctions of grains and vegetables at home before introducing the meal to hungry hikers on the trail. Health-food stores carry a wide variety of grains, dehydrated fruit and vegetables, even cheese and tomato powder. Ask a clerk at the store for recommended trail food items.

OF CANYONS, PLATEAUS, AND MOUNTAINS

It's your choice: a gentle saunter along a babbling stream deep in the forest, a rigorous trek up a rock-and-flower mountain slope, or a sandy walk past ancient sites and thorny cacti. Hikes in Utah cross the biologic, geologic, and even historic spectrum. Having even a tad of understanding about these worlds makes each visit all the more memorable.

Utah, with its variety of terrains, comprises three distinctive topographic zones. Sprawling across almost half of the state, incorporating the south and east, is the Colorado Plateau. The Great Basin, also known as the Basin and Range Province, lies across western Utah. The Wasatch and Uinta mountains, in the state's northeast, comprise the Middle Rocky Mountain Province.

Happy hikers munch lunch on a mountaintop.

Erosion is the shaper of the Colorado Plateau. Most of southern Utah's startling landscape consists of intricately carved and orange-hued layers of limestone and sandstone. Now standing as chapters in the earth's geologic history, these rocks formed from the silt and mud of the ancient seas that once blanketed most of state. As the layers of rocks began uplifting millions of years ago, rivers and streams carved deep canyons through them. Today the forces of wind, rain, and freezing temperatures are continually shaping the formations.

The mountain ranges within the plateau, the Abajos, La Sals, and Henrys, are laccolithic, or formed by molten lava that lifted the earth's crust and has since been carved into sharp peaks. In addition, numerous major uplifts within the plateau have resulted in several plateaus and cliffs. Among them are the Circle Cliffs; the Monument, Uncompahgre, and San Rafael uplifts; and the Aquarius and Sevier plateaus.

In the spring and fall Utah's southeast, commonly called Canyon Country, and its southwest, known as Color Country, make up a hiker's haven. It's a place where yucca and cacti dot the landscape, which folds into twisting canyons. Where sandy paths lead to ancient dwellings littered with pottery bits. Where bright green trees border meandering watercourses to powerful rivers or impressive rock formations. Where soaring cliffs edge a trail to a maze of intricately shaped spires. Where potholes pock giant slabs of slickrock offering panoramic views in every direction. This is also the area where the Ancestral Pueblo people formerly called "Anasazi" once dwelled. Please respect their ancient dwellings and artifacts by not touching or standing on them.

The Great Basin, named by explorer John C. Fremont, who noticed its rivers have no direct outlet to the sea, consists of broad valleys and mountain ranges that run north and south. Many of the communities surrounding Salt Lake City border on the eastern edge of the basin. Since pioneer days water from the Wasatch Mountains has been diverted to its valleys for use in farming and industry. Still, most of the Great Basin is desert.

However, in ancient times Lake Bonneville blanketed this area. From this massive inland sea the Great Salt Lake was formed. The base of the Wasatch Mountains and Utah's western ranges still bear the scars left by immense waves carving terraces or benches along slopes.

Hikers in the Great Basin are attracted to the remoteness and stark beauty of its mountains and plains. Few people venture into this relatively trailless terrain, but those who do enjoy activities such as exploring old mining communities, or walking a ridge top, or watching antelope bound across the desert.

Two mountain ranges straddle Utah's northeast corner. They are part of the Rocky Mountain Province. Popular and easily accessed, the Wasatch Mountains stand sharp and steep, rising above the Great Salt Lake to elevations towering over 11,000 feet. Glacial flows down its canyons have polished and etched many slopes here.

In contrast are the Uinta Mountains, which run east to west, a characteristic shared by few other mountains in North America. Their highest point is King's Peak, at 13,528 feet. Yet many child-friendly trails border the slopes and lakesides of this hiking gem.

Both ranges offer hikers beautiful alpine scenery, consisting of summits to ascend, rock walls to walk beside, wet meadows to edge, pockets of fir trees to enter, and sparkling ponds to fish or ponder.

HOW TO USE THIS BOOK

The hikes described in this guidebook represent the best of Utah's diverse terrains that are suitable for young hikers. All the trails selected are near or en route to popular destinations in the state. Thus, most of the hikes don't require driving far into remote regions, and all are two-wheel-drive accessible. The book is arranged into four zones, with eighteen to twenty-three trails in each.

The Wasatch and North zone includes trails in and around Salt Lake City, the Wasatch Mountains, and the Ogden and Logan Canyon areas.

The Uinta and Central zone consists of hikes in the Uinta Mountains, Flaming Gorge area, and Dinosaur National Monument. The central area includes a few hikes in the Strawberry Valley, and extends to the intersection of I-15 and I-70.

Zion and Bryce national parks are among the access points for trails in the Southwestern zone, which reaches from St. George in the southwest corner to Capitol Reef National Park in the state's south-central section.

Trails in Canyonlands and Arches national parks are included in the Southeastern zone. It encompasses Hovenweep National Monument in the southeast corner and Goblin Valley State Park, southwest of Green River.

Each hike description begins with an information block summarizing important trail facts on distance, elevation gain, maps, etc. Driving directions to the trailhead are described in the next paragraph. The hike directions and narrative are bordered by symbols for turnaround points, cautions, and environmental close-ups (see page 32 for a key to these symbols). Turnaround points indicate a fine spot to enjoy the view and turn around with a feeling of having completed the hike. A caution symbol indicates perilous cliffs, tricky crossings, or steep terrain.

Of special importance in these hike descriptions are the environmental close-ups, marked by an "e" symbol in the margin. Consisting of questions and observations, they are designed as tools for parents and trip leaders to involve children in learning from and respecting nature. Knowledge acquired is secondary to the wisdom and appreciation children gain from the comparing, listening, touching, even imaginative game-playing activities that are described at each "e." An "e" with an exclamation point indicates a fragile environmental close-up. Be extra careful around these special spots to avoid damaging the features.

Hikes are rated easy, moderate, and challenging. Rather than defining specific criteria that make a hike easy or challenging, I relied on a variety of factors. Elevation gain, trail condition, and distance were important factors when figuring this label. Equally important were what the hikers I met along the trail had to say about it. Also, because I was carrying, and in some cases prodding, my 2-year-old along the trail, my evaluations reflected a child's endurance. For this edition,

An increasing number of barrier-free trails opens Utah's natural areas to more visitors.

my 9-year-old son Niko and often his friend provided important feedback. Each hike, I can safely say, has been child-tested!

The "hikable" listing in the information block refers to the approximate months the trail is snow-free or open to the public. Winter snowfall and spring temperatures can alter these dates considerably. It's a good idea to call the nearest ranger station for an update on the trail's condition before attempting the hike early or late in the season.

All of these hikes can be completed in 1 day, and most range in length from 0.3 mile to 5.5 miles one way. (The climb up Mount Timpanogos, a *long* 1-day trek, is 17.4 miles, round trip.) Whenever possible, loop trips were selected. On these, the trail makes a circuitous route back to the trailhead. Turnaround spots marked in the trail description indicate ideal destinations for a short hike and/or lunch stop. Many of the hikes can be extended into overnight or backpack trips.

Hikers interested in learning more about using maps in the wilderness should refer to USGS maps. Not all the trails in the state are marked on these maps; however, the trails in this book with a USGS listing are provided for hikers who want to learn more about the region they'll be visiting. Trails Illustrated maps are listed for many trails. This relatively new series of topographic maps covers a broader area than USGS topographic maps. Waterproof and tear-proof, they are ideal resources for hikers at home and on the trail. It's a good idea to acquaint yourself with a compass while on a well-marked, perhaps familiar trail.

Wheelchair accessibility simply reflects portions of the trail are level enough for limited wheelchair use. Having spent enough time in a wheelchair to know I missed hiking, I now watch for barrier-free trails. At the time of this writing, Forest Service districts throughout the state were proposing numerous wheelchair-accessible trails. For a listing of most of Utah's wheelchair-accessible trails, see the Appendix. Before leaving, it's advisable to call the number listed with each trail to learn its current condition.

A NOTE ABOUT SAFETY

Safety is an important concern in all outdoor activities. No guidebook can alert you to every hazard or anticipate the limitations of every reader. Therefore, the descriptions of roads, trails, routes, and natural features in this book are not representations that a particular place or excursion will be safe for your party. When you follow any of the routes described in this book, you assume responsibility for your own safety. Under normal conditions, such excursions require the usual attention to traffic, road and trail conditions, weather, terrain, the capabilities of your party, and other factors. Keeping informed on current conditions and exercising common sense are the keys to a safe, enjoyable outing.

The Mountaineers Books

KEY TO SYMBOLS

 Day hikes. These are hikes that can be completed in a single day. While some trips allow camping, only a few require it.

 Backpack trips. These are hikes whose length or difficulty makes camping out either necessary or recommended for most families.

 Easy trails. These are relatively short, smooth, gentle trails suitable for small children or first-time hikers.

 Moderate trails. Most of these are 2 to 4 miles total distance and feature more than 500 feet of elevation gain. The trail may be rough and uneven. Hikers should wear lug-soled boots and be sure to carry the Ten Essentials.

 Difficult trails. These are often rough, with considerable elevation gain or distance to travel. They are suitable for older or experienced children. Lug-soled boots and the Ten Essentials are standard equipment.

 Hikable. The best times of year to hike each trail are indicated by the following symbols: flower—spring; sun—summer; leaf—fall; snowflake—winter.

 Driving directions. These paragraphs tell you how to get to the trailheads.

 Turnarounds. These are places, mostly along moderate trails, where families can cut their hike short yet still have a satisfying outing. Turnarounds usually offer picnic opportunities, views, or special natural attractions.

 Cautions. These mark potential hazards—cliffs, stream or highway crossings, and the like—where close supervision of children is strongly recommended.

 Environmental close-ups. These highlight special environmental elements along the trail and help children learn about and respect nature.

 Environmental cautions. These are warnings of fragile natural or historical features; be extra careful not to disturb these special spots.

WASATCH AND NORTH

1 OLD DESERET VILLAGE

Location	■ This Is the Place Heritage Park
Type	■ Day hike
Difficulty	■ Easy for children
Hikable	■ Year-round
Distance	■ 0.5 mile or more, one way
Starting Elevation	■ 4900 feet
High Point	■ 4900 feet
Maps	■ Trails Illustrated Wasatch Front and Strawberry Reservoir; Old Deseret brochure

Admission fee

 From Salt Lake City take Foothill Boulevard north, or 5th South Street east to Sunnyside Avenue (800 South). Drive east approximately 0.9 mile, to just before the Hogle Zoo, to the park's entrance on the left. Parking is provided at the visitor center and near This Is the Place Monument.

Witnessing and occasionally participating in the daily activities of pioneer life are what kids enjoy most about This Is the Place

A stagecoach driver awaits riders for tours of Old Deseret Village.

Heritage Park. Most of the buildings in this living history museum are structures used during Utah's settlement period from 1847 to 1869, when the railroad brought an end to pioneer life. Kids love hopping aboard the horse-drawn covered wagon that tours the village throughout the day.

Most families begin their walk through Old Deseret Village across the road from the visitor center. There's no need to follow an exact route along the dusty streets of the village. Simply allow your curiosity to lure you to each structure where individuals dressed in pioneer garb are stationed.

Deseret means "land of the honeybees," and it is the name Mormons gave to their new surroundings when they arrived here nearly 150 years ago. Children visiting Old Deseret Village witness Mormons "busy as bees" going about their daily chores.

Children of all ages are intrigued to discover that families as large as thirteen were raised in many of the village's one-room cabins. Remind your kids that homestead children had few, if any, toys. They probably had only one set of clothes, which were washed at night and hung out to dry in the desert air, and were ready to wear the next morning. The men and women at the homes can describe the jobs pioneer children had.

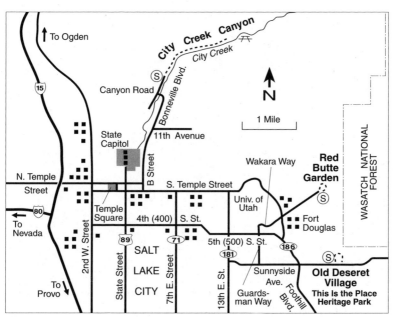

But most kids will find the chores, such as carding wool, weaving potholders from rags, or pumping the treadle-operated wood lathe, pure fun. Those are some of the daily activities held at the sites. The child in everyone is lured to the General Store, where a sampling of truly old-fashioned wooden toys, tin candle molds, cotton bonnets, and treats such as lemon drops and sarsaparilla soda are sold.

Do plan your visit to include the Blacksmith Shop, where all of the village's kitchen utensils, horseshoes, and nails are crafted. Children may get to use the blacksmith's bellows.

During their visit children will see a variety of occupations vital to the community. While walking among the sites, encourage children to imagine themselves as pioneers and ask them which job they would like to have. Is any job more important than the others?

The season for visiting Old Deseret is Memorial Day through Labor Day. Hours are 10:00 A.M. to 5:00 P.M. Old Deseret is closed during the winter months, except for such special events as the Pumpkin Harvest and the Christmas Candlelight Tour. Birthday parties can be scheduled by calling 801-584-8392.

Toilet and water facilities are available at the visitor center and in the village.

2 CITY CREEK CANYON

Location ■	Salt Lake City
Type ■	Day hike
Difficulty ■	Easy for children
Hikable ■	Year-round
Distance ■	0.5 mile to 6 miles, one way
Starting Elevation ■	4700 feet
High Point ■	4800 feet
Map ■	City Creek Canyon leaflet

Drive-through fee
Wheelchair accessible

From Temple Square drive east on North Temple to B Street. Proceed north (left), crossing 11th Avenue, then along Bonneville Boulevard to Canyon Road. Turn north (right) at the curve and go approximately 100 yards to the gate.

Utah's state capitol is a short walk from City Creek.

This quiet corridor close to Capitol Hill provides an enjoyable escape for hikers, bikers, moms pushing strollers, and eager-to-explore children (with energy to expend). Walkers are free to savor this lush preserve any day of the year because car and bicycle use is restricted on the narrow paved road along City Creek. They may also stroll the 3-mile dirt trail to the left of the road, just inside the park. Pets are not permitted in the City Creek corridor.

Following this trail, which begins on the road's left side about 50 yards from the entry gate, allows more opportunities to see wildlife. The trail follows an "edge," an area where two or more plant communities meet, such as the meadow grasses and streamside trees meeting here. After pointing out the stream alongside the road, ask children why animals would enter this area. What animals might they be? Explain that riparian zones such as City Creek provide essential water and food for at least 80 percent of all wildlife. What else might the trees and brush provide for animals? At some point along the walk, make a side trip to the stream to look for signs of wildlife.

Those who continue farther up the trail, a route better appreciated on cool days, cross sunny meadows and thickly vegetated areas offering numerous opportunities for discovering wildlife. During my midsummer trek, starting at the 3-mile point and walking back to the entrance gate, I saw numerous piles of scat (animal droppings)—territory markings left by coyote. In a brushy area, I came within 15 feet of a hawk gnawing on the remains of an animal. This canyon is indeed a slice of life.

Walking the narrow, paved roadway also has its benefits, including plenty of shade and close access to the stream. (Swimming is prohibited in this city watershed; fishing, however, is allowed.) Children's curiosity about what fish and other stream creatures eat can be explored by dipping a white cloth across a slow-moving section of the water's surface. Tiny brown particles—seeds, pollen, insect eggs, and larvae—become netted on the cloth, enabling children a look at just one component of the area's web of life.

Those large "elephant ear" leaves growing alongside the road are called burdock. They're edible, though not tasty. Children have fun looking for elephant ears of all sizes, including the "teeniest" and the one belonging to the king of the herd. No doubt, you will find the prodigious plant's seed dispersal mechanism: a burr stuck to youngsters' socks.

Another acquaintance they might make along the road is poison ivy. Growing just 100 yards beyond the gate, this display deserves distant examination so children will know to avoid it elsewhere.

The hike up the road extends from the entrance 5.75 miles, passing numerous picnic sites and the city's water treatment plant. For those who continue beyond the road's end, a 4-mile foot trail leads to a meadow. Two additional trails, the Pipe Line and North Fork, spoke outward from the foot track.

Water and toilet facilities are located near the trailhead and at a few picnic sites.

3 RED BUTTE GARDEN TRAILS

Location	■ Salt Lake City
Type	■ Day hike
Difficulty	■ Garden Loops, easy for children; Wildflower Meadow Loop, easy to moderate; RBG Natural Area, moderate to difficult
Hikable	■ Year-round
Distance	■ 0.5 mile to 4 miles, round trip
Starting Elevation	■ Garden Loops, 5025 feet; Wildflower Meadow Loop, 5025 feet; RBG Natural Area, 5100 feet
High Point	■ Garden Loop, 5075 feet; Wildflower Meadow Loop, 5150 feet; RBG Natural Area, 5467 feet
Map	■ Red Butte Garden brochure

www.redbutte.utah.edu
Admission fee
Wheelchair accessible throughout most of the gardens

From I-15, exit on the 6th (600) South Exit, traveling east. Continue to 7th (700) East and turn east (right), driving to 4th (400) South, which becomes Foothill Boulevard. Drive uphill to the intersection at Wakara Way. Turn left and continue on to Wakara Way to reach the Garden entrance. Ample parking is provided.

From kids to gardeners or hikers to landscapers—anyone visiting Red Butte Garden feels inspired, energized, educated, or simply at peace. This 150-acre natural haven is a four-season attraction. While its 30 acres of gardens fuel fantasies throughout the year, the Wildflower Meadow and 4 miles of mountain trails lure butterfly chasers and snowshoers. Kids are enchanted in the Children's Garden and can't resist the textures and scents of the Sensation Garden. Classes, concerts, guided hikes, and special exhibits encourage repeat visits to Red Butte Garden. Bicycles are not permitted here, adding another measure of tranquillity to this city hike.

The visitor center provides a map of the area and posts information on the day's classes or special events. The gift shop here features nature-based toys and books along with specialty garden items.

A friendly scarecrow greets visitors at the Children's Garden at Red Butte Garden.

Access to the first of a dozen different gardens begins on the paved walkway just outside the visitor center in the Courtyard Garden. Notice the fountain here shaped like Utah's state flower, the sego lily. The walkway leads to the Four Season Garden and the herb and medicinal gardens, all of which feature identifying placards near the plants.

Lingering in these oases may not be possible because your kids will probably find their way to the Children's Garden. There you may find them stepping across the pond or investigating the Pizza Plant Garden or quietly absorbed by a Discovery Box they found in the Sprout House. The Children's Garden, with its playful arrangement of sculptures, plants, caves, and fountains, is an imagination playground for anyone. Plant craft and nature investigation classes for kids are held here regularly. From this and other high points in the gardens, point out the spectacular view of Salt Lake City and the surrounding basin.

The upper path heading west from the Children's Garden leads to the Wildflower Meadow, the start of Red Butte's nature trails. The 1.25-mile loop circling the Wildflower Meadow consists of two trails: the Oak Tunnel trail on the west meets Zeke's trail, which returns to the area adjacent to the Garden Loops. Your kids will want to walk the Oak Tunnel located at the meadow's eastern end. Encourage your crew to find the secret staircase on the north side of the meadow. The reward for finding it is a visit to a cool streamside rest stop.

Access to the 4 miles of trails crossing the rolling hills of Red Butte Garden's Natural Area is from several points along Zeke's Trail. More information on these trails is available at the visitor center.

Pets, bicycles, and skates are not allowed in Red Butte Garden, which is open from May to September, 7 days a week, 9 A.M. to 8 P.M. and October to April, Tuesday through Sunday, 10 A.M. to 5 P.M.

Water and restroom facilities are available at the visitor center and the Children's Garden.

MORMON PIONEER NATIONAL HISTORIC TRAIL

Location ▪	East of Salt Lake City
Type ▪	Day hike or overnight backpack
Difficulty ▪	Easy to moderate for children
Hikable ▪	April through October
Distance ▪	4.3 miles, one way
Starting Elevation ▪	7420 feet
High Point ▪	6040 feet
Maps ▪	Trails Illustrated Wasatch Front and Strawberry Valley; USGS Big Dutch Hollow

www.nps.gov/mopi

From Salt Lake City take I-80 (Parley's Canyon) east to UT-65 (exit 134). Proceed north 8.2 miles to the top of Big Mountain Pass. The trailhead is on your right, on the left end of the cleared parking area. To pick up hikers or shuttle a vehicle, continue traveling east on UT-65 another 5.4 miles to the bottom of the hill where a dirt road joins on the right. Turn here and drive 3.3 miles to the "Mormon Flat" stone marker on the right. A parking area is provided here.

Retracing the last portion of the 1300-mile route Brigham Young and his followers took to what is now Salt Lake City instills more than an appreciation of history. This walk follows a creek where signs

The trailhead marker at Mormon Pioneer National Historic Area

of wildlife are abundant. Although most hikers prefer walking downhill to a shuttled vehicle awaiting them, some may opt for a more authentic pioneering experience by hiking the trail from the bottom to top, a 1380-foot elevation gain.

Before starting the hike, acquaint the members of your group with the historical importance of the path they'll walk. Depending on their knowledge of Mormon or Utah history, explain that in 1846 members of the Church of Jesus Christ of Latter-Day Saints (Mormons) began their journey west to build a Zion, or utopia, free from religious persecution. Their trek began in Nauvoo, Illinois, a town on the banks of the Mississippi River. In the following 22 years, 70,000 church members followed this trail. As you walk, encourage children to imagine carrying all their belongings in a wooden handcart, just as many poorer "saints" did on their travels.

The Donner-Reed party, a group of settlers heading to California, also used this trail. Theirs is a famous story of survival and exploration that ended during an early winter snowstorm in the Sierra Nevada Mountains.

Beginning from the east side of the parking area at Big Mountain Pass, the trail follows a powerline down through a meadow into a friendly fir forest. Signs and emblems for the Mormon Pioneer Trail mark this National Historic Trail. As the trail enters an aspen-spruce forest, it meets a creek, which under nondrought conditions runs all summer.

After about 1 mile, point out the different vegetation blanketing the north- and south-facing slopes. Discuss which side holds rain and snow longer and why different trees develop under these conditions. Ask, "What direction are we hiking in?"

At 1.8 miles downed aspen trees litter the forest floor. Note their beaver-chewed, cone-shaped ends. Soon old beaver dams crossing the stream can be pointed out. Within 0.5 mile the trail contours shallow ponds held in place by several stick-and-mud dams. Look for a lodge structure in the pond's center. Does it appear to have an entrance? Probably not. Beavers enter their homes from below the water's surface to store their winter food of aspen and cottonwood twigs. Discuss how this behavior affects the beaver's survival rate.

As the trail continues its descent from elevations where spruce-fir forests and then aspens naturally thrive, it enters a cottonwood-forested area. Beaver appetites took the lives of many cottonwoods here. Compare the value of cottonwoods with that of beavers. Point out that cottonwoods live 100 or more years, while a beaver's life is 15 to 20 years. Are beavers useful? Does the dam they build pool sufficient water to support enough wildlife to outweigh the loss of near-ancient cottonwoods? What other animals depend on the

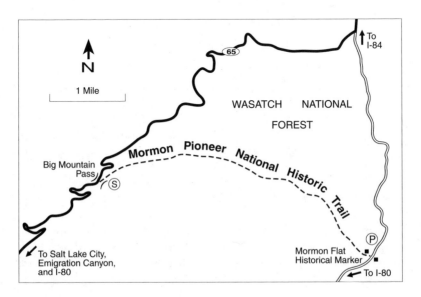

cottonwood for shelter or food? Help children understand the need for balance in nature, that both the cottonwood and beaver are necessary components of the web of life. Stop at the ponds to look for game trails leading to the water from the woods.

As the trail veers south out of the cottonwood area, look to either side of the canyon for piles of rocks standing 1.5 to 4 feet tall. These are what remain of the fortification the Mormon pioneers built in 1857 to defend themselves against what was known as Johnson's Army, sent to quell the Mormon rebellion. However, no shots were fired and both groups passed through here peacefully. By the time the army arrived in Salt Lake, Brigham Young had already sent the residents to Utah's south. Do respect these fragile, historic sites by not touching or climbing on them. The fortifications can also be seen from the parking area.

The final 0.5 mile weaves through a cottonwood sapling–choked marsh, then meets a footbridge spanning a stream. A stone Mormon Pioneer Trail historical marker is located near the trail's end.

No toilet or water facilities are provided at either trailhead.

𝟻 LAKE MARY TRAIL

Location ■	Little Cottonwood–Big Cottonwood Canyons
Type ■	Day hike
Difficulty ■	Easy to moderate for children
Hikable ■	Mid-June to mid-September
Distance ■	Up to 3.4 miles, one way
Starting Elevation ■	Little Cottonwood Canyon, 9400 feet; Big Cottonwood Canyon, 8800 feet
High Point ■	10,220 feet
Maps ■	Trails Illustrated Wasatch Front and Strawberry Reservoir; USGS Brighton

www.fs.fed.us/wcnf/slrd

To reach the Little Cottonwood Canyon trailhead, follow the Little Cottonwood Canyon Road 3 miles beyond Alta to the Albion Basin Campground. The trailhead begins near the campground's entry, opposite the trail to Cecret Lake.

For the Big Cottonwood Canyon trailhead, follow the Big Cottonwood Canyon Road to Brighton, where a loop drive passes the Mount Majestic Lodge on your right. Park in the lot near the lodge's fenced pool and the trailhead.

Winding through an alpine tapestry of rock-rimmed lakes, snow-studded cirques, flower-laced meadows, and quiet forests, this trail connects Big and Little Cottonwood canyons. Starting from either side, hikers view peaks standing sentry and encounter trails leading to their summits. Several turnaround points on the Big Cottonwood side enable families to customize the hike to their needs. Those with small children can hike a short distance to a lake, while older hikers can continue on to Little Cottonwood Canyon. Dogs are not permitted in either Big or Little Cottonwood Canyon.

From the parking lot at Mount Majestic Lodge, follow the short path to the main trail and turn left. Take this wide trail, which immediately narrows and veers into the trees before meeting a private road, where you jog left and proceed 50 feet. A sign for Brighton Lakes, Lake Mary, Catherine Pass, and Albion Pass marks the trail.

As the gentle climb begins up this mountain bike–restricted trail, watch for evidence of a porcupine dining here. This bark eater has ringed several trees along the trail's left side. Trees completely girdled by porcupines have had their nutrient and water supply cut off and will eventually die.

At 0.5 mile take the trail to the right, which climbs to a level clearing for views of Clayton Peak poking from the ridge on the far right.

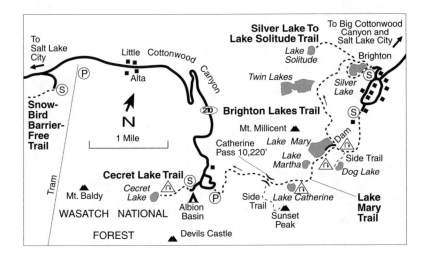

To its left is Twin Peaks, followed by Sunset Peak. A sign here indicates Dog Lake, a possible turnaround point for some hikers, 500 feet to the left. Continue straight ahead 0.25 mile for Lake Mary, 1.25 miles for Lake Catherine, and 2.5 miles for Albion Basin. Continue another 50 yards, turning left at the sign for Lake Mary, 0.25 mile, and Twin Lakes, 2 miles to the right. Those hiking the Brighton Lakes Trail take the trail to the right.

Approach Lake Mary, a popular and pretty rock-edged destination, by walking below its concrete dam. Point out that the dam is thicker at the bottom than at the top and ask why this is so. For those prephysics hikers with you, explain that the thicker, thus stronger, section of concrete is needed to support the greater pressure, or weight, of water at the lake's bottom. For some fun physics, stop to skip rocks at the lake. Because of watershed regulations, swimming and wading are not permitted in the lakes of Cottonwood Canyon.

Only 0.5 mile beyond here is Lake Martha, which sits in a forested basin. Gentle switchbacks climb above the lake. Take a breath-catching stop alongside the pair of limber pine that straddle the trail. Count the needles in each bunch and discover the branch's trademark bendability. Doing so will reinforce in youngsters the meaning of

White columbine, an alpine gem of the Lake Mary Trail

limber. Also, watch for a spring spilling left of the trail just after the viewpoint of Dog Lake.

At 1.8 miles a sign indicates Catherine Pass is straight ahead, while Catherine Lake is to the left. (By the way, the area's lakes were named for daughters in the Brighton family who homesteaded here.) Follow the trail to the right as it contours up the dividing ridge to the lowest point—Catherine Pass. Hikers can enjoy excellent views of Alta Ski Area, Albion Basin, and Little Cottonwood Canyon from here. It is even possible to see the Snowbird Tram in the distance. A hike up Sunset Peak (10,648 feet) begins by following the trail to the south.

The 1-mile descent to Albion Basin begins with a steep, forested section, then crosses a meadow, where it meets a jeep road before dropping into Albion Basin.

Toilet facilities for the Big Cottonwood side are about 100 yards from the parking lot, on the trail's left side. Water and toilet facilities on the Little Cottonwood side are at Albion Campground.

6 BRIGHTON LAKES TRAIL

Location ■	Brighton
Type ■	Day hike
Difficulty ■	Easy to moderate for children
Hikable ■	Mid-June through September
Distance ■	3 miles, one way
Starting Elevation ■	8800 feet
High Point ■	9440 feet
Maps ■	Trails Illustrated Wasatch Front and Strawberry Valley; USGS Brighton

www.fs.fed.us/wcnf/slrd

See directions for the Big Cottonwood Canyon trailhead in Hike 5, Lake Mary Trail.

Strolls along this mountain ridge lead hikers through a variety of alpine environments where spectacular views keep interest alive. Children like stopping at the lakes along the way, where they can throw rocks or look for Utah's version of the Loch Ness monster. Pets and swimming are not permitted in Big Cottonwood Canyon.

Begin this hike by following the trail from the parking lot at

Kids of all ages hike the Brighton Lakes Trail.

Mount Majestic Lodge. Take the short path up to a wide trail and veer left into the trees before meeting a private road. Jog left on the road and proceed to where a sign for Brighton Lakes, Lake Mary, Catherine Pass, and Albion Pass marks the trail. Follow this trail up a wooded slope as it bends to the right and reaches a viewpoint of the surrounding mountains. Another 50 yards beyond the clearing, turn right at the sign for Twin Lakes.

Cresting a short rocky slope, the trail passes a small, old cabin before it overlooks Lake Mary's northeastern edge. From the lake the trail descends into a spruce-fir forest webbed in faint, confusing trails. Stay on the main trail as it follows the tree line around a steep, boulder-filled slope. Just past a small creek, a trail sign indicates that Twin Lakes is straight ahead in 0.5 mile. Do not take the trail heading downslope from here.

After a brief wooded section, the trail meets another stretch of boulders blanketing the mountain slope. Look left where a path has been cleared through the rock rubble. Follow this dry pathway, listening to the water gurgling underneath your feet.

After crossing the stark, sun-drenched boulders, you enter brush consisting primarily of mountain willow. Watch for white-crowned sparrows, the little birds darting in and out of the dense greenery. Children who look carefully may discover a bird's hideaway, a nest. They may also notice that the air feels warmer in the brush. This slight temperature difference allows more eggs to hatch.

Views of the Brighton area and perhaps familiar ski trails command hikers' attention until they encounter Twin Lakes at 2 miles, just after the service road. Don't look for two lakes, as they merged into one after the concrete arch dam was put in place. Mount Millicent looms behind Twin Lakes.

Follow the service road 50 yards until another wide path leads to the ski off-ramp. Walk under the structure and meet the Brighton Lakes Trail, which turns right as it continues downslope.

At 2.4 miles the trail enters an open basin above the trees; Silver Lake can be seen sparkling below. Proceed another 0.1 mile to meet the trail that leads to the lake. After a few switchbacks through the meadow, the trail enters the trees, then meets the boardwalk around Silver Lake. Head back to the trailhead at Mount Majestic Lodge by turning right at the lake. Follow the boardwalk to the parking lot at Silver Lake and walk 0.4 mile on the road to your car.

Toilet facilities are located near both trailheads. Drinking water is available only at Silver Lake.

7 SILVER LAKE TO LAKE SOLITUDE

Location ■ Big Cottonwood Canyon
Type ■ Day hike
Difficulty ■ Silver Lake, easy for children; Lake Solitude, easy to moderate for children
Hikable ■ May through October
Distance ■ Silver Lake, 1 mile, round trip; Lake Solitude, 1.5 miles, one way
Starting Elevation ■ 8720 feet
High Point ■ 9040 feet (Lake Solitude)
Maps ■ Trails Illustrated Wasatch Front and Strawberry Reservoir; USGS Brighton

www.fs.fed.us/wcnf/slrd
Wheelchair-accessible loop

See directions for the Big Cottonwood Canyon trailhead in Hike 5, Lake Mary Trail. Access to Silver Lake and the parking area is on the right, 0.5 mile before the Brighton Lakes trailhead.

Walking around Silver Lake, which includes interpretive signs, then strolling the aspen forests to Lake Solitude, is a good "heals what ails ya" trek. Fishing is great at the first lake, and the second often provides what its name describes. Pets and swimming are not permitted in Big Cottonwood Canyon.

The trail around Silver Lake deserves a gold star; it's a stellar recreation site the entire family can appreciate. Recently redesigned with a boardwalk, this interpreted loop trail allows hikers who stroll, toddle, and wheel easy access to a diverse natural area.

The boardwalk winds through marshes, into pine forests, and along the lake's edge. The interpretive signs encourage readers to see how the environments here play a direct role in their own lives. Be prepared to play a naturalist's game of habitat hide-and-go-seek, as the signs suggest where and how to look for wildlife in this fragile wetland.

Two fishing docks along the boardwalk enhance wheelchair accessibility with built-in fishing-pole holders. Rainbow and brook trout are stocked here several times a summer. Plan to catch only as many "catchables" (9 to 11 inches) as you can eat fresh. Flies are encouraged for catch-and-release fishing. Silver Lake hikers may turn around at any point along the boardwalk, or continue following the boardwalk along the lake.

The trail to Lake Solitude begins at the northwest end of Silver Lake. Passing the first fork to the left, continue 0.1 mile to the next branch of the trail. Climb this 0.2-mile path through an aspen-fir forest to the Lake Solitude Trail and turn right. The route remains relatively level for the next 0.8 mile, heading northwest through an open area, then veering west through glens of towering aspen and a mixed forest.

Adults appreciate the therapeutic atmosphere these stands of aspens create with their serene white trunks that are topped in trembling green or golden tresses. And young children respond to this forest magic when you tell them fairies and rock gnomes live amongst the aspen trees. A hummingbird, an airborne green jewel hovering above a crimson paintbrush, may be the first of the "fairies" youngsters identify. Perhaps they'll consider a flittering gold-and-black butterfly or a tall, raggedy-topped mint as forest angels. Hands-and-knees explorers find such rock gnomes as caterpillars or "roly-poly" bugs. They may even consider lichen crusting a rock to be a gnome's house paint! Allow such imaginative activities as these to arouse children's interest in the natural world. They create a memorable

Mountain goats, reintroduced to the Wasatch Range, are frequently sighted on high, rocky slopes.

theme for treks in any environment. But do remind your companions that picking just one flower is against the law. Talk about why wildflowers are protected.

After passing a cross-country ski trail and under Solitude's Sunrise Lift, the trail turns south. Caution is advised along this area because mountain bikers access ski trails through here. Children's chatter can work like bear bells, warning bikers of your presence, but do keep the group walking close together to avoid any sudden, unpleasant surprises. Two more downhill ski runs are crossed before the trail climbs a short hill to the lake.

Stay on the existing path around the lake because the riparian area is fragile. The return route is via the same trail.

A vault toilet and water facilities are available at the Silver Lake area.

8

CECRET LAKE

Location ▪ Little Cottonwood Canyon
Type ▪ Day hike
Difficulty ▪ Moderate for children
Hikable ▪ June through mid-October
Distance ▪ 0.75 mile, one way
Starting Elevation ▪ 9460 feet
High Point ▪ 9880 feet
Maps ▪ Trails Illustrated Wasatch Front, Strawberry Valley, and Uinta National Forest

www.fs.fed.us/wcnf/slrd

From Salt Lake City drive south or east on I-215. Turn off at exit 7 and drive south on UT-210 to Little Cottonwood Canyon. From the mouth of the canyon drive 11.3 miles east to Albion Basin Campground. The 2.5 miles of gravel road beyond Alta Ski Resort are suitable for two-wheel-drive vehicles. Parking for trail hikers only is adjacent to the campground entrance.

It's no secret that Cecret Lake remains the gem of Little Cottonwood Canyon. Nestled atop a glacially carved mountain basin, this sparkling destination is popular with children, who are thrilled by the spectacular high country, and parents, who are enchanted by its wildflowers—Utah's finest display, which climaxes from mid-July to late August.

However, popularity can tarnish this alpine jewel. Hikers who pick "just one" flower along the walk or blaze a shortcut to the next switchback seriously impact this fragile land. Portions of the trail have recently been rerouted by the Forest Service to prevent further destruction in key areas. Dogs are not permitted in Little Cottonwood Canyon.

When starting out from the parking area, remind children (and grown-ups) that the alpine world's growing season is only 2 to 3 months. A flower stepped on doesn't have time to recover before winter sets in. A rock tumbled from its place exposes precious soil that erodes with the next rain. Ask your hike leader to avoid paths made by careless hikers. Encourage your companions to pocket litter found along the trail.

At the footbridge just below the campground area, point out the

Trails open to mountain bikers require hikers to be extra aware.

two mountaintops to the south: a dark, craggy peak and a rounded summit. Ask kids to judge which peak is Sugarloaf and which is Devils Castle. Expose Cecret Lake's hiding place, the depression on a flat ridge below and slightly left of Sugarloaf Mountain (11,051 feet). Observant hikers eyeing other maps of the area may notice Cecret Lake spelled as Secret, Cecret, or Seacret Lake. Named by early miners here, the lake is spelled differently in various documents. Ask your crew the correct spelling of *secret*.

Passing under the chairlift, look for the teeth and claw marks of a porcupine-gnawed tree. Decide if this tree has been girdled, or encircled, by the bark harvester. Do other parts of the tree appear affected by the porcupine's food selection?

A rainbow of wildflowers awaits summer hikers as the trail enters the moist environment of Little Cottonwood Creek. Get to know these mountain beauties by saying their color with their name: bright pink fireweed, lavender and white columbine, blue chiming bells, purple larkspur, orange or pink paintbrush, pink geranium, and white cow parsnip. Kids have fun matching flower colors to their clothing. Find out which flowers look like their names. Remember picking wildflowers is prohibited and there is a penalty for doing so.

Very young ones or easily winded ones may decide to turn around just beyond the flower showcase.

Where the trail forks at 0.3 mile, follow it uphill to the left. Potentilla flowers poke their petite yellow heads just above this rocky, inhospitable terrain. Kids who know some Spanish can count the plant's five petals and remember its common name, cinquefoil.

After a few switchbacks crossing the talus slope, the trail crests the ridge where the lake sits. Young anglers may hope to find fish in Cecret Lake until they feel its near-freezing temperature. Look for other forms of life adapted to the short, wet growing season along the lake. On sunny days pointing out to children the sparkling, diamond-studded lake stirred up by gentle breezes will add a feeling of magic to their visit.

On the return hike kids may notice tattered, "one-sided" spruce trees near the lake. The constant "pruning" action of the wind blows away protective snow, killing the exposed tree branches. It's easy to tell which way the wind blows up here! "Banner tree" is a more descriptive name given to the krummholz trees that develop at wind-swept elevations. Notice how the trunks of these trees appear old and twisted. Feel the square-shaped needles of a banner tree, and look for a stately version of the spruce tree near the campground. Has the tree's needle size been affected by life on the mountainside?

During the return hike, ask your companions to share their ideas on ways to protect the beauty of this area, yet allow people to visit it.

Toilet and water facilities are available at the campground.

 SNOWBIRD BARRIER-FREE TRAIL

Location ■	Snowbird Ski Area
Type ■	Day hike
Difficulty ■	Easy for children
Hikable ■	Mid-May through October
Distance ■	0.5 mile, one way
Starting Elevation ■	8080 feet
High Point ■	8150 feet
Map ■	Snowbird Activity Center brochure

Wheelchair accessible

Snowbird Ski Area is 6 miles up Little Cottonwood Canyon Road (UT-210), southeast of Salt Lake City. Follow the entrance road to Cliff Lodge, where parking for the trail is located.

This gentle interpreted trail winds through several alpine habitats to a picnic destination set at a spectacular mountain viewpoint.

Hikers and little riders enjoy the sights along the Snowbird Barrier-Free Trail.

Tucked in the ever-popular Little Cottonwood Canyon, this little-used walkway allows each hiker quiet opportunities to explore a truly natural environment. With luck, your little ones may spy a mountain goat sitting like a small cloud on the mountainside.

The trailhead is located opposite Snowbird's shops and aerial tram center. From the shop area follow the pavement across the bridge and turn right on the blacktopped walkway. The trail, which bars skates, bicycles, and motorcycles, bends to the right (west) and follows the base of Twin Peaks.

At the first interpretive sign, encourage kids to listen and watch for evidence of wildlife. Their accounting may include bees, birds, chipmunks, butterflies, even a mosquito. Ask your group, "What animals live here that we can't see? Where are they? What animals live here only in the summer?"

In the pillowy-soft duff of a towering spruce-fir forest near sign-posts 2 and 3 are found entries to ground squirrel homes. Point out the 2-inch-wide holes in the thick mat of pine needles and cone scales. Explain that these resourceful rodents use soil and the left-overs of their pine-cone meal, its scales, as a storehouse for the grasses, berries, acorns, and pine and flower seeds they've collected all summer. Chipmunks, or their larger look-alikes, golden-mantled ground squirrels, may hide away as much as twenty bushels of food in an area such as this. However, the swift rodents eat only a small amount of their stash. Using an available cone, allow children to try their hands at removing a seed for the squirrel. They'll learn their fingers are not adapted for gathering the forest dweller's cuisine. Can you find the remains of a recently descaled cone? Count the holes in the grass storehouse. Guess how many ground squirrels live here.

Upon reaching signpost 4, where a boardwalk leads to the elevated and fenced picnic platform, describe to kids the different environments they've walked past. Explain the word *habitat*, encouraging your companions to name the different places where animals and plants live.

At the picnic site binoculars can make the mountain views more exciting. During our visit here a mountain goat napped on a precarious cliff near Mount Baldy's summit.

Retrace your steps to return to the trailhead. The option of riding Snowbird's aerial tram 2900 feet up adds a special highlight to the day's adventure. Hikes down from the tram along the Peruvian Gulch Trail can be a bit long and steep for young children. I recommend they return to the base on the tram.

Toilet and water facilities are available at the base.

10 TIMPANOGOS CAVE

Location ■	American Fork Canyon
Type ■	Day hike
Difficulty ■	Moderate for children
Hikable ■	May to October
Distance ■	1.5 miles, one way
Starting Elevation ■	5638 feet
High Point ■	6730 feet
Maps ■	USGS Timpanogos Cave; Timpanogos Cave National Monument brochure

www.nps.gov/tica
National monument cave tour fee

The entrance to Timpanogos Cave National Monument is 10 miles east of I-15 on American Fork Canyon, UT-92 (exit 287).

Hiking the 1.5-mile trail with a 1065-foot elevation gain to Timpanogos Cave can be *almost* as much fun as seeing the cave's glittering stalagmites and spiraling helictites. Kids enjoy finding the numbered posts along the trail and at rest benches feel quite proud at seeing how much distance they've covered.

Come prepared with water bottles and treats. Also, for a child under 6 years old, it's a difficult hike to the cave, so plan on carrying him or her part of the way.

Entirely paved, the trail allows access to the cave to most any walker in good health. However, a baby in a stroller or any wheeled device is not allowed. For those intending to carry their toddler in a backpack, be aware that the cave's delicate features are easily harmed, so a frame pack must be carried in front of you while another person must haul, as I did, a wiggling and eventually sleeping child through narrow passages. This is not an enjoyable way to tour the cave.

Tickets for the cave tour are purchased at the visitor center or by calling the monument at 801-756-9193 in advance of your arrival. To minimize crowds at the cave entrance, your group's assigned time for departing on the walk is marked on the ticket. During summer months expect to wait an hour or more after buying the ticket to start this 1- to 1.5-hour hike. Use the wait time to view the introductory slide program or 25-minute videotape at the visitor center. Or experience the Five Sense Nature Trail along the 0.3-mile Canyon View Nature Trail across from the visitor center. A leaflet describing the trail's sensory approach to witnessing nature's forces is available at the visitor center.

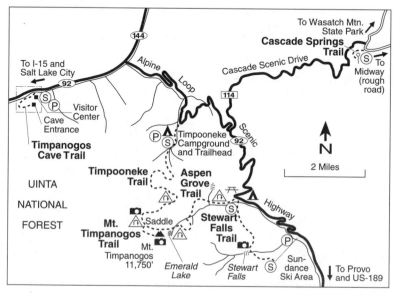

Plan frequent water breaks for hikers and passengers.

Before heading up the trail, let your companions know that in 1915 two 14-year-old boys discovered the entrance to Timpanogos Cave. Discuss how their hike would differ from today's walk. How would it be similar? Your tour guide can tell you more about the adventures of finding the three caves.

Continuing up the trail, look for tiny inholdings of plant life clinging to rock surfaces. In places where lichen adds a crunchy surface to smooth stone, find plants taking root nearby. Explain that lichen traps dust and eventually soil, laying the foundation for plants. It may appear impossible, but lichen actually breaks down the rock it clings to by producing a mild acid. Look for lichen of different colors and textures. Wildlife depends on many kinds of plant forms, including lichen. Please do not touch the plants along the way nor feed the squirrels; doing so is harmful to the animal, and it's against the law!

At the 0.25-milepost the rock has been blasted through to form a tunnel. Youngsters are thrilled to find holes in the rock where dynamite caps were placed to blaze the gentle path you are on.

Between signposts 5 and 6 take a few moments to acquaint yourselves with the area's trees; naming them while walking helps divert attention from the distance yet to walk. At signpost 9 stop to take in the views of the valley below. Point out the Oquirrh Mountains in the hazy distance. Ask your group, "In what direction are we facing?"

Signpost 12 features a slab made up of limestone and shale mingled together in thin layers. Touch a 0.25-inch layer and imagine that hundreds of millions of years ago this band of hard rock was the sediment of an ocean floor. Try to guess how many thousands of years are represented in the compressed layers of rock here.

At signpost 14 gaze out at the canyon below to decide if it is V- or U-shaped. Explain that a river initially carved a V route through here, marking it as a young canyon. If a glacier moved through here would the canyon become U-shaped?

Watch for the last switchback before the cave. Advice for groups with children afraid of the dark: During most tours the lights are turned off briefly so that visitors can experience the true darkness of the cave. The guide will warn you when this is going to happen, but it helps to prepare youngsters just before the tour starts.

Bring a jacket; the cave temperature hovers around 45 degrees Fahrenheit.

Because a trek to Timpanogos Cave has become a traditional event for Utahns, the park service has developed interesting themes for the cave tour. Photography displays, historic lectures, and flashlight are some of the specially arranged tours scheduled. Check with the monument for dates and times.

A restroom is located at the last switchback before the cave entrance.

11 MOUNT TIMPANOGOS

Location ▪	Uinta National Forest, Mount Timpanogos Wilderness
Type ▪	Day hike or overnight backpack
Difficulty ▪	Challenging for children
Hikable ▪	Mid-June to September
Distance ▪	17.4 miles, round trip
Starting Elevation ▪	Timpooneke trailhead, 7360 feet; Aspen Grove trailhead, 6850 feet
High Point ▪	11,750 feet
Maps ▪	Trails Illustrated Wasatch Front, Strawberry Reservoir, and Uinta National Forest; USGS Timpanogos Cave and Aspen Grove; Uinta National Forest map

Two trails, the Aspen Grove Trail and the Timpooneke Trail, lead to the summit of Mount Timpanogos. For accessing both trailheads, follow the directions for Hike 12, Stewart Falls Trails, to where the Aspen Grove Trail begins at the Theater in the Pines picnic grounds. The Timpooneke Trail begins at the Timpooneke Camp-ground, 6 miles northwest of Aspen Grove. Hikers planning to be-gin at either the Timpooneke or Aspen Grove trailheads and ending at the other should arrange for a shuttled vehicle to meet them, oth-erwise it's an additional 6-mile hike. See map with Timpanogos Cave, Hike 10.

Utah's most popular and spectacular climb is tested annually by thousands of children. However, the all-day trek up and down Mount Timpanogos is designed for healthy, prepared, and supervised kids.

Preparation begins with being well rested and properly equipped. Nothing fancier than sturdy hiking shoes, rain gear, sunscreen, a sweater, high-energy food, and at least 2 quarts of water per person is required. Preparation also means starting the hike around sunrise and spending most of the day on the trail. Warn your companions that they'll have to head back should clouds start blanketing the sky. Sud-den and severe weather changes are routine above tree line and cause life-threatening hypothermia for the unprepared.

The route we selected was up the Timpooneke Trail and down the Aspen Grove Trail. Timpooneke is a wide, well-designed route that ascends at a steady pace. Hikers going up this trail have the advan-tage of starting 500 feet higher. The Aspen Grove Trail is a bit rockier and has numerous switchbacks, which makes it a better route down. Along both trails to the summit we found ideal turnaround points for younger, inexperienced hikers.

From the large parking lot and stock loading ramp at Timponeeke Campground, the trail begins in a wildflower meadow and passes through an aspen forest and stream. Those wanting a shorter hike can walk 1.5 miles to a rustic overlook with a view of Scout Falls.

Next comes the Giant Staircase, a long, though easy, set of switch-backs through broken-down talus that passes several small waterfalls. During breath-catching stops orient your hiking companions to the northeast, where Park City and Heber can be seen.

Incidentally, experienced mountaineers recommend that climbers breathe at an even pace, adjusting the number of steps taken with each inhale and exhale according to terrain. But keep the rest stops brief, no more than 90 seconds long. Longer breaks not only increase time spent on the trail, they also diminish motivation. This is be-cause the drive to get started again diminishes as the cardiovascular system slows down. Hikers have to start all over again to attain the efficiency their muscles had before stopping. A group that stands dur-ing its rest stop will want to keep moving.

Hikers rest at the summit of Mount Timpanogos.

As the trail climbs higher, it leaves behind aspen and coniferous forests and opens up to increasingly magnificent views. At 5 miles you see the peak straight ahead. Another comfort, a vault toilet, is located near here. Use it rather than a bush to lessen the impact of the 200 to 400 hikers a day on this mountain.

Unfortunately, erosion damage caused by shortcutting the switchbacks is evident here. When your companions know that delicate alpine plants require many summers before flowering, they will respect the need to stay on the trail.

The option to hike to Emerald Lake, 1.5 miles from here, with a 500-foot descent, is best saved for the return trip from the summit.

At 6.1 miles a saddle is reached where views of Utah Lake and Provo, 6000 feet below, can be appreciated. Binoculars are useful here, especially if your home is in the area. From the saddle to the summit, the 1.5-mile trail takes a steep, steady ascent, veering slightly southwest of the ridge to reach the summit. Look for the small, open, metal, hutlike structure placed here by the county as a triangulation marker.

After a summit snack have your mountaineers determine north, south, east, and west by locating identifiable landmarks such as Utah Lake, Provo, and Salt Lake City. They'll enjoy seeing Deer Creek Reservoir in the east, the Great Salt Lake (if the air is clear) to the north, and in the south, the split between the Mount Timpanogos Wilderness and the Mount Nebo Range. Cirques (rounded valleys with steep walls occurring at upper ends of glaciers) and moraines (accumulations of rocks left by glaciers) are signs of glaciation that can be pointed out here.

Descending from the saddle, pass the first trail to Emerald Lake and continue another 0.1 mile to the second, easier trail on the right. After 0.4 mile cairns mark the route as it winds south then east before reaching Emerald Lake at 10,300 feet. Caution: Sliding down the perennial snowfield (not a glacier) above the lake can be extremely dangerous.

Keep your eyes open or binoculars poised for the herd of mountain goats commonly seen near the lake. During our visit they were too distant to photograph, but we could hear their catlike calls across the slopes. Presently there are two herds consisting of about forty goats in all. You may also spy one or more of the twenty-five bighorn sheep released in the Timpanogos area during January 2000.

From the lake take the leftmost trail from the outflow and continue descending, staying on the main trail as it passes a spur. Numerous campsites dot this lightly forested section of the Aspen Grove Trail. In fact, we recommend those preferring an overnight trek to the summit to camp at a site along this trail and climb the peak the next day. Campfires are no longer permitted here.

As the trail continues its descent via seemingly endless switchbacks, it meets a paved path near a waterfall. This flat, 1.25-mile final section serves as an ideal first-time trek for babes in strollers or backpacks. Families starting their hikes from the Aspen Grove Trail can use the waterfall as a turnaround point for the little kids and let the big ones hike on.

This hike requires a full day's commitment; start at about 7:00 A.M. and return by 6:00 P.M.

Toilet and water facilities are located at both trailheads.

12 STEWART FALLS TRAILS

Location	■ Uinta National Forest, Sundance Ski Area
Type	■ Day hike
Difficulty	■ Easy to moderate for children
Hikable	■ June to early October
Distance	■ From Theater in the Pines trailhead, 2 miles, one way; from Sundance Ski Area Ray's Lift, 3 miles, round trip
Starting Elevation	■ Theater in the Pines, 6850 feet; top of Ray's Lift, 7150 feet
High Point	■ 7200 feet
Maps	■ Trails Illustrated Wasatch Front, Strawberry Reservoir, and Uinta National Forest; USGS Aspen Grove; Sundance Recreation Map

www.sundanceresort.com/nature/hiking
Chairlift fee

From Provo travel east 6 miles on Provo Canyon Road (US 189), turning north (left) on the Alpine Scenic Highway (UT-92). Proceed 3 miles to the turnoff for the Sundance Ski Area, or continue another 3 miles to the Theater in the Pines picnic area on the left. Ample parking is provided at both trailheads.

Either way you approach these grand falls, the trails to them provide rewarding forest visits. Those starting at Sundance Ski Area ride Ray's lift, where magnificent views of the Mount Timpanogos Wilderness begin their looped hike, which descends via the Stewart Falls Trail. Hikers beginning at the Theater in the Pines trailhead enter tall, quiet spruce stands, spectacular maple glens, and fields of wildflowers en route to the 200-foot cascading waterfalls.

Hikers opting for the **Sundance route** begin their trip by riding Ray's Lift at the base area. Within 15 minutes they reach the top, where a hawk's-eye view of surrounding mountains and cirques captures everyone's attention. To the northeast is Heber Valley, and beyond it are the Uinta Mountains.

From the chairlift follow the trail as it traverses Top Gun Bowl through an old growth forest to junction #25 on the trail map. Turn

Two trails lead to views of Stewart Falls.

left and follow the trail across the meadow to junction #2 at the entrance of Dry Lakes Basin. In the clearings watch for Stewart Falls spilling its white cascade beneath the east face of Mount Timpanogos. The trail circles west and traverses to the base of the falls. Revegetation efforts may prohibit entering the falls area, so plan to make this site a visual, not tactual, treat.

To ride the chairlift back down, follow the same trail back to Ray's lift, which runs until 6:00 P.M. Be aware that the lift closes during storms.

Those completing the loop walk cross the creek and follow the Stewart Falls trail as it crosses junctions #34 and #23. Stay on the trail as it follows the creek through dry meadows and oak brush. Compare this with the north-facing slope's blanket of spruce and fir trees. Talk about why this occurs. The skier in your group knows the best powder conditions can be found on north-facing slopes. How does this explain the different plant types?

Turn right where the trail meets junction #22 and descends to the creek. Follow the trail to the bridge and across the road to the base of the lift.

For information on the lift schedule or to include a performance of Sundance's children's summer theater in your visit, call 801-225-4107.

The **Theater in the Pines** trailhead for Stewart Falls Trail begins at the Aspen Grove Trail and veers left, alongside the parking area. Massive Mount Timpanogos hovers high overhead, 5000 feet in the sky. It disappears from sight as the trail turns left up a short, steep hill. Don't let this section deter you; the terrain is gentle most of the way to the falls.

Rapid-fire rat-a-tat-tats of squirrels and chipmunks announce your passing through the dark, friendly confines of a fir forest. Sharing the forest floor here is thimbleberry, identified by its raspberry-like fruit and five-lobed leaves. Ripening in late July, these berries taste bland compared to their familial look-alike.

Views of the ski area's runs mark 0.5 mile, where the trail turns west into a forest medley of oak, fir, aspen, and maple. Note the various sizes of the maple trees' leaves. Find out if this occurs in oak and aspen leaves. Your youngsters may also notice matted grassy areas. Tell them a deer probably slept there recently.

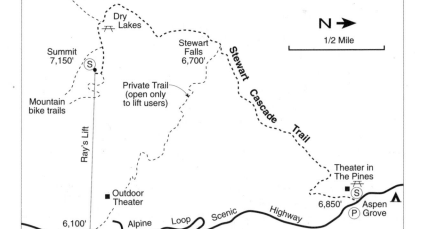

Ferns are another prolific forest-floor covering along this section. Spring hikers find the fronds curled tightly like snails, unfurling as they grow. In late summer, visitors will discover the undersides of the fern fronds are dotted with black sori, tiny packages of the plants' spores.

The minty aroma here is attributed to giant hyssop, or horsemint. Giant indeed, this 4- to 5-foot-tall lavender-headed flower can also be identified by rolling its square stem between fingers.

The trail continues into meadows, one of which is filled with cone-flowers. Lacking any ray flowers, these brown cones bob with the wind, seemingly aware that cows, deer, even elk or bear won't eat them. Ask, "What purpose do these plants have?"

After the trail crests to another view of Sundance Ski Area at 1.2 miles, it drops about 0.6 mile and leads to the first look at the falls. Follow the trail to the next viewpoint. Several steep, potentially dangerous trails to the falls web this area. It's advised to stay on the main trail before heading back on the same route.

Toilet and water facilities are available at both trailheads.

13 CASCADE SPRINGS

Location ■	Uinta National Forest
Type ■	Day hike
Difficulty ■	Easy for children
Hikable ■	May through October
Distance ■	0.6 mile of loop trails
Starting Elevation ■	6270 feet
High Point ■	6350 feet
Maps ■	Trails Illustrated Wasatch Front, Strawberry Reservoir, and Uinta National Forest; USGS Aspen Grove

Area includes 0.25-mile wheelchair-accessible trail

Follow the directions for Hike 12, Stewart Falls Trails, continuing about 4 miles past the Theater in the Pines picnic area to the crest of the Alpine Scenic Highway, to the intersection with Road 114 (Cascade Scenic Drive). Turn east (right) and drive 6.5 miles to the parking lot for Cascade Springs.

This interpreted oasis loops around a series of springs that cascade

Numerous trails weave around the wetland jewel of Cascade Springs.

and pool into a diversely vegetated area. Boardwalks span much of this delicate ecosystem, offering intimate views of a rarely seen environment. Wheelchair accessible, this fascinating trail is suitable for all hikers.

At the parking lot a map shows the area's three trails. The main trail starts from the gazebo on the left and includes a short, steep descent, which is unsuited for wheelchair users without well-muscled help. The wheelchair-accessible trail to the right follows a gentler route to the springs. Both trails meet in a grove of box elder trees adjacent to a creek. The Springs Loop trail begins at the bottom of the hill and circles a hillside gurgling with spring flow. Rest benches and paved trails or boardwalks are provided throughout.

Upon reaching the bottom of the hill, the two trails meet, then cross the creek. The boardwalk around the lower springs begins here. The signs along this state-of-the-art interpreted trail introduce terms such as microenvironments, plant succession, and adaptation and offer an understandable explanation of how the springs formed.

Young children may be more interested in kneeling down on the boardwalk to peer at trout darting in travertine pools beneath them or to examine the freckle-faced yellow monkey flower. Most kids simply explore this lush area on their own, then stop for close examination at a few of the interpretive signs. During our visit we learned a moose had been "camping out" at the springs for several weeks. Youngsters were excitedly looking for the moose's bed and the willow tops he had nibbled on.

 During the walk along the sun-exposed hillside of the Springs Loop, look for ways this area differs from the lower loop. Listen for birdsong. How many different springs can be counted? Does it seem possible that 7 million gallons of water flow from this source daily?

Ask kids their thoughts on why the Forest Service made these springs available for visitors of all abilities to see.

Toilet and water facilities are provided at the trailhead.

14 NEBO BENCH TRAIL

Location	▪	Uinta National Forest
Type	▪	Day hike
Difficulty	▪	Moderate for children
Hikable	▪	June to mid-October
Distance	▪	2.8 miles, one way
Starting Elevation	▪	9253 feet
High Point	▪	9800 feet
Maps	▪	Trails Illustrated Uinta National Forest; USGS Mona and Nebo Basin

 Take I-15 to Nephi, turning east on UT-132 (at the light on 100 North). Proceed 6.1 miles and turn left on the Nebo Loop Road. Follow this road 12 miles to the Monument trailhead on the west (left) side of the road, where ample parking is provided.

Wilderness solitude and pristine beauty envelop hikers on this eas-ily accessed trail along Mount Nebo (11,928 feet), the highest peak of the Wasatch Range. Visiting this little-used area entails walking through a variety of forest environments, including basins blanketed with wildflowers and grassy meadows walled by mountainous terrain. Superb views of the San Pitch Mountains to the south and Nebo's two sister peaks elevate this hike to "really cool" status, according to a pair of 12-year-old hikers we met here. The first 2.8 miles of the 8.5-mile trail is described here for day hikers.

The trailhead is located at the parking lot's southern end, with the register box 30 yards beyond. Be sure to sign the register; your signa-ture helps to justify more funds for the area's maintenance. Follow the fork in the trail, turning right where you see a sign for Mount Nebo and Andrews Canyon.

At this junction the trail gently descends, contouring through as-pen stands for 1 mile. Flowers of every color grab most every hiker's interest along this riparian section of the trail. Giant hyssop, best known for its minty smell, can also be identified by its height, which reaches 5 feet, its shaggy-mop lavender flower, and its square stem. Another tall show-off is purple larkspur, distinguished for its tubular spur at the flower's base. Probably the most common, but no less pretty, flower is the sticky geranium, with its pink petals thinly veined in dark purple. Unlike its purple companion, larkspur, which is poi-sonous to livestock, geraniums are favorite forage for deer, elk, bear, and moose. When kids hear your outrageous or descriptive names for the flowers, they'll be inspired to create their own titles.

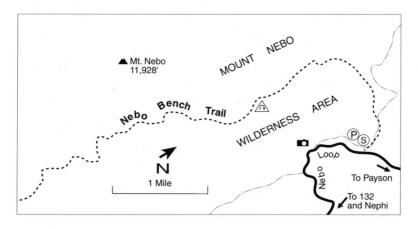

Golden mantled ground squirrels look similar to chipmunks but are larger.

But do look up and west for views of Mount Nebo's cirques, circular gouges in its side that are reminders of the glaciers that once carved this area. During heavy snowfall winters, these depressions may hold snow throughout the year.

After crossing a creek at 0.8 mile and entering another aspen forest, take note of the trees' bark, where names and interesting shapes are carved in the trunk 15 feet up. These "arborglyphs" are probably the historic etchings made by shepherds on horseback more than 50 years ago. The trail then enters a meadow where tall grasses reach the shoulders of many a young hiker.

At 1.4 miles avoid the unmaintained trail. Take the high route to the right, which crosses another creek and begins a climb up Nebo's bench—a flat, barely discernible ridge on which this massive mountain appears to sit. The ragged, wind-worn spruce trees here are pioneers in a harsh environment. For their brave attempt at establishing tree growth here, they're given the name "banner trees."

Your companions will understand why the name was given when you point out a tree shaped like a flagpole with a banner flapping to one side. Ask them, "From which direction does the wind blow here?" Discuss with your group why it's hard for plants to root and thrive near a mountaintop. *Krummholz*, the German word for "crooked wood," is often used to describe these hardy, wind-sculpted trees.

Continue walking along this windy ridge, enjoying the views of Mount Nebo and its two sister peaks. Ask kids to point out the highest peak in the group. A turnaround point can be anywhere along here; however, a logical place is at 2.7 miles, where the trail begins descending. The San Pitch Mountains come into view directly south at this point, as does a rocky tree-slide area east of the trail in an otherwise forested area.

Toilet facilities are provided at the trailhead. No water is available here.

15

OGDEN NATURE CENTER TRAILS

Location ■	Ogden
Type ■	Day hike
Difficulty ■	Easy for children
Hikable ■	Year-round
Distance ■	0.25 mile to 1.5 miles, one way
Starting Elevation ■	4275 feet
High Point ■	4275 feet
Map ■	Ogden Nature Center brochure

www.ogdennaturecenter.com
Admission fee
Wheelchair accessible

From I-15 take exit 347, 12th Street, and proceed east 0.5 mile. Ogden Nature Center is located at 966 West 12th Street, on the north side of the road. Ample parking is provided.

A set of trails looping around a tapestry of marshes, meadows, and ponds allows youngsters endless opportunities to discover wildlife in their natural habitats. Many parents report their children enjoy seeing the center's rehabilitated hawks and owls or examining snakes and turtles housed at the interpretive center as much as their hike around the 127-acre nature reserve.

From the parking lot follow the foot trail canopied by Russian olive trees to the interpretive center—a visit here being the best way to begin the hike. The center's entrance area is invitingly landscaped with a lily pond edged by commonly available trees, shrubs, and flowers while a small waterfall adds a gentle tone to the setting.

Once inside the center the tone turns to intrigue. During our visit we watched a gopher snake swallow a mouse provided by the volunteer animal handler. Tarantulas, owls, and lizards are among the caged animals we watched during feeding time. Special animal and insect exhibits are ever changing at the Center, promising a new experience for repeat visitors.

At certain times of the year the Center's naturalist guides, most of whom are volunteers, are on hand to show children safe ways to handle the caged animals. The guides are also trained to serve as interpreters

A rehabilitated tortoise receives special attention at the Ogden Nature Center.

for any size group. Advance arrangements (call 801-621-7595) and a small fee are requested.

Before leaving the Center pick up the "Habitat Trail Guide," a booklet that guides visitors, big and small, along the Habitat Trail. This 0.25-mile, fully accessible trail weaves through four different habitats: aquatic, riparian, upland, and wetland with "observation stops" along the way. The booklet describes the characteristics of each habitat and suggests a "just for kids" activity at each stop.

Follow the trail in a counterclockwise direction, first stopping at the bridge over the Plain City Canal—a wetland habitat. Summer visitors may enjoy watching dragonflies zip around the cattails. The trail continues along the canal before it crosses between an open field and a forested area, also called an ecotone. The trail then enters a riparian area via a bridge over the canal. Just beyond here, the longer, nonaccessible portion of the 1.5 mile trail begins. This graveled foot trail enters a tunnel of trees leading to Blackbird Pond, which is edged by large, old trees.

Leaving the riparian area of the pond, the trail then enters an upland, an open area dominated by teasel, a 4- to 6-foot-tall plant with a menacing barbed head. Children are fascinated to know that this overwhelming plant was actually brought here by pioneers planning to use the quilled top for carding wool or brushing hides. Some reports say they were used to comb hair! It's best not to try using one this way.

The sounds of birds calling and frogs croaking signal your arrival to Teal Pond, a wetland attraction for Canada geese, great blue herons, ducks, and western painted turtles. Red-winged blackbirds, easy for your youngest bird-watcher to identify, nest in the marshes here. Follow the trail to return to the interpretive center.

Allow time to visit the birds of prey housed in the Ogden Nature Center's mews, located southeast of the interpretive center. Injured birds or those unable to hunt in the wild, like the red-tailed hawk, golden eagle, prairie falcon, and northern goshawk, are on display with permission from the U.S. Fish & Wildlife and the Utah Division of Wildlife.

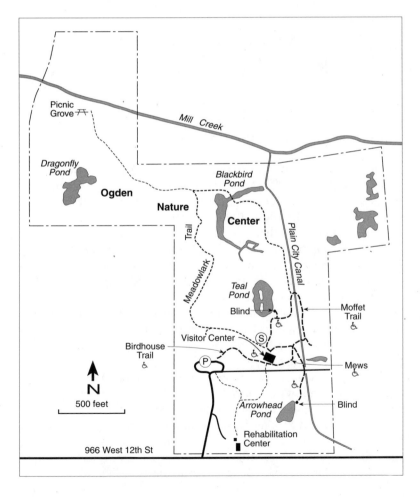

Ogden Nature Center is open from 10 A.M. to 4 P.M. Monday through Saturday. Call 801-621-7595 for information on extended summer hours.

Water and restroom facilities are available at the center.

16 NORTH ARM OF THE PINEVIEW RESERVOIR

Location ■	Ogden
Type ■	Day hike
Difficulty ■	Easy for children
Hikable ■	May through October
Distance ■	0.5 mile total, loops and one-way trail
Starting Elevation ■	4890 feet
High Point ■	4890 feet
Map ■	None

Wheelchair accessible with support

 From the junction of UT-39 and UT-203 in Ogden, drive east 7.2 miles on UT-39 to UT-158 at the Pineview Reservoir Dam. Turn left and drive 3.8 miles to the North Arm parking area on the right, near the North Fork of the Ogden River.

This trail network through the Pineview Reservoir's North Arm gives kids an opportunity for dry-land exploration of a wetland. Hundreds of habitats can be discovered here. The likelihood of seeing the area's inhabitants is high for edge-of-light hikers—those visiting during the sunrise and sunset hours.

The trailhead map shows the area's three short trails; the right and middle trails form loops that connect, while the left trail parallels a marsh. A platform for viewing the reservoir is planned for the end-point of the marsh trail.

Beginning the habitat hunt on the right fork, watch for birds darting from the willow thickets. Yellow warblers and white-crowned sparrows are common summer residents here.

 Those who find a fingertip-size swelling, called a gall, on a willow branch have discovered the home for an insect's larvae. When laying eggs, the mother produces enzymes that cause a plant's stem section to grow abnormally. As the young insect matures, it literally eats itself

Teasel towers over most hikers at the North Arm of the Pineview Reservoir.

out of house and home. Notice if other galls appear to be dwellings of the same insect variety.

Where the right fork veers left, tall cottonwoods draw attention skyward. Look for nests of sticks poised in the crotches of dead limbs. Lower down on the trunk keen-eyed observers may see a woodpecker's 2-inch-wide entry hole to its nest.

Near here the trail forks in several directions. A few short paths branch off the middle fork and lead directly to a unique habitat. The main trails circle this riparian zone and return to the origin.

Children who explore this wildlife domain on their own discover the quiet satisfaction of observing nature. Remind them to stay on the trail and to remain quiet. Deer and moose are drawn to the site for food and water.

After the group gathers at the trailhead again, walk the left trail along the marsh. The lake level directly affects the extent of the marsh.

The marsh music along this trail is worth tuning in to. Try identifying the instruments. Experiment with listening skills by blindfolding a hiker who is guided by a leader. Compare the marsh sounds with those heard along the right and middle trails.

This short trail leads to a viewing area of the Pineview Reservoir. Return via the same route.

No toilet or water facilities are provided at the trailhead.

17 AMERICAN WEST HERITAGE CENTER

Location	■ Logan
Type	■ Day hike
Difficulty	■ Easy for children
Hikable	■ June through August, plus special Saturdays in winter and spring
Distance	■ 0.5 mile or more, round trip
Starting Elevation	■ 4500 feet
High Point	■ 4500 feet
Map	■ American West Heritage Center brochure

www.americanwestcenter.org
Admission fee

The entrance to the American West Heritage Center is 6 miles southwest of Logan on US 89-91. Parking is provided at the north entrance.

Walks to the barn to milk the cow, to the summer kitchen to churn butter, or to the village to make candles are some of the hiking experiences available at the American West Heritage Center, a working family farm that has preserved a slice of the Cache Valley's past. Utah State University students and volunteers operate the farm using horse-drawn farming implements, copying the methods used in 1917. Children who join the day's events, be it turning the cider-press wheel or riding the hay wagon to the barley field, get a fun lesson in history. For those who prefer strolling around a farm, 68 of the farm's 159 acres offer access to meadows rimmed by streams and the Wellsville Mountains.

A map available at the information kiosk near the parking area shows the farm's layout. However, most kids linger around the large shed where vintage tractors and a tall steam-powered thrasher sit protected from the rain and snow. Direct questions about the farm and its tools to any of the workers, identified by their turn-of-the-century clothing.

The farm's major source of power—1800-pound Shire workhorses—draws special attention, especially if your visit coincides with horse harnessing or pulling. Children are equally intrigued by the farmhouse, root cellar, and smokehouse. While visiting the farmhouse, kids enjoy sitting on the straw-filled ticks (mattresses) in the children's bedrooms and discovering how food was "put up" in the days before refrigeration.

The Victory Garden, the main source of food for the family at home during World War II, still supplies about 1600 quarts of fruit and vegetables a year. Depending on the time of your visit, children may participate in planting, weeding, harvesting, or canning at the farm.

Special events, like Baby Animal Day, Apple Harvest Day, cabin raising, and sheep shearing are among the themes planned for Saturdays from April through December. Those who miss Saturday's events can sample them during the following week.

For more information contact the American West Heritage Center, formerly known as the Jensen Living Historical Farm, at 1-800-225-FEST or 435-797-1143.

18 RIVERSIDE NATURE TRAIL

Location ■	Logan River Canyon
Type ■	Day hike
Difficulty ■	Moderate for children
Hikable ■	May through October
Distance ■	1.5 miles, one way
Starting Elevation ■	5020 feet
High Point ■	5084 feet
Map ■	Bridgerland Hiking Trails brochure

From Logan drive 4.3 miles east on US 89 to the Spring Hollow Campground road on the right. Drive across the Logan River to the restroom and parking area on the left. The trailhead is across the campground road, near the lower picnic area. The trail destination at Guinavah Campground is 1 mile east on US 89. Turn right just past the campground entry and proceed left 0.1 mile, following signs for the amphitheater. Turn right at the parking area; the trailhead is on the right.

Starting at Spring Hollow Campground, this interpreted trail follows the Logan River's gentle course through marshes, meadows, and forests. Sightings of a porcupine-chewed tree trunk or a dipper bobbing along the shore enliven the hike for children and grown-ups alike. A large Forest Service sign describing riparian zones marks the trailhead.

Bordering the first portion of the trail is burdock, with its showy elephant-ear leaves and bristly seedhead. Undoubtedly, this prolific plant's burrs will demonstrate their seed-dispersing ability by clinging to a hiker's sock, or worse, his or her hair! Stop to examine a burdock burr to see where the inventor of Velcro got his idea. Compare the Velcro found on your hiking gear with the natural hook found here.

As the creek follows a marshy area, pay attention to birdcalls. Is one bird communicating with another? What might be the warning?

Crimson patches on sleek, black wings easily identify red-winged blackbirds, frequent visitors and breeders at marshes. Their liquid "konk-la-ree" call advises the listening hiker that water is ahead. If you happen to see a red-winged blackbird perched on a cattail, watch its wing movement. The bird's mating display in spring months includes spreading its wings while singing. Two birds flashing their wings wildly are battling.

Pausing at a stream means "feeling nature" for this hiker.

Along this section, walk quietly and look for animal tracks in the mud, a feather floating on the water, a stump of tree gnawed on by a beaver. Discuss with your companions why animal signs are more easily found here than along the trail's first section.

Climbing above the river into a forest of maples and firs, ask children if they see any plants here that were growing near the river. What makes this area different from the river's edge? This is a good spot to watch ducks, perhaps to see, as I did, a mother teal and her ducklings.

A rest bench near the Logan River's clear waters provides an ideal place to watch trout dart from shadow to shadow. Explain to your beginning anglers that when a fish surfaces, it feeds on insects. And just like humans, they have taste buds. Knowing these fish have taste buds, located both inside and outside their mouths, makes it easy to understand why trout are selective about the flies anglers toss at them.

Just beyond here look across the river and halfway up the canyon wall for the Wind Cave. It was formed as water and wind eroded a pocket in the limestone. Tell your companions the rock wall they are looking at once was ocean bottom. Over millions of years the soft sediment hardened into limestone.

Along the trail here watch for trees scarred by two different animals. What might they be? Cone-shaped tree stumps are the beaver's trademark. The leaves and stem of the beaver-toppled tree, stashed in a riverbank den, were probably the hibernating animal's winter foods. The gnawed-off bark of a ponderosa pine indicates a porcupine dined on the tree's sweet inner bark. In winter the porcupine feeds on tree bark, while its summer diet consists of grasses. Was the snow deep when the porcupine peeled away the tree bark? How can we tell?

Dippers frequently perch on rocks along the river. Beginning bird-watchers readily identify the dull gray bird by its bobbing motion. Also known as a water ouzel, it dives underwater to feed on insects and fish. Count the seconds the dipper stays dipped.

Listen for different birdcalls while walking along the river. Song sparrows defend their territory with three or four short, clear notes followed by a buzzy "toweee" call. If you see a brown-gray bird with a streaked white chest pumping its tail in quick, short flights, the song sparrow is giving you further warning that you've invaded its territory. Name other creatures that have property to defend here.

The final portion of this section of the Riverside Trail rises above the river into a mixed forest of bigtooth maple, juniper, and fir. The

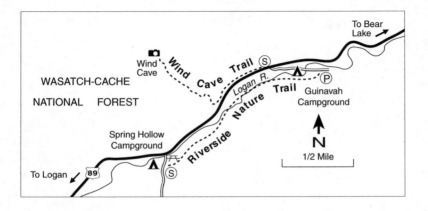

0.1 mile descent to Guinavah Campground is steep. Careful, slow stepping may be required of little ones and their big companions. Toilet and water facilities are available at both campgrounds.

19 WIND CAVE

Location ■	Logan Canyon
Type ■	Day hike
Difficulty ■	Moderate for children
Hikable ■	Late April to early November
Distance ■	1.7 miles, one way
Starting Elevation ■	5100 feet
High Point ■	6010 feet
Maps ■	USGS Mount Elmer; Bridgerland Hiking Trails brochure

 From Logan, starting at Lady Bird Park (0.5 mile east of Utah State University), drive 7 miles on Logan Canyon Road (US 89). The trailhead is on the left, 100 yards before the entrance to the Guinavah

An insider's view of Logan Canyon from Wind Cave.

Campground on the right. Parking is provided in the graveled area alongside the road.

As one of the first trails in the area to open and the last to close, Wind Cave is a spring and fall favorite. Spring wildflowers and maple trees ablaze in the fall are but a few of the attractions this popular trail offers. Summer hikers to the Wind Cave should begin their hike early in the day and bring plenty of water.

From the parking lot the trail ascends a rocky slope, quickly losing the sound of cars racing below.

A sound to be very alert for here is that of a rattler. Though more often seen than heard, rattlers will not attack unless provoked. If you are lucky enough to spot one, keep a safe distance (4 yards or more) when trying to see the rattles at the end of its tail. (In rattlesnake terri- tory, remind children to place their hands and feet only in areas they can see; surprised rattlesnakes are often aggressive!) The rattles con- sist of several interlocking coils, with each coil representing a molt, not 1 year as is commonly believed. Because snakes molt, or shed their skin, more than once a year, and strings of rattles often break in as little as 6 months, it's rare to find a twelve-ringed rattler in the wild.

As the trail reaches the top of the telephone pole at 0.2 mile, look across the canyon to see the China Wall. Named after the ancient 1500-mile-long fortification in northern China, this rock formation continues halfway up Logan Canyon on both sides of the river. The Crimson Trail's switchbacks, climbing 800 feet above the riverbed, can also be seen in this limestone wall across the highway.

After a slight descent at 0.4 mile, the trail bends right and heads up a canyon draw flocked by big-toothed maples. Remain on the main trail as it heads northwest; the Wind Cave tucked in the China Wall on this side of the canyon can be seen along here. Resist cutting across the switchbacks here because doing so causes serious erosion.

While continuing the climb up the base of the China Wall, point out the dramatic differences in vegetation on both canyon sides. Why is the north-facing canyon thickly blanketed in *coni*ferous (*cone*-bearing) trees, while sage, maple, and juniper thinly cover the south side?

As the trail reaches the top of the China Wall, make sure little ones who tend to wander are close at hand.

Maintain adult supervision near and in the cave, which is actually a series of alcoves 20 feet high formed by water and wind erosion.

Observant hikers may find crinoid fossils embedded in the lime- stone boulders here and along the China Wall. Deposited millions of years ago, when northern Utah was a warm, shallow sea, a crinoid is actually the broken skeleton of a sea lily, an animal similar to corals found in today's oceans. Can you find other reminders of the area's ancient past?

Return via the same trail.

Water and toilet facilities are located at Guinavah Campground.

20 TONY GROVE NATURE TRAIL

Location ■	Logan Canyon, 27 miles east of Logan
Type ■	Day hike
Difficulty ■	Easy
Hikable ■	June to mid-October
Distance ■	1.25 miles, loop
Starting Elevation ■	8050 feet
High Point ■	8055 feet
Map ■	None

From Logan drive 30 miles east on US 89 (Logan Canyon Scenic Byway) to the turnoff for Tony Grove Campground—milepost 393.8. Turn left (west) on this paved road and proceed 7 miles to the Fisherman's Loop, past the campground turnoff where parking for hikers is provided. The campground here provides 37 campsites.

Formed by glaciers, fringed by wildflowers, and frequented by wildlife, it's no surprise that the Tony Grove Lake is considered the "crown jewel" of the Bear River Range. As the trail edges the lake, it crosses marshes via boardwalks, threads clusters of glacially tumbled boulders, and weaves through towering stands of purple monkshood. Wildlife sightings here may include the petite pika or the massive moose. For more information on the glacial beginnings of this lake, see the trail description for White Pine Lake, Hike 22. As for its nominal beginnings, Tony Grove was so named because of its popularity with Logan's "tony" or high-living uptown set during the 1880s and 1890s.

From the parking lot head north (right), circling the lake in a counterclockwise direction. Tall stands of horsemint border this section of the trail, nodding their lavender-to-white shaggy flower heads. Stop to feel the plant's square stem—a sure sign that it belongs to the mint family with its 5000 different species worldwide.

Logs and boardwalks encourage hands-and-knees investigations along Tony Grove Lake.

A boardwalk spans the lake's marsh area, allowing kids and parents to hands-and-knees investigate this secluded section of the lake. Trampled or torn plant life may indicate a moose had entered the lake to cool off or graze on willows and grasses.

A wildflower wonderland flourishes along the lake's marshy shores. Bright red fireweed, purple monkshood, rosy paintbrush, and the white umbrella-like flower cluster of the cow parsnip tower over many hikers' heads. It's fun to play a game of matching clothing colors to flower colors in this kaleidoscopic environment.

Late summer visitors notice bunches of miniature red apples found on bushy plants near the lake. These berries are the fruit of the mountain ash, providing food for birds and mammals through the winter.

As the trail weaves through the boulders tumbled from the lake's cliff side, listen for the high-pitched whistle of a pika. This small, round-bodied relative of the rabbit spends most of its days gathering bundles of grasses as foods for the winter. To see a pika, sit quietly and watch for quick movements among the rocks. The sound of a babbling brook or a hummingbird's whirring may also be noticed during this quiet pause. During our visit we watched the lake's beaver lodge, hoping to see movement in its surrounding waters. Your chances of seeing this largely nocturnal animal increase during the sunset to dark hours.

As the trail loops around the lake's southern end, it enters the quiet darkness of an old forest. Point out that few plants grow under the spruce trees here and why this has occurred.

Continue on the trail as it completes the loop back to the parking lot. Toilet and water facilities are available at the campground.

21 MOUNT NAOMI

Location ▪	Logan Canyon
Type ▪	Day hike
Difficulty ▪	Moderate to challenging for children
Hikable ▪	July to October
Distance ▪	3.2 miles, one way or longer
Starting Elevation ▪	8043 feet
High Point ▪	9980 feet
Maps ▪	USGS Naomi Peak; Bridgerland Hiking Trails brochure

See directions for Hike 20, Tony Grove Nature Trail.

Climbing the highest peak in the Bear River Range is an adventurous day hike even for experienced hikers. The rewards come early and late in this trail, as it winds through flowered meadows and forested slopes to a phenomenal full-circle view of northern Utah's mountains and valleys.

Beginning at the Tony Grove Fisherman's Loop, the trail to Mount Naomi shares the route to White Pine Lake for 0.25 mile. A sign here directs mountain climbers to the left, lake visitors to the right. Don't be misled by the prominent peak ahead of you. Mount Naomi makes its first appearance near the final ascent.

Within the first 0.1 mile the trail enters a forest medley of fir, spruce, aspen, and pine. While the aspen is obvious, the other three coniferous trees require close-up examination to name. Find the tree with the most bendable branches. It's a limber pine, whose needles come packaged in fives. The fir's needles are flat and flexible. Notice how the white fir's cones stand up. A Douglas fir's cones hang down. How does the bark on the two fir trees differ? If you find a spruce tree, you'll notice its needles aren't friendly; rather, they are stiff and spiky.

As the trail crests open meadows, it retraces the route glaciers took as they carved this region, dragging boulders along their path. Look for large piles of rocks called moraines left along a glacier's edges. Count on seeing the best wildflower display here in late July and early August.

You may be sharing the trail with four-legged inhabitants of this wilderness region. Watch for tracks in the trail. Although moose

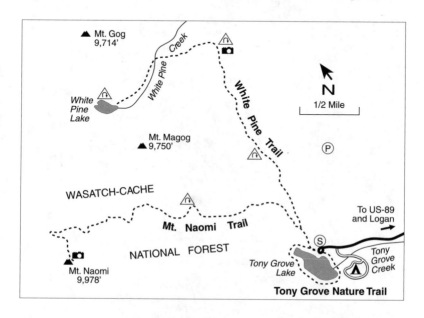

sightings are common around Tony Grove Lake, remember the summer diet for moose is primarily cottonwoods and willows. It's unlikely they'll roam far from a reliable source.

As the trail ascends to a rocky ledge above a basin at 1.25 miles, notice that fewer trees are taking root in the meager soil. At 1.9 miles you reach a saddle where mountains to the north fill the horizon. Continue crossing the rock ridge to another edge of a rock basin, where Mount Naomi comes into view at 2.1 miles.

The trail ascends rocky mountain-goat country where limber pine and Englemann spruce wear the windblown look of alpine trees with-

The view northwest from Mount Naomi

standing the harshest of temperatures and winds. Their small stature is deceptive. A tree with a 3-inch-wide trunk rooted at tree line (10,000 feet) could be more than 300 years old. The same tree planted in a moist, subalpine zone could grow to a trunk size ten times that. How old might these trees be? Do limber pine or spruce appear to be the tree pioneers of this alpine terrain?

Clark's nutcrackers patrol this terrain in search of their favorite food, pine nuts. If you see or hear one of these bold, noisy gray birds here or at the campground, it may look like it has the mumps. It's not contagious; a nutcracker can carry over 100 seeds in its throat pouches.

At 2.9 miles you reach the saddle of the highest ridge, where the Mount Naomi Wilderness begins. A sign marks Cherry Peak to the right, Mount Naomi close by to the left. The trail to the summit may be a bit faint, but it is well worth the effort. Landmarks in all directions are a delight to identify.

Return via the same trail.

Toilet and water facilities are available at the campground.

22 WHITE PINE LAKE

Location ■	Logan Canyon
Type ■	Day hike or overnight backpack
Difficulty ■	Moderate for children
Hikable ■	July through October
Distance ■	4 miles, one way
Starting Elevation ■	8000 feet
High Point ■	8800 feet
Maps ■	USGS Naomi Peak; Bridgerland Hiking Trails brochure

See directions for Tony Grove Nature Trail, Hike 20.

Nestled in a glacially carved limestone basin, White Pine Lake serves as a rewarding destination for family day trips or beginners' backpacking adventures. Hikers enroute to the lake follow the crest of several glacial basins where wildlife sightings are common, especially if this popular trail is explored midweek or during prime moose feeding hours (early morning or early evening).

A yellow-bellied marmot alert to intruders

The trailhead is located at the Fisherman's Loop's north side. It shares the route with the Mount Naomi trail up a canyon draw for 0.25 mile, to where a sign directs White Pine walkers to the right, Mount Naomi hikers to the left.

From the sign the trail initially climbs before leveling out along a glacially scoured basin. Point out the large pile of rocks, or moraine, on the left. Explain that glaciers over the last 2 million years packed the area's valleys, pushing rocks as they moved. In some places huge boulders gouged the path, resulting in deep lakes such as Tony Grove Lake. When the glaciers retreated, or melted, they left behind their grinding tools, now called moraines. The rocks that stubble the path you are walking remain as evidence of the great glaciers that carved and sculpted the mountain flanks during the last ice age more than 10,000 years ago.

Following the trail's northerly route cresting glacial basins, be sure to stay on the main trail. Several spurs have been blocked off to prevent further erosion to this area popular with both two- and four-footed animal species. Remember, the human animal is a visitor here. Talk and walk softly where wildlife reside.

At 1.25 miles the trail edges another large, shallow basin, which can serve as a turnaround point for those interested in a short hike.

Continuing through aspen glens and fir forests, the trail meets a narrow, glacially carved crease in the terrain, climbing its east-facing side to the trail's high point at 2.8 miles.

The two prominent knobs viewed from here and at White Pine Lake below you are Mount Magog on the left and Mount Gog on the right. They were named for Old Testament biblical characters from the Book of Ezekiel.

The trail switchbacks, then heads west on its 1.2-mile, 400-foot descent to White Pine Lake. Before reaching the lake the trail levels near a creek crossing and meets the sign directing horse traffic to the right and hikers to the left. Just before the lake, a sign indicates toilets and camping to the right. To simply view the lake, follow the trail straight ahead. Please stay on the trails, remembering that high-altitude plants have only a few days in the year to root, grow, and possibly flower. Plans to protect this heavily impacted fragile environment include banning campfires and designating dispersed campsites.

How does this lake compare to Tony Grove Lake? Point out that both have a limestone wall edging one side. Do they appear to be the same size? The same depth? (The deepest points measured in 1962 were 18 feet for White Pine and 50 feet for Tony Grove.) Explain that they are cirque lakes. Thousands of years ago, a glacier formed here from accumulated snow. As it retreated, it left behind this rock-rimmed basin filled with water. Could the water filling the lake still be glacier water? Why? Find the inflow and outflow streams.

To return, follow the same trail back. During breath-catching stops near the summit, stop to examine the needles of the area's namesake, the white pine, more accurately called white fir. Look for examples of three different coniferous trees—pine, fir, and spruce.

Toilet and water facilities are located in the campground.

23 LIMBER PINE TRAIL

Location ▪ Wasatch-Cache National Forest, Logan
Type ▪ Day hike
Difficulty ▪ Easy for children
Hikable ▪ May through October
Distance ▪ 1 mile, loop
Starting Elevation ▪ 7780 feet
High Point ▪ 7960 feet
Maps ▪ USGS Garden City; Bridgerland Hiking Trails brochure

From Logan drive 35 miles east on US 89 to the Limber Pine rest area on the right (south), just past the Bear Lake summit. Ample parking is provided here.

Only a few short, easy trails lead hikers through as many intriguing forests with stunning viewpoints as does the Limber Pine Trail.

A family poses with a "granddaddy" limber pine.

Starting from a highway picnic site, the recently rerouted trail loops through a variety of forests on its route to what was once considered the area's oldest and largest living landmark, a limber pine tree. For families traveling east of Logan, this trail has become a favorite lunch and leg-stretching spot.

In addition to the interpretive signs that highlight the natural features of the Limber Pine Nature Trail, the following suggestions may heighten the hike's fun factor for kids and provide them with an opportunity to gain a better understanding of and appreciation for the environment.

- Get to know the trees of this cool, dark forest by feeling their needles. Discover how the *flat*, *flexible* needles of a *fir* tree won't roll between fingertips, while the *spruce* tree's *square*, *spiky* needle will. Compare cones (please don't remove a cone from the tree), noticing which tree points its cones up, and which tree lets them hang down. Tell kids to find a tree with "snake tongues" all over its cones. No worry, the tongues are actually the three-branched bracts of a Douglas fir cone.

- Look for "restaurant rocks," the name we give to rocks and tree stumps that look like the picnic table of a chipmunk or squirrel. Bits of pinecones, including their cores and scales, are all that remain of a forest dweller's efforts to eat the cone's seeds.

- Between signposts 3 and 4, "chair trees" grow on either side of the trail. Heavy snow loads formed these growing aspen trees into a shape that invites some hikers to sit on them. However, ask your young climbers to try their skills on less handicapped trees.

- Look for evidence of another forest animal's meal—rows of tiny holes drilled in tree trunks. Sapsucking woodpeckers bore these holes, which drip a sap that traps its insect meal. Explore ideas of how the bird removes the sap from the tree using its long tongue.

- Near signpost 8 a very large Douglas fir fell in 1993 providing a fine example of decomposition. Trace the tunnels made by ants and beetles under the tree's bark. Feel the tree's trunk, finding where it has softened and is joining the soil around it.

Ancient branches of a limber pine surround a young treeclimber.

- At the valley overlook near signpost 9, point out the sinks, or depressions. Explain that under the blanket of grasses and sage lies a layer of rock that formed 400 million years ago, when oceans covered Utah. As water dripped through cracks in this layer, the rock dissolved, causing large sections to sink.

- Upon reaching the giant limber pine cluster at signpost 10, ask kids to count the separate trees here. At one time this cluster was considered the oldest and largest living limber pine tree. Look for other limber pines grouped together. A large white fir stands nearby. Compare its needles and branches to the limber pine's. The giant limber pine tree attracts the climber in every kid and serves as a great setting for family photographs.

- As the trail heads downhill watch for 2-inch holes in the thick loose bedding under trees. Golden-mantled ground squirrels or chipmunks have stashed their winter cache in these middens, the holes being their entrances. Talk about what foods a squirrel might keep here.

- Near signpost 12, Bear Lake shimmers blue in the distance. Tell kids to imagine what it was like here nearly 200 years ago when mountain men, Indians, trappers, and traders gathered at the lake for a "rendezvous." Furs were traded for supplies and hunters showed off their skills in rowdy contests.

The trail circles back to the trailhead.

Toilet and water facilities are provided at this trailhead.

Opposite: *Every hiker should know and avoid this plant – poison ivy!*

UINTA AND CENTRAL

24 CRYSTAL LAKE LOOP

Location ∎	Mirror Lake Area, Wasatch-Cache National Forest
Type ∎	Day hike
Difficulty ∎	Easy for children
Hikable ∎	Mid-June to mid-October
Distance ∎	3 miles, loop
Starting Elevation ∎	10,000 feet
High Point ∎	10,160 feet
Maps ∎	Trails Illustrated Wasatch Front and Strawberry Reservoir; USGS Mirror Lake; High Uintas Wilderness map; Kamas Ranger District "4 Great Day Hikes" brochure

Recreational use fee for all vehicles parked in the Mirror Lake Demonstration area. No charge for traveling UT-150.

 From Kamas drive 26 miles east on the Mirror Lake Highway, UT-150. Turn left on the Trial Lake Road and proceed 1 mile west on the road past Trial Lake to the turnoff for Crystal Lake. The trailhead is located to the right of the horse loading ramp. Ample parking is available in the paved lot.

This easy access to the Uinta's Lakes Country edges creeks to wade or investigate, lakes to fish or contemplate, and views to appreciate. Newcomers to backpacking find this route an ideal introduction, generally planning their hike to Meadow Lake, 5 miles beyond the destination for this half-day walk. Groups with two cars like having a second car at the Trial Lake parking area, which is closer to the trail's end.

The trailhead sign introduces you to destinations along the Notch Mountain Trail (the first portion of the hike): Wall Lake, 1 mile; Ibantik Lake, 4 miles; Meadow Lake, 5 miles. The trail immediately enters the dark quiet of a spruce-fir forest. Two timid lakes hiding behind trees on either side of the trail support a lily pad community.

Notch Mountain is viewed straight ahead, while Reids Peak, the pyramid-shaped dome, and Bald Mountain, the longer mass of rocks, appear on the right. The trail continues following a very easy grade through the coniferous forest for less than a mile. Then the sound of

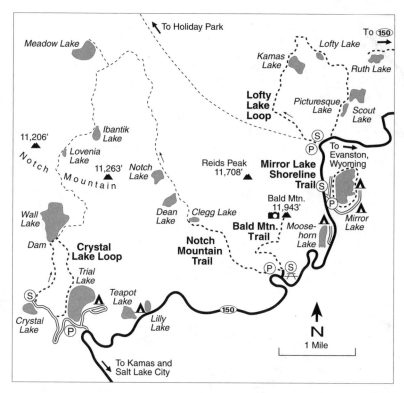

water splashing quickens everyone's pace and soon a creek with water splashing along its rock runway becomes visible on the right, as does the wall it spills from. Cross the dam that spans Wall Lake's outflow. As your group walks past the wall of rocks retaining the lake's water, they'll see the source of its name.

Before turning right at the sign for Trial Lake Loop, stop for lunch or wading at Wall Lake. A sandy shore near the trail encourages hikers to take off their boots and rest their feet.

As the trail descends gradually from Wall Lake, point out how the creek flows quietly as it meanders along the flat sections of the forest floor. Known as a riparian zone, the area is lush with plant life flourishing in rich, wet soils along the creek. When children count the different flowers or note how tall the grasses and shrubs are here, they may recall the first half of the hike being much drier, with fewer plants, and certainly no creeks to cross. Ask them to explain why they think the two areas are so different.

Children enjoy the hike's latter half because logs for balancing on span the creek in several places. Be sure to avoid play in marshy areas, where many plants and insects suffer the impact of feet, no matter how little they are.

If you warn your little ones about herds of little red elephants, they'll giggle with you, as our 2-year-old did, when you show them this pink, elephant-headed flower. Also watch for the sturdy, long footbridge at about 1.6 miles, where youngsters can hang their feet over the edge and launch their leaf boats "downriver."

At 2 miles little anglers may want to venture off the trail to where the rocky banks of Trial Lake boast hundreds of couch-sized rocks to fish from.

After passing the lake, the trail veers to the right and passes two privately owned cabins before meeting the road to the Trial Lake parking lot on the left and the Crystal Lake parking lot on the right. If your car is parked at Crystal Lake, the driver will need to walk about 1 mile up the road to the trailhead.

A vault toilet is available at the trailhead. No water facilities are provided.

25　NOTCH MOUNTAIN TRAIL

Location ■	Mirror Lakes Area, Wasatch-Cache National Forest
Type ■	Day hike
Difficulty ■	Easy for children
Hikable ■	Late June through September
Distance ■	1.5 miles or more, one way
Starting Elevation ■	10,715 feet
Ending Elevation ■	10,500 feet
Maps ■	Trails Illustrated Wasatch Front and Strawberry Reservoir; USGS Mirror Lake; High Uintas Wilderness map

Drive 29 miles east of Kamas on the Mirror Lake Highway, UT-150, turning left at the Bald Mountain trailhead picnic area (see Hike 26). Ample parking is provided near the trailhead.

This gently descending trail contours the base of Bald Mountain, then meanders a variety of meadows before reaching several small

Herds of little red elephants flower in marshy alpine areas.

lakes. The trail's changing terrain provides your little ones with plenty of knee-high discoveries. The extent of these stops often determines the hike's length.

The Notch Mountain Trail starts at the trailhead for Bald Mountain (see Hike 26), then veers to the left. (Mountain climbers head right.) Stop to appreciate this close-up view of the peak. Sharp rocks tumbled from Bald Mountain pierce the path, requiring careful footwork for the first 0.2 mile.

Crooked, elfin trees along this windswept section often elicit sympathy for their bedraggled appearance. However, they are brave pioneers, these krummholz trees, forging life in an otherwise inhospitable environment. Point out how the crippled-looking fir trees help block the wind, allowing their neighbors of the same fir species to grow in stature. Explain that krummholz trees often take root where a branch touches the soil on the side protected by its own trunk. Look for tree seedlings formed where a branch might touch down. As your group continues down the trail, note the progressively larger trees as the wind decreases.

Wildflowers begin vying for hikers' attention as the trail ventures into alpine meadows, starting at 0.7 mile. While brilliant pink paintbrush and soft lavender bluebells are eyed for their beauty, the yellow daisy-flowered heartleaf arnica is commonly overlooked. Have children unfold the plant's leaf to discover the shape that gives the plant its first name. They are also surprised to learn this flower has been used as a medicine to raise body temperature and to prevent infection of wounds. Remind them that wildflowers shouldn't be picked, and eating them can be dangerous.

A footbridge spans a brook at 1 mile; different plant varieties can be found thriving in the surrounding marsh. Tell your little ones to watch out for herds of little red elephants here. Imaginations need little prompting when a plant stalk covered with pink-purple flowers, each shaped like the head of an elephant, is pointed out.

Towering over your shortest hiker in these wet areas is false hellebore, commonly referred to as skunk cabbage. Its large pleated leaves protrude from stalks 3 to 6 feet tall, topped by a branched cluster of yellow-green flowers. Youngsters enjoy peeking from behind these tall stands. Big kids, however, are interested to know that American Indians used the plant to lower blood pressure. Again, remind them that trying such self-medication can be fatal.

Leaving the marsh areas the trail edges the trees. Explain that this route protects the fragile meadow from harm caused by foot traffic. Dry meadows along the trail's right side serve as ideal lunch stops.

At 1.5 miles the trail meets Clegg Lake on the left, a destination for some groups. Dean Lake, located within the next 0.8 mile, is worth aiming for. It is quite possible to make a loop for an overnight backpack trip because Notch Mountain Trail eventually ends up at Trial Lake, the end of the Crystal Lake Loop.

Return via the same trail.

Toilet and picnic facilities are available at the trailhead, but not water.

26 BALD MOUNTAIN SUMMIT

Location ■	Mirror Lakes Area, Wasatch-Cache National Forest
Type ■	Day hike
Difficulty ■	Moderate to challenging for children
Hikable ■	July through September
Distance ■	2 miles, one way
Starting Elevation ■	10,715 feet
High Point ■	11,943 feet
Maps ■	Trails Illustrated Wasatch Front and Strawberry Reservoir; USGS Mirror Lake; High Uintas Wilderness map; Kamas Ranger District "4 Great Day Hikes" brochure

Recreational use fee for all vehicles parked in the Mirror Lake Demonstration area. No charge for traveling UT-150.

See directions for Hike 25, Notch Mountain Trail.

The trail to this mountain summit enables most any hiker to claim with pride, "I made it to the top!" As in any high-altitude adventure, plan this trek for early in the day to avoid afternoon thundershowers and life-threatening lightning. Families with some younger hikers may divide at the trailhead, with the less experienced members investigating the meadows along Notch Mountain Trail.

At the trailhead, which is directly north of the parking lot, a Forest Service sign describes plant and animal adaptations to life at timberline. This information proves useful for investigative breath-catching stops as the trail ascends, gradually traversing the peak's broad, rocky base.

Initially, the only suggestions of life seem to consist of American

bistort, the white, cotton-topped flower, and cinquefoil, the yellow flower with five petals. (After a moment spent counting its petals, those with even limited Spanish skills will remember its name.) However, if you are especially lucky and/or keen-eyed, you may spot a mountain goat ambling across distant, almost vertical slopes here. Because isolation is their main defense, mountain goats are rarely seen. A viewscope at Mirror Lake allows for close observation.

The view toward Mirror Lake from the top of Bald Mountain

At 0.5 mile several of the many lakes dotting this region come into view. When we hiked this trail in mid-July, we crossed a snowfield here; there was also one closer to the summit. Wind power shaped the first snowfield into an overhanging mass of snow, forming what is called a cornice. Does wind have the same effect now?

As the trail reaches what appears to be the top of the world, look for tree line, the highest elevation that trees will grow. Does it appear to be at the same height on all surrounding mountains? What causes it to be higher in some places than others? Consider wind (winter winds dry trees at a time when no replacement water is available), water, soil, and sun exposure as key factors influencing tree growth. If a line were drawn along tree line, an average summer temperature of 50 degrees could be expected. What does today's temperature feel like? Notice the difference in air temperature when a cloud blocks the sun's warmth.

At 1 mile the trail flattens on a false summit. During this 0.3-mile walk, views of the area's Lakes Country and the Uinta and Wasatch mountains occupy everyone's attention. Point out how the Wasatch Mountains run north–south, while the Uintas run east–west. This is the only place in North America outside of Alaska's Brooks Range where mountain ranges run perpendicular to each other. The Uintas, named after the Uintats, mountain-dwelling Indians, also hold the honor of being Utah's highest range. They contain Precambrian rocks over 600 million years old that were uplifted from the earth's core. Most of Utah's mountains are igneous, formed of molten rock that was eventually elevated. Do they look different than other mountain chains you've seen? How?

The jagged peak in front and to the left is Hayd (feet), named after Ferdinand Hayden, the first surve   much of the West. The rounded peak is Mount Agas

With the wind blasting from all directions, a loc   Lake with tiny cars winding along its antlers' curv   Other views include Reids Peak, the pyramid-shaped hump on the left, and Mirror Lake, the larger lake next to Pass Lake.

Bald Mountain has a flat top, and the last 10 minutes of scrambling across the top is level, with no real trail to follow. When your group reaches the summit, you'll see much of the area's trail network, including part of the Lofty Lake Loop (see Hike 28). Try counting all visible lakes. Before heading back on the same trail, stop to saturate your senses in this top-of-the-world environment.

Toilet facilities are available at the trailhead. Nearest water is at Mirror Lake Campground.

27 MIRROR LAKE SHORELINE TRAIL

Location	Mirror Lakes area, Wasatch-Cache National Forest
Type	Day hike
Difficulty	Easy
Hikable	July to October
Distance	1.5 miles, loop
Starting Elevation	10,000 feet
High Point	10,000 feet
Maps	USGS Mirror Lake, High Uintas Wilderness Map, Mirror Lake Scenic Byways brochure

Recreation use fee for all vehicles parked in the Mirror Lake Fee Demonstration Area. No charge for traveling UT-150, Mirror Lake Scenic Byway.

Located between mileposts 31 and 32, drive 31 miles east of Kamas on UT-150. Watch for the turnoff for Mirror Lake Campground on the right (east) side of the road. Ample parking is provided.

This interpretive trail edges a glacially carved lake located in

Paddlers stroke the waters of Mirror Lake.

Utah's most scenic watershed—the Uinta Mountains. The trail is accessible from several sites within the Mirror Lake Campground and is popular with anglers of all sizes and most expectations. The first 0.2 mile of the trail is accessible for those in strollers or wheelchairs.

An information kiosk at the trailhead acquaints hikers to the significance of the Uinta watershed. Your kids will be wowed when you tell them that snow here often reaches 20 feet—enough to cover the windows of most two-story homes! This knowledge will help them understand that almost all of Utah's water comes from these mountains.

Several interpretive signs along the trail feature the animals of this region. The three-dimensional signs encourage hikers to feel the size and depth of each animal's tracks. At one sign children experience the size of a soaring eagle by placing their arms on the bird-of-prey's life-sized, spread-winged silhouette. The interpretive signs are posted along the trail's first 0.3 mile.

A wooden boardwalk crosses over several marshes alongside the lake offering kids close-up opportunities to examine life in these waters. As the trail reaches its final portion, a boardwalk spans a marsh where herds of "little red elephants" show their rows of pink spikes to admirers who kneel close. "King's Crown" with its fleshy leaves and maroon top hat also reigns over wet mountain soils. (Remember, picking wildflowers is prohibited in this and all national forests.)

Water and toilet facilities are available near the trailhead.

28 LOFTY LAKE LOOP

Location ■	Mirror Lakes Area, Wasatch-Cache National Forest
Type ■	Day hike or overnight backpack
Difficulty ■	Moderate to challenging for children
Hikable ■	July through September
Distance ■	3.8 miles, loop
Starting Elevation ■	10,080 feet
High Point ■	10,840 feet
Maps ■	USGS Mirror Lake; High Uintas Wilderness map; Kamas Ranger District "4 Great Day Hikes" brochure

Recreational use fee for all vehicles parked in the Mirror Lake Demonstration area. No charge for traveling UT-150.

Drive 32 miles east of Kamas on Mirror Lake Highway (UT-150), continuing 0.8 mile past the road to Mirror Lake Campground. Turn left at the Pass Lake trailhead sign. Ample parking is provided in the lot.

This alpine tour of the area's prettiest lakes and vistas includes equally alluring views right at your feet. Fishing's best at Lofty Lake, while overnight backpacks to Kamas Lake are remembered as stellar events. As in all high-altitude explorations, start this loop hike early in the day and don't begin it if the sky looks threatening.

Best walked in a clockwise direction (for a gradual ascent and steep descent), the hike starts at the trailhead, 40 feet left of the parking lot's center. The sign indicates Holiday Park, Meadow Lake, and Cuberant Lake—all destinations reached at a split in the trail at 0.3

Anglers at Lofty Lake

mile, where the trail forks, directing hikers going to distant Holiday Park to head left, while people in pursuit of Lofty Lake veer right.

From here the trail descends 0.1 mile to a marshy area of the forest. A subalpine forest of Englemann spruce and Douglas fir shades the trail for the next 0.5 mile. Stop to compare these two compatriots tending the tundra's edge. Note differences in their bark, shape, color, and even odor. Shake their hands (a branch, that is), noting the fir's needles are flat and flexible, while the spruce's are sharp and spiky. Which tree is most common here?

This gentle descent through forest opens to lovely Reids Meadow, where flowers seem to compete for "best of show" in late July. Your visit will coincide with some version of the display, so try some flower-naming or -comparing games to arouse your children's interest. They might nominate candidates for "oddest shape," "prettiest color," "funniest smell," or the tiniest or biggest, and so on.

The trail traverses the right side of the meadow, which is easily harmed by foot traffic. Views of Bald Mountain on the left and Reids Peak on the right fill the horizon as the trail ascends back into a subalpine forest. At 0.9 mile you pass a small lake on the left before reaching a sign for Kamas and Lofty lakes to the right, Cuberant to the left. Note the numerous minipools in this forested area. They don't appear to have inflow or outflow streams connecting them. Ask your companions to imagine how the depressions were formed as glaciers moved through here. Look for signs of animal life in or near them.

At 1.5 miles meet beautiful Kamas Lake, ringed by rock and talus. The power of wind here helps explain why its few coniferous trees are curiously deformed and small. Called *krummholz*, the German word for "crooked wood," these pioneer trees are weathering the storms, showing their age, not by wrinkles, but by the thickness of their trunk. Find the oldest krummholz. Note if it is the most exposed tree bracing itself against the wind. Also look at how the tree's twigs on the windward side are sheared off by the wind, while the leeward branches reach out like a flag on a staff. This distinctive shape has earned the krummholz trees the name "banner trees."

As you leave the lake following its left side, the trail crosses over a very small outflow and then climbs a short (0.2 mile), steep draw before it crosses a meadow marked by cairns. As your group ascends this minipass, tremendous views of the mountains tapering off into the plains occupy your breath-catching moments. The peak in front is Hayden Peak.

Via switchbacks the trail continues its climb to Lofty Lake at mile 2.2. Tiny flowers peeking through the rock rubble that's known as scree add a pleasurable diversion to the continued ascent. Enjoy the grand view at the summit (2.4 miles) before the steep descent to Scout Lake at 3.3 miles.

Just past the sign for the Pass Lake trailhead at Scout Lake, the trail crosses a small service road and follows along the right side of a smaller, narrow lake called Picturesque Lake. At the end of this lake the trail is obscure; however, bear to the left and downhill, avoiding the many fainter trails that invite you to the small cliffs on the right.

lake's drainage and contouring to the right, the trail
Creek trailhead.
facilities are available at the trailhead. The nearest
or Lake Campground.

29 RUTH LAKE

Location	■ Mirror Lakes Area, Wasatch-Cache National Forest
Type	■ Day hike or overnight backpack
Difficulty	■ Easy to moderate for children
Hikable	■ July through September
Distance	■ I mile, one way
Starting Elevation	■ 10,200 feet
High Point	■ 10,800
Maps	■ USGS Mirror Lake; High Uintas Wilderness Map, Mirror Lake Scenic Byway brochure.

Recreational use fee for all vehicles parked in the Mirror Lake Demonstration area. No charge for traveling UT-150.

Drive 35 miles east of Kamas on UT-150. The parking area is on
the left (west) side of the road, near milepost 35.

The sounds of a babbling brook accompany hikers on this gentle
amble to an alpine lake. The trail follows a staircase route climbing
granite boulders and edging lush marshes. Ideal as a day hike in the
mountains, Ruth Lake also serves as a perfect destination for beginning backpackers and fishing trips. Several other lakes are within 0.75
mile from Ruth Lake. Four interpretive signs along the way help explain the dynamic forces of this rich ecosystem.

Before stepping foot on the trail, show your companions a map of
Utah or the High Uinta Wilderness Area. Explain they are entering
one of the few mountain ranges in the world that runs east to west.
Both the Wasatch and Rocky Mountains are oriented north to south,
a trait shared by most other ranges.

Glaciers formed during the last ice age carved the lakes of these
mountains, which now hold most of Utah's water. Despite their
lovely and pristine appearance, the water in these lakes, streams,

False hellebore, also known as skunk cabbage, is a poisonous plant commonly found in moist areas.

and waterfalls should be purified before drinking.

As the trail climbs up through spruce trees and over granite boulders, the sound of a brook leads to a child-size waterfall. The trail then edges a marsh. This pattern of climbing over rocks and then walking alongside a marsh or a lake is repeated several times on the hike. It is a natural staircase created by glaciers. As the large masses of ice retreated, or melted, they carved out basins for lakes and left rocks in their path. As you continue the hike, count the "steps" of this ice age staircase.

Also, watch for gouges or scrapes in the rock. These were made more than 10,000 years ago as the glaciers moved, carrying with them rocks that scraped against other rocks. Stop to feel these ice age markings and imagine this place blanketed in massive blocks of ice.

As the trail contours the shallow pond (or third "step"), encourage your companions to look ahead to the clearing just beyond the trees. Heighten their pathfinding skills by asking, "Where might Ruth Lake be located?" The answer to their question lies just a short walk ahead. Five or six campsites edge this alpine tarn, a small lake created during glaciation.

Following the trail around the lake in a counterclockwise direction leads to what my 9-year-old companion declared was a natural rock dam. Ask your companions how glaciers may have left this formation, called a moraine.

Return via the same trail.

Toilet facilities are located in the trailhead parking area for Ruth Lake. Water is available at Mirror Lake Campground, between mileposts 31 and 32.

30 FOREMAN HOLLOW NATURE TRAIL

Location ▪	Uinta National Forest, Heber City
Type ▪	Day hike or cross-country skiing
Difficulty ▪	Moderate to challenging for children
Hikable ▪	April through October, skiable in winter
Distance ▪	4.3 miles, loop
Starting Elevation ▪	7700 feet
High Point ▪	8200 feet
Maps ▪	Trails Illustrated Wasatch Front and Strawberry Reservoir

 From Heber City travel 14 miles southeast on US 40 to the Lodgepole Campground on the right. Turn right at the entry for Loop B and proceed 0.2 mile to the first road on the left, which is blocked off. For those not camped here, parking is available along the loop drive adjacent to the RV sanitary site, which is across from the campground host site.

Starting and ending at Lodgepole Campground, this little-used nature trail winds through the forests of a hillside's north- and south-facing slopes. Interpretive signs explain principles of forest ecology and point out interesting aspects of commonly overlooked plants. When the aspens showcase their fall colors, hikes here are memorable events.

The Foreman Hollow trailhead is 0.7 mile from the campground road. Follow the abandoned road up a drainage called Foreman Hollow, veering right as it passes a small corral on the right. The road appears quite faint at this point. Watch on the right for the trailhead marked by a Forest Service sign and rock stairs set into the hillside.

Shaggy-topped mint plants nod their lavender heads as hikers climb this first steep portion of the trail. Breath-catching breaks can be enhanced by a strong whiff of any of several varieties flowering throughout the summer.

Interpretive signs along the way introduce such common plant residents of a south-facing slope as chokecherry, Gambel oak, and sage. Aspen shades the trail through brushy undergrowth until an open area at 1.2 miles. Near the signpost, stop to compare the forested canyon to the north with the dry, sparsely vegetated hillside where you are standing. By closely examining a leaf, discover how a sage plant protects itself from the sun's drying rays. Minute hairs on the leaf surface act as a sun block, reducing evaporation of the leaf's vital fluids. For those preferring a shorter hike, this viewpoint of Daniels Canyon can be a turnaround point. (Skiers may want to head back here to avoid the steep descent beginning in less than a mile.)

Grand stands of aspen lure hikers to follow the trail as it veers north. Fluttering in the slightest breeze, aspen leaves provide a gentle rhythm to your walk. Stop to show children why the leaves "quake" so readily: Each leaf stalk is longer than the leaf itself and is attached to the branch at a right angle, acting as a pivot. Kids will understand why aspen leaves quiver in the slightest breeze when they blow gently on a leaf they hold by its stem.

Fall hikers curious about how trees change colors should read the description in Hike 57, Deer Creek Lake to Chriss Lake Loop.

Springtime skiers here appreciate seeing aspen wear their woolly

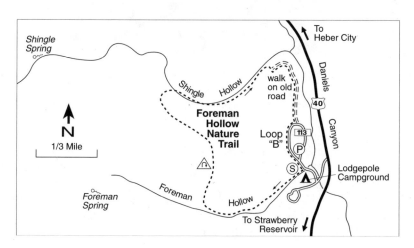

Aspen forests surround hikers on the Foreman Hollow Nature Trail.

earrings—the tree's 3-inch catkins that appear before the leaves do. Catkins are compact spikes of flowers, found only in the spring on willows and poplars. Aspen, a member of the willow family, bears the scientific name *Populus tremuloides*. Children finding catkins on the ground have more fun naming them just as they appear: fuzzy worms.

At 2.1 miles, just past the sign about a spring, point out the small pond on the trail's left side. Decide if a man or a beaver made it and why. If a beaver was the builder, where did it get the lumber? Look for tracks in the mud along the water.

An earnest descent to a slice in the canyon called Shingle Hollow begins just past this point. Hollow, by the way, is a term applied to drainages. Both Foreman and Shingle hollows are named after the springs that trickle down them. The stream crossed at 2.5 miles began as Shingle Spring less than a mile west of here.

As the trail traverses the slope, passing from shady nooks to sunny slopes, call attention to the differences in temperature. Point out mosses carpeting the base of trees. Based on this natural sign, see if your hike leader can tell you in which direction the group is hiking.

Regal monkshood, with its lovely purple crowns worn by 4- and 5-foot-tall stalks, decorates this north-facing passage. Entering the dark, quiet confines of a towering spruce forest, look for holes dimpling the thick carpet of needles. Ground squirrels enter their storehouses through these underground passages. Imagine the contents of their collection.

The trail meets an abandoned road at 3.5 miles. Turn right, crossing a fence, and continue 0.7 mile to the campground, entering at campsite 16. Another 0.1 mile to the left leads to the campground host sites and the main road.

Toilet and water facilities are provided at the campground.

31 FIFTH WATER TRAIL

Location ■	Spanish Fork
Type ■	Day hike
Difficulty ■	Easy to moderate for children
Hikable ■	Year-round
Distance ■	2 miles, one way
Starting Elevation ■	5600 feet
High Point ■	5720 feet
Maps ■	Trails Illustrated Wasatch Front and Strawberry Reservoir; USGS Rays Valley

From the junction of I-15 and US 6 in Spanish Fork, drive 10.7 miles southeast on US 6 to the Diamond Fork turnoff (Forest Road 29). Turn left and drive 10 miles on this paved but narrow winding road to the Three Forks sign. Turn right here, to where ample parking is provided.

Hot springs and cool waterfalls spilling into family-size pools create a delightful destination all ages will enjoy. This popular site for visitors on foot, mountain bike, and horse can get congested on weekends and holidays throughout the year; quiet getaways are more likely to occur midweek. Be aware that nudity is increasing among users at the "hot pots," which may make this hike unsuitable for some children.

The trailhead is located across the wooden bridge in the parking area. Sixth Water Creek roars on the trail's right side as it follows a branch of Diamond Fork Canyon for 1 mile. Flowing from Strawberry Reservoir, during the summer this creek rages through the canyon, causing serious consequences for anyone who tumbles into it. Little hikers who tend to wander need to be carefully supervised along this first portion of the hike and on the return trip. However, fences placed by a group of individuals concerned about trail safety are in place at many precipitous locations.

Another note of caution, though minor in comparison, is that poison ivy graces the trail's left side. Get kids familiar with it by pointing out its three-leaf arrangement. They'll see it at several spots along the trail.

Note the rock walls of the canyon. Your youngest scientist may tell you that they are conglomerate. Explore ideas of where the rounded rocks compressed in this formation originated. Does erosion appear to be taking its toll? Are the canyon's rocks the same kind as those in the creek?

At 1 mile the trail crosses a wooden footbridge where it meets the docile Fifth Water Creek on the right. This is an ideal treat stop before the trail increases its gentle climb to the pools and cascade.

At 1.4 miles the smell of sulfur, or "rotten eggs," wafts through the air. Although several inviting pools and waterfalls are found along this portion of the hike, do continue on.

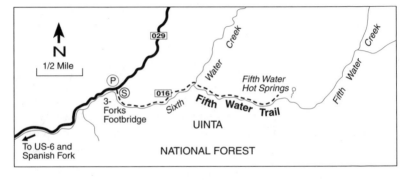

At 2.0 miles, just past an area where springs have trickled across the trail and tall, yellow morning glories nod with your passing, the trail forks. Views of the waterfall straight ahead make it obvious that you are to follow the right fork.

Rules of safety can't be overapplied here, where sharp, slippery rocks edge the pools. Before kids scatter in this wet play yard, warn them that painfully hot water is present. It's best to first have an adult survey the pools to find the ones "too hot" or "too cold" or "just right."

Return via the same route.

No toilet or water facilities are available at the trailhead.

3₂ **MAPLE CANYON**

Location	▪ West of Moroni
Type	▪ Day hike
Difficulty	▪ Moderate to challenging for children
Hikable	▪ June through mid-October
Distance	▪ Arch, 0.7 mile, one way; Canyon Loop, 3 miles
Starting Elevation	▪ 7500 feet
High Point	▪ 9000 feet
Map	▪ None

In Fountain Green from UT-132 turn west on 400 South. Drive 6.1 miles, following the curve to the left (road name changes to County Road 283) to an unmarked paved road. Turn right and continue 0.5 mile to a gravel road. Turn right and proceed 3 miles to the trailhead. Limited parking is provided along the roadside near the picnic area and trailhead.

In a little-used portion of Uinta National Forest, this maple-shaded trail leads to a large arch youngsters can easily reach. Experienced young hikers enjoy completing the entire loop, which circles up and around an amphitheater of conglomerate crags overlooking grand vistas of the valley.

At the trailhead, which is located near the group picnic area, a map sign shows the trails of this canyon, Middle Fork being the hike described here.

At 0.1 mile a massive boulder alongside the trail's right seems placed to satisfy awakened curiosities. Hikers can get a close-up examination here of the area's unique geology, which looks like towers of rock rubble compressed together by coarse cement. Point out that the rocks are all rounded. They are remnants of the ancient seas and rivers that once (many millions of years ago) blanketed this area.

The trail continues through the shade of canyon maples, which are also called bigtooth maples. The sweet sap of this western relative of the sugar maple can be used to make maple sugar. In the fall its showy red and gold leaves appease many a visual appetite.

At 0.2 mile, after crossing a dry creekbed that occasionally flows in the spring, the trail begins a short but serious ascent. It levels a tad, then veers left slightly to meet the sign for the arch at 0.7 mile. Turn left here and climb a rocky hill via switchbacks. When your eyes can be diverted up from the trail, you'll see the arch, a rock span 50 feet wide. Most arches are made of sedimentary sandstone; it's quite rare to see an arch composed of conglomerate rock.

The area directly under the arch is steep and contains many loose rocks, so your visit here should be brief. Exploring the area is not suggested. However, before heading down explain that arches are created by wind and water erosion, not by flowing water. The opening here started in a thin area of the preexisting wall where the bond holding the rocks together was weak. Over a long, long period of time, the freezing and thawing of rainwater fractured the rocks. Eventually, wind blew the rock particles away and the larger ones fell

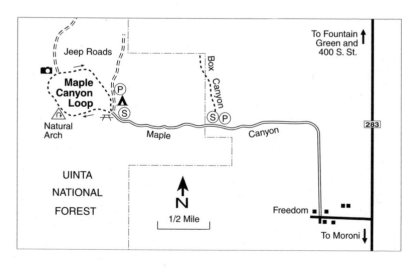

down the slope. Examine the rocks below the arch. Did any belong to the original rock wall that stood here millions of years ago?

When descending from the arch, send kids down one at a time. Wait until one child has reached a safe place at the bottom before allowing the next to proceed. This will prevent tumbling rocks from injuring a hiker. Those continuing on the longer loop, turn left at the arch sign; arch hikers retrace their steps back to the trailhead.

Pathfinding skills are needed for several parts of the longer trail as it veers left to an amphitheater, then right to climb up to its crag-edged rim, and then down the opposite side to complete the loop. When we hiked the trail, blue survey tags tied to trees marked the route in areas where the trail was faint. Wooden signs also mark strategic points along the route.

The first questionable portion of the trail occurs at 0.9 mile, where the trail winds to the left through meadow grass, then oak brush. Blue survey tags are reassurances you're on the trail. Just when you might think you've lost the trail, a big, bold sign for Maple Canyon and the loop trail appears at 1.1 miles. Turn right here, climbing north through the heart of a spectacular crag-crested amphitheater. Do stop to catch your breath and enjoy the vista and to appreciate the ascent already accomplished.

Bigtooth maples, also known as canyon maples, flock Maple Canyon.

Hearts a-beating, hikers reach the serene, white-trunked symmetry of an aspen grove at 1.3 miles. Watch for an aspen tree on the right with the words "Loop Trail" carved in it. Turn right here where the trail climbs to a crest of the amphitheater, then traverses to a high point. Awesome views of this canyon's conglomeration of conglomerate walls reward the climber at 1.5 miles. The valley beyond is dotted with gleaming roofs housing gobs of gobblers, reminding hikers of the drive to Maple Canyon through Utah's turkey-raising center.

e

For another 0.1 mile the trail follows the amphitheater's highest ridge, affording continuous and changing views. Manzanita flourishes in this sun-drenched landscape. Note how the oval leaves of this brushy ground cover face straight up, not flat to the sun. Ask how this feature affects the plant's adaptation to sun exposure. Are there any other plants or trees here with leaves as wide?

CAUTION

A jeep road accesses the loop trail at 1.6 miles, where there's another viewpoint and a rest bench. Cross the road and descend a very, very steep trail. In some places yellow spray-painted rocks identify this perilous route. Also watch for tree blazes, cuts made into the bark to mark the trail. The trickiest section begins just below the last viewpoint and continues for less than 0.1 mile as the trail drops into the trees. As the trail becomes easier your conversation might include the many ways the Forest Service met the challenge of signing this trail.

At 2.4 miles maple trees are once again your companions—particularly helpful companions when tagged by a blue survey ribbon to mark less obvious trail sections. At 2.7 miles the trail joins the gravel road above the Maple Canyon Campground. Follow this to the right for 0.3 mile to reach the trailhead.

Indian paintbrush is found in alpine and desert landscapes.

Toilet facilities are provided at the campground.

33 BOX CANYON

Location ■	West of Moroni
Type ■	Day hike
Difficulty ■	Easy to moderate for children
Hikable ■	June through mid-October
Distance ■	0.2 mile to 0.5 mile or more, one way
Starting Elevation ■	7500 feet
High Point ■	7500 feet
Map ■	None

See the directions for Maple Canyon, Hike 32. On the gravel road travel 2.3 miles to Box Canyon on the right, just before the Uinta National Forest Sign. Limited parking is available alongside the road.

This cobblestone walkway in a slot canyon teases imaginations and tempts the climber in everyone. Box Canyon is an ancient riverbed with rock-studded walls reaching 200 feet in height and standing 6 to 20 feet apart. Hikers here, drawn by the quest for what's next in this rocky vein, often climb, crawl, and hoist each other up to the next boulder or cave in the wall. Sturdy hiking shoes are recommended in this ankle-twisting terrain.

Box Canyon also appeals to rock climbers. Caution is advised when many climbers have gathered here (especially on fall weekends) because of the increased chance of loosened or falling rock.

Cooling shade and steady breeze often welcome hikers into this slot in the canyon wall. Point out how all the rocks here are rounded and smooth, like those along rivers. But what happened to the river? Tell your kids that long ago, way before the dinosaur age, these rocks lined the rivers and lakes that covered much of the West. Over millions of years other rock layers covered this area and all the land moved. In some places it lifted up and in others it sank. The rocks of this ancient river are now "glued" together by minerals from another layer of rock. Stop to feel the difference between the rocks and the binding layer. In geologic terms, a limestone deposit percolated through this ancient riverbed, which was later uplifted and eroded to form the canyon.

Within the first 0.3 mile the explorers in your crew will spy a cave in the wall, about 50 feet up. Most kids will scramble up, but will need a boost for the last 5 feet. There's enough room for two to three people in this rocky alcove, but supervision is advised here.

Boulders lodged in between the canyon walls will appear to block your passage. However, you can get around them, as each boulder becomes a climbing challenge or a fun scramble. There's even a 20-ton rock lodged 10 feet overhead that you can walk under! No worries, this canyon was not featured in a Harrison Ford film, and the boulders won't chase you down the canyon.

Your group's scrambling skills will determine the distance of this hike. However, within 0.5 mile, technical skills are required to continue this exploration safely.

Return via the same route. Along the way listen and watch for the bubbling of a small creek. Notice where it disappears underground. Where does it resurface?

Toilet facilities are located in the campground near the trailhead for Maple Canyon.

34 CLEVELAND-LLOYD DINOSAUR QUARRY

Location ■ 33 miles south of Price, San Rafael Swell
Type ■ Day hike
Difficulty ■ Easy to moderate
Hikable ■ March through September
Distance ■ 100 yards to 1.5 mile, one way
Starting Elevation ■ 5800 feet
High Point ■ 5980 feet
Map ■ Park brochure
www.blm.gov/utah/price/quarry.htm
User Fee

From Price drive south 12 miles on UT-10 to the Cleveland/Elmo turnoff. Follow the "dinosaur" signs to the quarry, heading east on twisting unpaved roads. When wet these roads are slick. Continue through an open gate and over the cattle guard to the visitor center—a small brown building with an American flag flapping from a tall pole.

It's Utah's own Jurassic Park, a dinosaur deli preserved in stone.

Bones and tracks of the best-known dinosaurs litter this National Natural Landmark located in the San Rafael Swell—a scenic sandstone uplift covering 2000 square miles.

Kids to scientists come here to see the world's only known dinosaur "predator trap"—now a quarry of dinosaur bones. They also enjoy the exhibits at the visitor center and the ranger-guided walks past sauropod and theropod tracks and other prehistoric formations. This remote destination features an interpreted rock trail, a picnic area, and a trail to a 360-degree view of the swell. Several nearby sites of archaeological and geologic interest complement a visit to the dinosaur quarry. Ending the day on the beach at Huntington State Park tops the trip.

Because of its proximity to Cleveland, Utah, and the early work done here by Princeton University and financed by Philadelphia lawyer Malcomb Lloyd, the area became known as the Cleveland-Lloyd Quarry. Bones and full skeletons from this rich source of dinosaur fossils are on display in over 60 museums worldwide. Fortunately, the nearest dinosaur destination is in Price at the College of Eastern Utah's Prehistoric Museum—a must-see for all dino fans.

A grinning allosaurus skeleton greets you as you enter the visitor center. A diplodocus head, a camarasaurus leg, and many more dinosaur

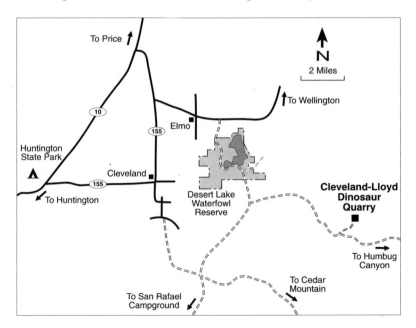

Ancient claws meet little paws at Cleveland-Lloyd Dinosaur Quarry.

bones are on display all over the center. They represent a small fraction of the 12,000 bones that have been excavated here. A bone map on the wall shows what kind and where the bones were found. The color mural on the opposite wall depicts life here 147 million years ago.

Imagine this place as a land once covered by shallow lakes and streams. The quarry's stark surroundings have no resemblance to yours or the mural's image, but remnants of prehistoric stream channels can be seen in the red sandstone layer west of the quarry buildings. During a ranger-guided hike you may see tracks left by a stegosaur or find fossilized mud cracks from 140 million years ago.

A short walk (100 yards) from the visitor center leads to the quarry buildings. The roofs of these metal sheds protect the dinosaur predator trap. About a dozen different species have been found here and an estimated 50 to 100 bones per square yard are buried in this partially excavated site. Scientists are uncertain how large predators became trapped at this site. Some believe it was "sticky mud," others say it was a "steep-sided mud hole," and others contend a "pocket of poisonous gas" killed the dinosaurs. Encourage your promising paleontologists to describe what they think caused the mass of dinosaurs to die. What would they need to find to prove their theory?

In the shade of the quarry buildings is a good place to explore fossils with your companions. Explain that the dinosaur bones they are seeing are actually bones that have become rocklike over millions of years. Fossilization began when thick layers of sand, mud, and volcanic ash buried the bone, weighing heavily on it. Seas often covered the land. Over a long, long period of time, groundwater passed through the bone, taking tiny parts of the bone and leaving minerals in its place. Eventually, minerals replaced the bone tissue, which then hardened into a rock. In many ways the dinosaur bone served as a mold for a rock that formed over millions of years. No bone material is actually in the fossils found at Cleveland-Lloyd.

The 1.5-mile Rock Walk starts on the east side of the buildings. This interpreted trail features dinosaur bones and several unusual rock formations. Wear sturdy walking shoes for this 0.75- to 2-hour hike. Trail brochures are available at the visitor center.

The 1.25-mile hike to and from Raptor Point leads to a spectacular viewpoint that includes the Book Cliffs and the Wasatch Plateau. Keen-eyed hikers may see the white rumps of antelope in the distance.

The quarry is open 10:00 A.M. to 5 P.M daily, Memorial Day through Labor Day, and weekends (Friday to Sunday), beginning late March through September. If you begin either hike after 4:00 P.M., park your vehicle outside the gate at the visitor center. Please do not remove any plants, rocks, or fossils from this protected site.

Water and toilet facilities are available at the visitor center. However, water is limited and visitors are encouraged to bring water with them.

35 CURRENT CREEK NATURE TRAIL

Location	■ Uinta National Forest, Heber City
Type	■ Day hike
Difficulty	■ Moderate for children
Hikable	■ May through October
Distance	■ 1.25 miles, loop
Starting Elevation	■ 7700 feet
High Point	■ 8100 feet
Maps	■ Trails Illustrated Wasatch Front and Strawberry Reservoir

Wheelchair-accessible fishing ramp near trailhead

From Heber City drive east 45 miles on US 40 to Current Creek Junction, a road on the left (north) identified by a gas station and small hotel. Proceed 19.8 miles on this gravel road that nearly circles Current Creek Reservoir, ending at the campground. Bear left to Loop D. Follow the road to the Tot-Lot on the left; parking and the trailhead are on the right. The wheelchair-accessible fishing ramp is located 0.2 mile north of here, near the trailhead.

Walking the nature trail above Current Creek Reservoir is like taking the family on a forest safari. Deer dart across the path, hawks soar overhead, and beavers ripple the waters of a nearby pond. Equally abundant are the interpretive signs, thirty-two of which identify the natural features along this loop trail.

From the trailhead walk 0.1 mile and turn right at the junction. Following the loop in a counterclockwise direction allows a shorter ascent and gentler descent.

Ascending through groves of milky white aspen trees, children enjoy hunting for signs of deer and elk. Their findings might include matted grassy areas where a deer bedded down for the night, saplings with leaves nibbled off, deer scat, faint trails aimed toward water, or scars on the aspen trunks. As any hunter or nature photographer knows, the best chances of seeing a deer or elk occur at dawn and dusk.

Within 0.5 mile, views of the Current Creek Reservoir provide an excuse to catch your breath. Become acquainted with plants of this dry area by starting with the limber pine (near signpost 10). Gently shake its branch. Notice how flexible it is? Ask kids what it means when a person is limber. Sniff a cluster of sage leaves (signpost 11) to learn its distinct scent. Bitterbrush (signpost 12), despite having a not-so-pretty name, is worthy of smelling because it is endowed with tiny, fragrant yellow blossoms. This is a favorite browse, or food, of mule deer; look for deer tracks and droppings near the plant. In this same area, June and July hikers will recognize Utah's state flower, the sego lily. Its walnut-sized bulbs provided essential food for many Mormons during their early lean years in the state.

Having read the Latin names of so many plants, you'll find it appropriate that the area near signpost 13 is named *altimus maximus* (highest point). From here the loop begins its descent.

Before leaving this point explain to youngsters that the Current Creek Formation, as with other rock layers, was named by geologists for the area where it was first identified. The sign shows a "submarine sandwich" of the area's rock strata. Ask kids to point to the oldest and youngest rock shown on the sign and in the view.

Also look to the right and down the slope for activity in the beaver ponds. Is the lodge or dam visible?

The high-pitched "keee-ah" of a red-tailed hawk may turn heads upward. Those fortunate enough to see the broad-winged bird soar in circles are watching it close in on its prey. Ask your beginning bird-watcher what rodents a hawk might catch in this forest.

As the trail continues its descent, stop at signposts 17 and 18 to compare white fir and subalpine fir. How do their needles differ? In what ways are their cones similar? What tree might make a perfect Christmas tree for your home? A shopping center? The forest?

Those interpreting the lumber-value chart at signpost 25 may need to calculate a tree's age. One method, though not very accurate, is to count the number of branches on one side of a tree. Each branch is the equivalent of 1 year. Make up a game of finding trees of different ages, perhaps matching each member of your group with a tree his or her age.

After passing the last interpretive sign, the trail rejoins the common trail for 0.1 mile before reaching the trailhead.

The adjacent Tot-Lot playground area and nearby fishing access add to this destination's appeal to families with young children.

Toilet and water facilities are available at the campground.

36 ROCK CREEK TRAIL TO YELLOW PINE ACCESSIBLE TRAIL

Location ■	Ashley National Forest, Duchesne
Type ■	Day hike
Difficulty ■	Rock Creek, moderate for children; Yellow Pine Accessible, easy for children
Hikable ■	May to October
Distance ■	Rock Creek Trail, 4 miles, one way; Yellow Pine Accessible Trail, 0.5 mile, loop
Starting Elevation ■	8100 feet
Ending Elevation ■	7500 feet
Maps ■	USGS Twooroose Pass; Ashley National Forest Travel Map

Wheelchair-accessible trail at Yellow Pine Campground

From Duchesne drive 14 miles north on UT-87 to UT-131. Follow this road north 2.7 miles to Mountain Home's post office. Turn left at the intersection here, and continue driving north and west 23 miles on the paved road through state, reservation, and Forest Service land. The Rock Creek trailhead is on the right side of

Ravens are intelligent birds that are often seen in Utah's canyons.

the road as it nears the dam and crosses the bridge. Parking is provided across the road from the trailhead. Shuttle a car to the trail ending at Yellow Pine Campground, 3.4 miles south of here. Turn left into the campground where an overflow parking area is provided on the right, just inside the campground entrance.

The variety of terrains and abundance of wildlife signs along this streamside stroll fascinates hikers of all sizes. A vehicle shuttled to the trail's end allows time for creek-splashing fun near Yellow Pine Campground. Groups with small children may choose to walk the nearby Yellow Pine Accessible Trail while older siblings explore the Rock Creek Trail.

Beginning from the trailhead just below the Upper Stillwater Reservoir dam, the rock-studded trail climbs above the creek. July-ripe raspberries flourish in the disturbed soil of this area. While the dam's mechanical hum fills the air, tell children the water stored behind the concrete dam remains there all summer. During the fall and winter it flows underground 30 miles through a series of tunnels southwest to Strawberry Reservoir. Ask your companions why reservoirs are built. How do they benefit animals or people? In what ways do they change an area that once was a stream?

As the lodgepole forest gives way to an aspen glen, point out the number of downed white-trunked trees. Closer inspection shows beavers have toppled them. Ask your companions for their theories on why the beavers left these logs here. Talk about how the forest's loggers move trees from here to a dam site downstream.

Just before crossing the first wooden footbridge spanning a marshy area at 0.5 mile, look to the left where a mudslide has smothered the vegetation. Do you see grasses and seedlings reclaiming the area?

At 1.2 miles another wooden footbridge spans a gurgling spring where yellow-faced, red-freckled monkey flowers thrive. These are among my favorite wildflowers, and I've watched many a smile form on the face of a youngster who stooped to see its freckles.

Look for the telltale V-shape rippling the still waters of the beaver pond complex at 1.5 miles. The best way to see beavers, who are mostly nocturnal, is to sit quietly by the pond at sunrise or in the early evening.

At 2.2 miles, after a footbridge spans a significant stream, the trail enters a lodgepole forest and briefly climbs to a small meadow. Rock Creek flows at its slowest pace here, and the number of beaver lodges and dams holding the water explains why. When asked why beavers build dams, show children that water is slowed behind the dam. This raises the water level surrounding the lodge high enough that winter ice will not reach all the way to the stream's bottom. Explain that beavers do not hibernate and therefore need to ensure winter access to their food supply stashed in the lodge, which they reach via an underwater entrance. Look at the mud-and-stick structure to see how the fur-bearing rodent constructs its home.

One-half mile beyond the beaver subdivision, the trail rejoins the vigorous stream. Besides being a prime habitat for beaver, the willows and grasses of this riparian zone attract moose. They are solitary and tend to linger in thick willow stands, hiding from view. However, their large tracks of two ovals leave quite an impression in the mud—and in young minds. If your eye catches the bounding of a large dark creature in a thicket, you've probably seen a moose, just as we did the evening we hiked this trail. Look closely: Broken ends of branches or a naked limb stripped of its leaves could be signs of a moose dining here.

At 3 miles the trail crosses a gate opening in a barbed wire fence, then follows the creekside through a ponderosa and lodgepole forest as it veers left. Rocks rim either side of this faint portion of the trail, which then swings right to parallel the stream.

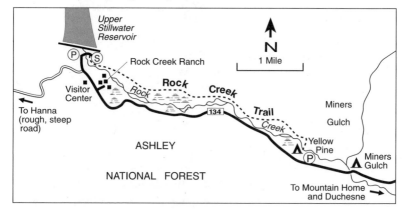

At mile 3.8 a shallow, grassy depression and an abandoned beaver lodge in its center stand as remnants of wetter years. Allow children to take advantage of this rare opportunity for a close-up and dry investigation of a beaver's home. Prohibit any climbing on the mud-and-stick structure, and keep hands out of any openings. Perhaps another creature has taken up residence here!

Sage and stands of pinyon and juniper trees mark the last 0.2 mile before the junction for Yellow Pine Campground on the right. The trail descends to Rock Creek, where numerous shallow pools near the footbridge serve as fantastic finales for heated hikers.

After crossing the footbridge, meet the Yellow Pine Accessible Trail by turning left onto the walkway. Follow the pavement a short distance to a log cattle-guard gate that precedes the first interpretive sign.

This sensory-oriented loop trail helps visitors attune their noses to the maple scent of a ponderosa pine, their ears to the quivering of aspen leaves, and their fingers to the feel of beaver-gnawed trees. Geology, forest management, trees, and riparian zones are among the natural features described.

Yellow Pine Campground provides both drinking water and toilets.

37 McCONKIE RANCH PETROGLYPH TRAIL

Location ▪	Vernal
Type ▪	Day hike
Difficulty ▪	Moderate, with some challenging climbs
Hikable ▪	Year-round, except after heavy snows
Distance ▪	0.5 mile to 2 miles, one way
Starting Elevation ▪	6200 feet
High Point ▪	6280 feet
Maps ▪	Vernal One Day Self-Guided Tour #3, Indian Petroglyphs–Dry Fork Canyon

Donation requested

From US 40 in Vernal (175 miles east of Salt Lake City) turn north onto 500 West Street. Proceed to UT-121 and turn left, driving 3.5 miles to 3500 West Street and then turn right. Travel 6.5 miles to the turnoff on the right for the McConkie Ranch. Follow this paved road about 1 mile to the parking area on the left that is marked by hundreds of deer antlers hanging from the wire fence.

Hikers encounter intriguing symbols and square-shouldered deities at every bend as they walk along a sandstone wall above a family's homestead. This rock art collection is "some of the best rock art in the United States," according to the president of the American Rock Art Research Association. Visitors here also see the cabins and artifacts of the Dry Fork Canyon settlers. It's indeed a lively look at the prehistoric and pioneer life of the region.

This is a privately owned ranch. Please respect the privacy and property of the homeowners in the area by hiking only on designated trails. Supervision is recommended at all times along the trails here.

Before setting foot on the trail, which begins directly across the road in front of the parking area, acquaint children with the era and art they are about to see. Explain that the rock art was made by Fremont Indians hundreds of years ago, long before Columbus arrived in this country. Remind them not to touch the art. Even though rock art appears indestructible, acids from skin oils will cause it to deteriorate.

The first 50 feet up a steep hill leads to the sandstone wall where prehistoric people displayed images of their gods, events, symbols, and perhaps signatures. Can you see the mountain lion, the hummingbird, and the Indian hanging on to a rock?

Follow the path along the rock wall for 1 mile or more. Ladders lead to impressive petroglyphs at several points along the way. At the time of this writing, small signs and yellow survey tags marked the safest route to each site. Please respect the personal efforts the McConkie family has made in opening their property to the public by following the marked trail.

When examining each drawing look for different artistic styles, observe where paint was used, and try to find drawings made one on top of another. Children like to look for the so-called "headhunter" amongst the many big-shouldered beings. And they notice the styles of necklaces, belts, and headgear displayed on the classic Fremont figures. Kids are naturals at interpreting and naming the scenes.

On the left at 0.8 mile the trail meets a lower, easier-to-follow trail that can be used to return to the parking area. Those who continue walking along the canyon wall another 0.5 mile discover more rock art.

The Three Kings, famous for its detail and regal features, reigns 100 feet above the McConkie Ranch, just 0.5 mile southeast of the parking lot. The easier and more direct route to it starts on the

Stick roof shelter shades hikers at McConkie Ranch.

opposite side of the fence, just past the beige house. Look for a stair-case ladder that climbs over the fence. Follow the fence line marked by red survey tags to an iron post standing upright in the sage field. Look up about 100 yards to see the life-size beings carved into a sand-stone panel. Those with binoculars will see the kings' adornments. Note the figure at the far right that projects slightly from the rock surface. This style, called bas-relief, is rare in this kind of rock art.

CAUTION An equally interesting array of rock art decorates the sandstone walls en route to The Three Kings. Please stay on the trail here. The Three Clowns, the first rock art seen on this hike, shows clowns with different headgear—either crowns or flat bars—which reflect their differences in status. Next, a pair of ladders about 20 feet apart lead to more displays. The ladders are easy to climb, though precarious to step around at the top. Note the many circular shapes—are they tribal symbols? Names? Letters?

The canyon wall breaks for a short distance where you pass the Giant's Club, a rock pinnacle. Proceeding along the canyon wall be-gins to feel like a walk in an art gallery. A flat area at the end of this rock span provides perfect viewing of The Three Kings. Return on the same path.

Do allow time to visit the McConkie homestead cabins near the beige house. Ancient remnants found in the area are housed in some of the old dwellings. There's also an excavated basketmaker pit house near the museum cabin and many manos and metates on display. The Saloon Cabin and Trading Post both contain artifacts of settler life in this area at the turn of the century.

The best way to make a trip here meaningful is to have a McConkie family member guide you. If you arrive between 11:00 A.M. and 4:00 P.M., someone may be available. Group leaders can contact Jean McKenzie at 6228 McConkie Ranch, Vernal, Utah 84078.

No public toilet facilities are provided. Bring water; the visitor center here sells bottled water and soda.

38 DRY FORK NATURE TRAIL

Location ▪	Ashley National Forest, Vernal District
Type ▪	Day hike
Difficulty ▪	Easy for children
Hikable ▪	May through October
Distance ▪	0.5 mile, loop
Starting Elevation ▪	7720 feet
High Point ▪	7720 feet
Maps ▪	Trails Illustrated Flaming Gorge National Recreation Area and Eastern Uintas

See directions for Hike 37, McConkie Ranch Petroglyph Trail. Continue 2 miles past the ranch turnoff, bearing right at the fork, and proceed 4.6 miles to the pavement's end. Continue another 2.4 miles to the fork, bearing left, and drive 0.7 mile to the clearing on the left where the trailhead is located.

This gentle, interpreted walkway loops around a mixed forest's most interesting features. It's an ideal leg-stretching break during the scenic drive into the High Uintas called the Red Cloud Loop Tour, or it makes a pleasing destination after visiting Dry Fork Canyon's petroglyphs.

Fifteen interpretive signs along this looped trail offer insight into the characteristics of a healthy forest. However, after the first few numbered stops children's interests generally wander in a different direction. Instead, try a multisensory approach to "sensationalize" the visit. The following activities and investigations at each site provide a fun approach to sampling nature and provide opportunities for your crew to gain a better understanding of and appreciation for the environment.

- At station 1 stop to smell the sagebrush. Crumpling a few leaves releases the fragrance of the West. Very close examination of a sage leaf reveals the thick layer of fine white hairs that protect it from the sun. Scrape off the hairs to discover the sage leaf's true colors.

- The juniper berries on the tree near station 2 also wear a sun-protecting makeup. Called "boo-berries" by our toddler who saw them as blue, the berries' true green color was revealed after he'd rubbed off the white-blue powdery film. Ask a young hiker to crush one of the berries between his or her fingers to discover its distinctive odor. Imagine eating a raw juniper berry, as many American Indians once did. They also cooked, dried, and ground the bitter, dry fruit into a flour.

- Just past station 3 stop for some "aspen power powder" by placing your palms on the tree's trunk. Kids enjoy face painting themselves with this white dusting, which, in a pinch, can be used as a sunscreen.

- Gently shaking the hand (branch) of a limber pine at station 4 explains why it was so named. What's another word for limber? Could the tree be called "flexible pine"?

- The best way to meet a ponderosa pine (at station 5) is to hug and smell it. (Watch out for sap!) Describe the ponderosa's aroma. How do the needles of this pine compare to the limber's?

- Around the downed logs near station 6, look for signs that soil is forming around them. Does the wood feel soft and broken down? Have insects begun burrowing in it?

- Listen between stations 7 and 8 for the sounds of a chickadee's descending call, or the rat-a-tat-tatting of a red-napped sapsucker drilling holes in a tree in search of insects.

- Feel a square-stemmed needle of the Englemann spruce at station 9. Notice it is stiff with a sharp spikey tip. In comparison, fir needles feel flat and flexible.

Look, but don't pick!

- Near signpost 10 watch for red soil washed down from the flood of 1997. Talk about how floods sometimes help a natural area by bringing soil and seeds to an area.

- The rounded rocks of the Dry Fork streambed near station 11 suggest a past of wetter years for this waterway, which is now dry except during spring melts. Ask, "Why aren't the rocks sharp and angular? Why are rocks in rivers always rounded and smooth?"

- Near signpost 12 look for charred tree stumps. Careless campers caused a fire here in 1994 that burned 185 acres. Look for tree seedlings in this area.

- Encourage youngsters to feel the crusty lichen texturing the boulders between signposts 12 and 13. They'll be fascinated to hear that lichen is actually two microscopic plants that support each other. They slowly break down rocks by producing an acid that human hands can't feel.

- Compare the needles, bark, and cones of the Douglas and subalpine firs at station 14. How are the fir trees similar to the spruce? How are they different?

- After a hands-and-knees look at the holly grape at signpost 15, hikers can follow the trail as it loops back to the parking lot.

No toilet or water facilities are available at the trailhead.

For information on the Red Cloud Loop Drive call the Vernal Chamber of Commerce at 435-789-1352.

39 HOG CANYON

Location ■	Dinosaur National Monument
Type ■	Day hike
Difficulty ■	Easy for children
Hikable ■	Year-round
Distance ■	0.5 mile, one way
Starting Elevation ■	5400 feet
High Point ■	5400 feet
Maps ■	Tour of the Tilted Rocks brochure; Trails Illustrated Dinosaur National Monument; USGS Dinosaur Quarry and Split Mountain; Dinosaur National Monument brochure

www.nps.gov/dino
National monument entrance fee

 From Vernal (175 miles east of Salt Lake City on US 40) proceed another 13 miles east to Jensen. Turn north on UT-149 and drive 6 miles to the entrance and parking area for the Dinosaur Quarry at

Fossilized dinosaur bones get close-up inspections at Dinosaur National Monument.

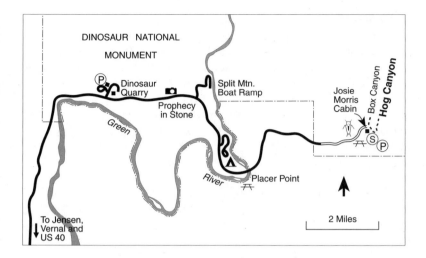

Dinosaur National Monument. Follow Cub Creek Road 10.1 miles east to the Josie Morris Cabin.

After an exciting visit to the Dinosaur Quarry, your youngsters may hardly be interested in a homesteader's hog haven. Yet this short, shaded trek up a canyon of historical interest offers a delightful respite in Dinosaur National Monument's high desert terrain. This hike is also a pleasant conclusion to the Tour of Tilted Rocks interpretive drive along the Cub Creek Road.

Exploring the remains of Josie Morris's homestead occupies every hiker's interest. The dilapidated structure that remains is a mere skeleton of the lively, yet simple life she crafted by herself in a very remote location. Why settle here? Take a quick walk up Box Canyon, directly across from the cabin, to see where she corralled her livestock. Look for other features this area has that might appeal to a homesteader.

Many plants around the cabin are living remnants of Josie's work. Ask youngsters to identify which trees she probably planted.

The trail begins at the east end of the property, near the spring. Mint plants scent the air here and in several spots along the trail. Encourage your group to look for other mints, which can be recognized by their fragrance and square-shaped stem (roll it between your fingertips). I discovered five different mints during my hike to Hog Canyon.

After passing the chicken coop, the trail enters an open area from which Cub Creek Canyon can be viewed. Follow the trail to the left and into a cluster of trees. As the trail reaches the base of Hog Canyon, it veers left into a meadow. A rare orchid has been located in this area, and walking here is restricted to the trail. It's not likely you'll see the flower, but knowing about it makes the meadow seem especially significant while passing through.

 As it enters the boxed-in area of the canyon, the trail crosses a small creek several times. Explain that Josie fenced the canyon's narrow, open ends to take advantage of its walls to enclose her pigs. During the return walk on the same trail, keep an eye out for fencing, gates, and other landmarks that might be remnants of a homesteader's life.

For the dinosaur fans in your group, we recommend a visit to the Prehistoric Museum of Eastern Utah University in Price. Exhibits here include a recently excavated woolly mammoth found during the construction of a dam in a nearby canyon.

Restroom and drinking water facilities are located near the parking lot for the entrance drive to the Dinosaur Quarry.

40 LITTLE HOLE NATIONAL SCENIC TRAIL

Location ▪	Flaming Gorge National Recreation Area
Type ▪	Day hike
Difficulty ▪	Easy to moderate for children
Hikable ▪	May to October
Distance ▪	Up to 7.2 miles, one way
Starting Elevation ▪	5605 feet
Ending Elevation ▪	5530 feet
Maps ▪	Trails Illustrated Flaming Gorge National Recreation Area and Eastern Uintas; Flaming Gorge National Recreation Area brochure

 Flaming Gorge National Recreation Area is 38 miles north of Vernal on US 191. (Vernal is 175 miles east of Salt Lake City on US 40.) The trailhead is located at the boat launch ramp, accessed on a winding road 0.2 mile east of the dam to the right. Ample parking is provided above the boat ramp. Shuttle of vehicles to the trail's end at Little Hole can be arranged through the service station/river trip center in the town of Dutch John. Little Hole is the boat launch ramp 6 miles east of Dutch John on Forest Road 75.

Kids find endless diversions along this trail that edges the Green River's clear, spirited flow from the dam. They'll be on the lookout for river otters at play on the shores, and in doing so will learn to read the river for its many signs of wildlife. Little anglers are amazed at the sight of large trout feeding in what writers of outdoor magazines deem the "best stretch of fishing river in this country."

A fun theme to add to this 7.2-mile walk is to ask your little ones to find seven wonders, one for each of the miles numbered on the trail.

Beginning the trail near the dam's boat launch, the first wonder everyone must avoid is poison ivy. Take a few moments to acquaint youngsters with this unwelcome plant's shiny, deep green leaves grouped in threes.

Perhaps the finest wonder I'll remember from this walk, is watching a river otter family play amongst rocks on the riverbank. Recently reintroduced to the Green River, this member of the weasel family once swam every waterway in the continent. Trapping, then pollution and land development nearly eliminated the otter by the mid-1800s. Active all year, otters dive through holes in the ice to fish. They are swift swimmers identified by the ripple they send across the water's surface. Discuss the value of reintroducing the river otter. Let youngsters know that otters benefit streams by eating primarily carp, chub, flannelmouthed suckers, and crayfish, all of which compete with trout for limited amounts of food.

Between mileposts 2 and 3, point out the landslide on the opposite side of the river. Ask the kids if the landslide could have caused

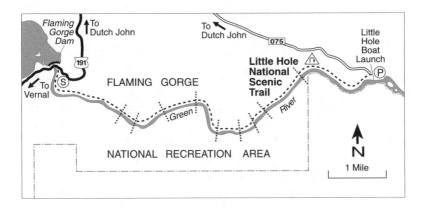

Rafters paddle the Green River as seen from Little Hole National Scenic Trail.

the rapid here. Ponderosa pines along this section deserve a hug for their aroma. Find the 4-foot-wide pine that's been cut to clear the trail. Count its tree rings to find out its age when it was sawed. Look for trees of similar age, twice as old, and half as old.

Green algae thickens large sections of the waterway, suggesting why the river was named the Green. However, anyone who has seen this river winding slowly through eastern Utah's desert land knows it as a brown river. The Green flows true to its name near its headwaters in Green River, Wyoming. On its route to Utah it turns brown as it picks up sediment from desert canyons. By dumping the sediment in the lake behind the dam, the river runs clear again, only to return to its brown state just a few miles downriver in Dinosaur National Monument.

The very clear, calm pools between mileposts 3 and 4 may look inviting for a swim, but a little toe test will remind you that this water spills from the lake's bottom. Talk about why the water is so cold. What other changes to the river are due to the dam (clear water, controlled flows)?

The crystalline waters are ideal for viewing another wonder: huge trout (brook, brown, rainbow, and cutthroat). To show children what trout eat, have them dip an open white handkerchief or T-shirt across the water's surface. Insect larvae will remain on the cloth.

The towering red canyon walls around milepost 5 rate a "wonder" ranking because these rocks are Precambrian (over 600 million years old). Generally found deep underground, most of the world's oldest rocks are seen only by those who walk or raft river gorges such as the Green's. Erosion and uplift over tens of millions of years caused this rock's exposure here in Red Canyon.

At mile 5.5 there are primitive toilets. This can be a short turn-around point for hikers starting at the Little Hole end of the trail.

Look for the spring that feeds the ferns and bushes of this lush area. What animals might come here for cover or food?

Prickly pear, pinyon, and juniper freckle the dry terrain for the last mile. Many large birds, including bald eagles, survey the river corridor, so keep on the lookout for wonder number seven.

Rafts are available for rent in Dutch John. Any number of hiking/rafting combinations is available for experienced white-water rafters using the available shuttle services. For more information stop at the visitor center at Flaming Gorge Dam.

Water and toilet facilities are located at both ends of the trail.

41
UTE MOUNTAIN TRAIL TO BROWNE LAKE

Location ■	Ashley National Forest, Flaming Gorge
Type ■	Day hike
Difficulty ■	Easy for children
Hikable ■	May though September
Distance ■	1.6 miles, one way
Starting Elevation ■	8834 feet
Ending Elevation ■	8300 feet
Maps ■	Trails Illustrated Flaming Gorge National Recreation Area and Eastern Uintas; USGS Jensen Butte and Leidy Peak

From Manila on the west side of Flaming Gorge Reservoir, follow UT-44 south 5.5 miles, turning right (west) on the Sheep Creek Geologic Loop. At the tour's end (about 8 miles), turn right (west) at the signs for Spirit Lake (Forest Road 218) and drive 1.3 miles to the road to Ute Mountain Tower, Forest Road 005. Turn left (south) and proceed 0.8 mile to the road's end at the tower, where a parking area is provided. Low-clearance vehicles are not recommended on many of this area's rough roads.

To reach Browne Lake return to Forest Road 218 (which is called

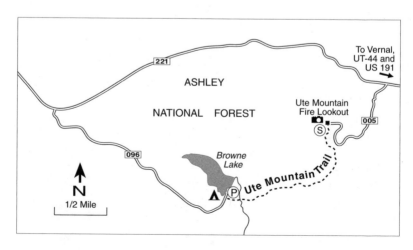

A ranger adjusts the fire finder from the lookout tower near Ute Mountain trailhead.

Forest Road 221 where it meets Forest Road 005) and turn left (west). Drive 3.5 miles to Forest Road 096 on the left. Turn left (south), going 1.5 miles to the road's ending at the Browne Lake campground.

A visit to Utah's first and only operating fire lookout tower highlights this easy walk starting at the top of Ute Mountain. The trail winds through stands of aspen, fir, and pine, ending in the meadows of Browne Lake, where fishing and camping are available.

The Sheep Creek Geologic Loop, a fascinating look at rock formations spanning 600 million years, ends a few miles west of the fire lookout tower. Children will enjoy the drive's look at a rare sampling of earth's history, especially if they read the "Wheels of Time" chart (available at any area visitor center) as they ride past the highway interpretive signs. While scanning the slopes they'll be excited to spot bighorn sheep, reintroduced here in the 1980s. Late summer and fall visitors see the water of Sheep Creek flow brilliant crimson because of the kokanee salmon spawn.

Before setting foot on the trail, which is located left of the lookout tower, carefully climb its stairs and knock on the door overhead. (Have your youngest count the steps.) The Forest Service fire lookout will be on hand most everyday throughout the summer to explain the work of fire detection and prevention.

Little ones and their bigger counterparts will be intrigued to learn how a person lives for weeks at a time in a 14-foot-square room 50 feet above ground. Seeing how the fire finder works or walking the catwalk around the tower room gives them a sampling of the observer's work. Ask why more fire lookout towers are not in use. What's being done to replace them? Find out what causes fires, what the lookout does when he or she spots a fire. How does the lookout cook, wash, and spend his or her free time? On the way down the stairs, talk about the books and projects you would bring while working at a fire lookout.

The Ute Mountain trail to Browne Lake is signed with blazes cut in the lodgepole pines. This rocky trail descends steadily into a young aspen forest littered with decaying lodgepole. Forest regeneration can be explained here by pointing out the aspen seedlings growing in place of the pines. Explain that aspens are among the first trees to rebuild a forest. Sprouting from previously established root systems that remain unharmed by fire or disease, these fast-growing, sun-loving trees live for about 100 years. A fire occurred here in 1985. Ask your young hikers how old they think these trees are. Look in the undergrowth for other tree seedlings.

Views of the Uinta Range fill the horizon as the trail descends into spruce forest shared by aspens. (Did the fire occur here?) Explain that the Uinta is the only major mountain range running east and west in the continental United States. How do these mountains appear different from the Wasatch Range?

Clusters of tiny, yellow star flowers dress up the forest floor like bracelets of sunshine as the trail enters the meadows of sage. Called stonecrop, this succulent plant has fleshy stems and leaves. Squeeze one of its leaves. The water that oozes explains the plant's method of conserving water in its very dry home. Other flowering companions are yarrow and pussytoe. Their technique for holding the minimal moisture here is to wear a sunscreen, a covering of fine hairs on their stems and leaves. Look closely and use a fingernail or pocketknife to scrape away the plants' fine fur to examine this adaptation.

Point out the different grasses and flowers as the trail nears the creek outlet from Browne Lake. Here I saw a group of youngsters having a great time wading and splashing in the shallow waters.

Fishing is reportedly good at Browne Lake and a campground is located nearby.

Water facilities are not provided at either trailhead. Toilet facilities are provided at the Browne Lake campground.

42 FREMONT INDIAN STATE PARK TRAILS

Location ■ South of Richfield
Type ■ Day hike with nearby camping at Castle Rock
Difficulty ■ Easy to moderate for children
Hikable ■ Most trails open year-round
Distance ■ Parade of Rock Art Trail, 0.4-mile paved loop; Canyon Overlook Loop, 1 mile; Hidden Secrets, up to 2 miles
Starting Elevation ■ 5800 feet
High Point ■ 6000 feet
Maps ■ Park brochures, interpretive guides

www.nr.state.ut.us/parks/www1/frem.htm
State Park Admission fee
Wheelchair-accessible trail to rock art

Located just off I-70 between Richfield and the intersection of I-15 and I-70, Fremont Indian State Park and Museum is accessed via exit 17 if traveling east on I-70, or exit 23 if traveling west on I-70. Follow the signs to the visitor center where ample parking is provided. Castle Rock Campground is located 2 miles southwest of the visitor center, across I-70.

It's hard to resist thinking the prehistoric people of Clear Creek Canyon created over 500 panels of rock art close to the state's central highway so more people could see them. In the same tradition, the folks at Fremont Indian State Park and Museum designed the trails and museum displays to appeal to all visitors, from neophyte desert hikers to veteran canyon country explorers. The numerous trails at the park combined with camping at Castle Rock Campground provide a complete getaway for families. At the visitor center, strollers, wheelchairs, and binoculars are available for use in the park. During the summer months a volunteer guide leads interpretive walks on the Parade of Rock Art trail.

A walk through the park's interpretative museum offers an ideal introduction to the ways Fremont people lived, ate, dressed, and played. The museum houses many of the artifacts collected during the construction of I-70 through Clear Creek Canyon. Chi'kee, the full-size statue of a Fremont woman dressed in rabbit skin and jewelry, captivates children with her taped tale of life in the canyon 1000 years ago. Kids can try their hand here at grinding corn using the mano and metate on display. They can also become a Junior Ranger at Fremont Indian State Park by completing the activities described in the park's activity manual available at the visitor center.

A cluster of easy to moderate trails threads the region around the visitor center. The barrier-free Parade of Rock Art trail leads to numerous rock panels before it meets the Court of Ceremonies trail at the top of the loop, which heads back to the visitor center.

In addition to interpreting the various designs and images, encourage kids to call them petroglyphs if the image appears pecked into the stone, or pictographs if paint has been applied. Do any rock images show both characteristics? Ask your little interpreters to look for different styles or perhaps a repeated figure. Name the animals. Look for maps, hunt scenes, clan symbols, or any theme that children can identify.

The Court of Ceremonies trail parallels several rock panels noted for their human figures. Ask your pictograph-petroglyph scout to count the number of people images he or she sees. For a short hike back to the visitor center, follow the trail over a small footbridge; turn right, climbing a rough rocky slope before leveling in a pinyon-juniper stand and then descending a small hill.

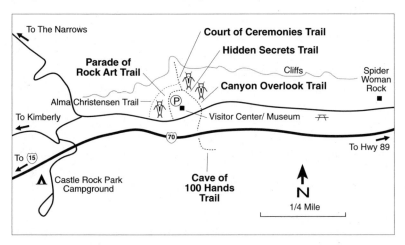

Petroglyphs of hunt scenes and clan symbols etch many rock surfaces at Fremont Indian State Park.

Views of the thickly forested Tushar Mountains across the interstate to the south stand in contrast to the thin grass, brush, and cacti of this area's high desert. Stop in this sparsely vegetated landscape to look, as perhaps a Fremont woman once did, for food—the seed from Indian ricegrass, cactus in fruit, juniper berries, or the nuts from a pinyon cone. Let kids know the Fremont were hunters and farmers who grew corn, beans, and squash. From here they will see the granary (prehistoric food storage room) and a pithouse with a ladder entry at the base of the hill and will race down the trail to investigate. The pithouse is a replica of the kind found at Five Finger Ridge, the remains of a hill on the other side of I-70 where the largest Fremont village was excavated.

 Hidden Secrets trail is accessed from the Court of Ceremonies just past marker 4 and at the fork near the top of the ridge near marker 5. Consisting of three short, connecting loops, this trail gives hikers a chance to discover signs of prehistoric life on their own. One secret not to miss is the petroglyph panel on a conspicuous south-facing cliff. Look for a shield figure and detailed drawings of desert bighorn sheep. The shield may represent the year's lunar cycle. Ask your companions why this calendar shows thirteen circles.

Canyon Overlook trail meets Hidden Secrets trail, giving hikers panoramic views and a close-up look at rock art panels on a cliff face. Clear Creek Canyon was and continues to be a major transportation thoroughfare. Fremont people, pioneer settlers, and gold miners all hiked this corridor. Wagon leaders once paid a quarter to travel the road through here, which was replaced by a rail line, then an auto road, and finally an interstate highway. At the overlook, don't miss the petroglyph panels on the cliff to your left.

Cave of 100 Hands is another recommended trail in the park. But don't walk the 0.25 mile to the cave expecting fifty pairs of hands to greet you; much fewer decorate its wall. While walking near the I-70 overpass look for deer footprints in the mud and swallow nests in the bridge overhead. A natural spring flows in the area directly in front of the cave. What clues would thirsty travelers find here telling them water is available? It is not advised to drink from this area and do watch out for stinging nettle.

CAUTION

After your kids count the number of hands in the cave, let them know archaeologists have excavated the site and found evidence that people once lived here. Ask your explorers their theories on how and why prehistoric people left their handprints on rock walls. The trailhead to Cave of 100 Hands starts on the south side of the frontage road, opposite the visitor center. The moderate trail leads through sage country under I-70, then east.

Detailed drawings of desert bighorn sheep and other animals and people can be seen at Skinner Canyon, 2.2 miles east of the visitor center on the frontage road. Before heading out, ask at the visitor center about the Curse of Spider Woman Rock. Before I-70 construction this rock had several rock panels that told parts of the Hopi creation legend. Spider Woman Rock got its name from the petroglyphs on it describing the Hopi legend of Spider Woman.

Water and toilet facilities are available at the visitor center. The park's museum, visitor center, and gift shop are open daily 9 A.M. to 6 P.M. during the summer and 9 A.M. to 5 P.M. from Labor Day to Memorial Day. Castle Rock Campground is located 0.75 mile west of the visitor center.

HIDDEN PINYON TRAIL

Location ■ Snow Canyon State Park, St. George
Type ■ Day hike
Difficulty ■ Moderate for children
Hikable ■ Year-round
Distance ■ 1.4 miles, loop
Starting Elevation ■ 3400 feet
High Point ■ 3616 feet
Map ■ USGS Santa Clara

www.nr.state.ut.us/parks/www1/snow.htm
State park admission fee

From St. George drive north on Bluff Street past Sunset Drive, turning left at the signs for Snow Canyon Parkway. Continue 6 miles to the campground entrance on the left. The Hidden Pinyon trailhead is 100 yards south of the campground and fee station.

Hidden Pinyon Trail treats hikers to an adventurous walk through a diverse slice of canyon country. Kids enjoy rock scrambling on the trail, and their parents will appreciate the area's magnificent views. Sturdy shoes are recommended for this interpreted loop trail, where sandy terrain and rock-stubbled paths require careful footing. Make sure to follow the signs because other trails cross the Hidden Pinyon Trail.

A brochure highlighting the plants and rock formations of Hidden Pinyon Trail is available at the trailhead.

At the trailhead, basalt nodules perforate the sandy path. These volcanic-like chunks are the product of a relatively recent volcanic flow—only 10,000 years ago. The black lava layer scattered across the ridge above the campground to your right is 1 million years old. Ask your hikers how the two rock forms appear different.

Stop to look (don't touch!) and compare the lichen and moss bonded to opposite sides of the rock at signpost 4. Children might describe lichen as crusty and hard, while the moss is soft and velvety. Remind them that lichen, despite its lifeless appearance, actually produces its own food. Mosses, however, thrive in the shade and depend on moisture and small amounts of soil to survive.

After the trail takes you through a narrow passage, it leads to a rock ledge. Hikers of all sizes may need help here.

Helping hands along a slickrock slope at Snow Canyon State Park

At signpost 5 the trail bears right, gradually ascending through sand and boulders to an open area where the trail forks to the right. (Following the left fork leads back to the trailhead.) Slickrock slopes between signpost 6 and 13 may lure some hikers off the trail; how- ever, please stay on the trail and off these dangerous areas.

Shortly after signpost 16, turn left to the Hidden Pinyon Over- look up a short hill on the left. Here is a lovely view of West Can- yon—worthy of the trek indeed.

Desert varnish stripes many of West Canyon's sheer walls. Explain that the black coating, which is common to rock surfaces throughout the Southwest, develops over many centuries. Scientists who study minerals in rocks long assumed that desert varnish consisted of a rust that formed from the iron oxides in rock. In the late 1970s, however, they discovered that fine, airborne clay particles make up the major- ity of the coloring, the rest being iron and manganese oxides and sand grains. When a dusting of clay sticks to a surface of wet rock, the water evaporates, concentrating the clay and the dark staining minerals that have been oxidized by microscopic bacteria living on the rock surfaces. Shiny varnish occurs on smooth surfaces and is rich in manganese. Look for areas where the rock is not painted by desert varnish. Do they appear to be protected from wind and rain?

After the view, retrace your steps back to signpost 16 and follow the easy scramble over red rock past signposts 17, 18, and 19. Upon reaching the soft sand beyond signpost 19, look for the hidden pinyon.

The trail loops back to its beginning near signpost 9. Watch for the marked trail that veers to the right between signposts 6 and 5, which leads back to the trailhead.

Toilet and water facilities are available at the campground.

 SPRING CREEK CANYON

Location ■	South of Cedar City
Type ■	Day hike or overnight backpack
Difficulty ■	Easy to moderate for children
Hikable ■	April through November
Distance ■	2 miles or more, one way
Starting Elevation ■	5600 feet
High Point ■	6100 feet
Map ■	USGS Kanarraville

 From Cedar City drive 9 miles south on I-15, turning off at exit 51 (Kanarraville). Proceed south 4.5 miles on a paved road through the town to its south end, passing the last house, and turn left on the dirt road. Follow this road 0.7 mile to a fork where a parking area is provided. High-clearance vehicles may continue another 0.4 mile to the left before parking in a clearing on the right. Parking is limited here.

This is a delightful introduction to hiking a canyon's "narrows" because the access is easy and exploring opportunities abound. Though not maintained, the trail is well defined as it passes through Bureau of Land Management (BLM) wilderness study areas and sections of Utah state land.

 This creek was dry during my late-June hike here; however, any streambed can become dangerous during the area's mid- to late-summer flash-flood season. Call ahead (435-586-2401) for current conditions. If rain threatens, slot canyons such as this should be avoided.

As Spring Creek Canyon narrows, it lures hikers into a beautiful rock recess.

Beginning at the first parking area, follow the old jeep road as it crosses Spring Creek and reaches a level plateau along its west side. Continue on the trail through open areas and stands of scrub oak for 0.8 mile to the mouth of the canyon.

Upon reaching the canyon entrance, cross the creek to the right and follow the footpath over the creekbed again and again. The canyon widens initially, with maples shading the rocky route to where

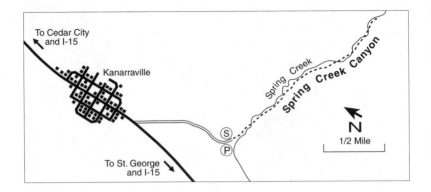

another side canyon enters on the left. Follow the footpath that veers left and up a short hill to an interesting arched alcove. This can be used as a primitive shelter or campsite.

Continuing into the heart of the canyon, watch for a spring bubbling from a sandstone slab on the right at 1.5 miles.

Just before the walls appear to reach their narrowest slot at 1.6 miles, look for sandstone blocks tumbled in a pile on the right side of the trail. While some hikers will prefer the challenge of climbing this natural obstacle course, others will ponder how recently the squares broke off this wall. What caused it? Are other areas of the sandstone wall unstable?

Climbing up and over rocks and logs becomes increasingly difficult as the span between canyon walls becomes arm-lengths wide. However, this is the allure of exploring canyon narrows, where every hurdle climbed leads to another exquisite sight of smooth-sculpted sandstone washed in slanted rays of sunlight. No plants inhabit this starkly beautiful rock recess, and the slice of blue sky overhead serves as a comforting cap.

Depending on your group's cooperative climbing skills, the exploration can continue safely for another mile before the canyon forks. High ledges in both canyons require technical climbing skills and equipment.

Thirsty summer hikers may want to try moistening their mouths by sucking on the red berries of the three-leafed sumac bush found in the open area just past the canyon entrance. The dry, somewhat sticky berries growing on bushes with small oak-shaped leaves have a distinct lemon flavor. This was commonly used by Native Americans to flavor pemmican.

No toilet or water facilities are provided at the trailhead.

45 MIDDLE FORK OF TAYLOR CREEK

Location	■ Zion National Park, Kolob Canyon
Type	■ Day hike
Difficulty	■ Moderate for children
Hikable	■ April through October
Distance	■ 2.7 miles, one way
Starting Elevation	■ 5500 feet
High Point	■ 5760 feet
Maps	■ Trails Illustrated Zion National Park; USGS Zion National Park; Zion National Park brochures

www.nps.gov/zion
National park entrance fee

Zion National Park's Kolob Canyon Visitor Center is accessed from I-15 via exit 40, 19 miles south of Cedar City or 34 miles north of St. George. From the visitor center drive 2 miles east on the paved road to the signed Taylor Creek Trail parking area on the left.

Following an ever-changing canyon streambed, the trail to Double Arch Alcove features rewarding destinations, such as historic cabins

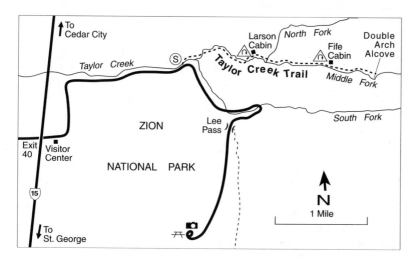

A Western collared lizard perches on a rock cairn.

and exquisite waterfalls. Quiet, observant hikers frequently spy a deer bounding through the brush or a golden eagle soaring overhead. The many wildlife signs in this less visited portion of Zion National Park add excitement to the trek. A flash flood in the spring of 1993 altered the trail, but it is now well established. A self-guiding trail guide to Kolob Canyon is available at the Kolob Canyon Visitor Center.

A short, steep descent from the trailhead leads to the canyon bottom. Walking this streambed shaded by cottonwood, river birch, and maple trees involves many stream crossings, which are made easy with strategically placed rocks. The counting experts in your group may have fun keeping track of the number of times the group crosses Taylor Creek's middle fork.

At the seventh creek crossing, at 0.3 mile, watch for the fascinating formation on the left consisting of rock layers folded on top of each other. Ask youngsters to imagine the force required to bend these layers. How much time did the process take?

Two life zones merge along this trail, one featuring sun- and heat-tolerant plants, the other bearing water-dependent trees and shrubs of the streambed. Ask your companions to point out plants from both zones. Explain that the stream creates a riparian zone, an important source of food, water, and shelter for the area's wildlife. A spider dangling from its web, a woodpecker drilling holes in a distant tree, bees landing on flowers, even a rattlesnake sunning itself are among the wildlife youngsters might discover. (When not surprised, rattlers assume a coiled, defensive position when approached. If left alone, they will crawl away and hide.)

Animal tracks are especially easy to spot because the path is sand most of the way. If you discover, as we did, a large cat or dog print, you may be looking at a resident bobcat or coyote's trademark. (Pets are not permitted here.) Also, stop to listen for a mule deer stepping on twigs, a squirrel chattering, or a canyon tree frog's bleating call.

The ponderosa pine stumps are remnants of the logging that took place here in the early 1900s, before the land became part of Zion National Park. Stop to savor the smell of a standing ponderosa's bark. Count the needles in a bunch. How long are they? Most of the trees seen now are young, having replaced the 2- and 3-foot-wide trees that once flourished here. Imagine how different this streambed must have been before logging took place.

At 1.2 miles Larson Cabin sits in a juniper forest. From 1930 to 1933 Gustav Larson homesteaded here, raising pigs. Do you suppose he fenced them or let them roam free to feed? On what? Of the many places along the streambed, why do you think he chose this one to build a cabin? The cabin's log walls are white fir, a tree with flat, flexible needles and silvery, smooth bark found farther upstream. The cabin can serve as a turnaround point. Do leave this historic site unaffected by your visit.

Following the trail through the junipers, stop to compare them to the ponderosa pines before meeting the north fork's stream. At this confluence of the north and middle fork canyons, Paria Point looms 7802 feet high on the right. Proceed to the right, following the narrowing slice between canyons. The stream crossings become a bit trickier in this last section, but a reward, a lovely 5-foot-tall waterfall at 1.6 miles, makes the work worthwhile.

At 1.7 miles, beneath an overhang on the left, look for inscriptions left by two explorers in 1871. Discuss why it is not acceptable anywhere, and is illegal in national parks and forests, to mark trees and rocks.

An agriculture professor who raised goats here built the Fife Cabin at 1.9 miles. Imagine the racket of pig squeals and goat bleats bouncing off these slickrock walls 60 years ago. Back then new trees were slowly filling in a forest left thin by logging. How would Arthur Fife's view from his cabin have differed from the view now?

Just beyond the cabin a tree-canopied interlude precedes the view of Double Arch Alcove, on the right. Stone steps lead to a good viewpoint of this geologic beauty. Youngsters will have fun experimenting with their echo here—our toddler did! Clumps of yellow columbine clinging to the rock wall's seep line flower in early summer. Before heading back, relax in this shady oasis to the music of dripping water.

Despite an apparent trail that continues upstream, do not proceed into this unsafe, rockfall site.

The nearest toilet and water facilities are at the visitor center.

46 EMERALD POOLS TRAIL

Location ■	Zion National Park
Type ■	Day hike
Difficulty ■	Easy, then moderate for children
Hikable ■	April through November, lower pool is reachable year-round except after heavy snows
Distance ■	First pool, 0.6 mile, one way; upper pool, 1.1 miles, one way
Starting Elevation ■	4276 feet
High Point ■	4708 feet
Maps ■	Trails Illustrated Zion National Park; USGS Temple of Sinawava; Zion National Park brochure

www.nps.gov/zion
National park entrance fee
Wheelchair accessible with assistance for first 0.5 mile

From Zion Visitor Center drive 0.7 mile north to the Zion Canyon Scenic Drive. From April through October the Zion Canyon Scenic Drive is closed to private vehicles. A shuttlebus transports all visitors to the Upper Zion Canyon, which includes the Emerald Pools and Riverside Walk. Those visitors on foot or bicycle or during

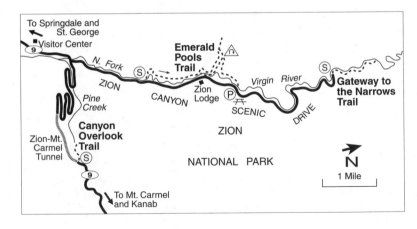

November through March turn left on the Zion Canyon Scenic Drive and proceed 3.0 miles to the turnoff to the parking area on the left. (Parking is also available at Zion Lodge, across the street.) The trail begins at the footbridge near the lot's northwest corner.

Everyone from wheelchair users to rock-climbing enthusiasts can immerse themselves in beauty along one of Zion's most popular sets of trails. Three pools, each spilling into shady, fern-fringed grottoes, serve as destinations that reward hikers of all abilities. Two options are provided for making a loop trail, both of which allow closer looks at Zion's delicate web of life.

From the parking lot, cross the footbridge spanning the North Fork of the Virgin River. Those turning left here hike directly to the middle and upper pools, thus missing the first waterfall and pool, and heavy foot traffic. This hike description follows the trail leading right from the bridge. This section of the trail is paved, though too steep to recommend for wheelchair users.

Children enjoy the sideshow along this lovely shaded walkway overlooking the Virgin River. Squirrels scamper about the trees, lizards dart across the walkway, and birds flicker in the brush. Remember not to feed the critters, regardless of how cute their pose for your photographs. It's against the law and harmful to them!

After a summer rainstorm or during heavy spring melt-off, the normally brisk-flowing Virgin River becomes the park's raging artery, picking up rocks, sticks, and debris. This river has been described as an "ever-moving strip of sandpaper." Ask your young geologist in what way this is so.

Quiet prevails as the trail veers left, away from the riverside and into Heaps Canyon (named after an early Mormon pioneer). With the river out of earshot, this is a good place to tune in to the numerous birdcalls.

The trail enters a cool chasm adjacent to the lower pool. Summer hikers can refresh themselves in the fine spray of the waterfall. As the trail dips behind the water, note the necklace of yellow columbine, or shooting star, flowering along the curve of slickrock. Perhaps a canyon wren will serenade you with its clear, descending melody. The rare canyon tree frog might sound off its sheeplike croak from either pool area.

The lower pool on the left appears enticing to many a hiker. However, swimming or wading in this or any park pool is not allowed. Body oils and walking on pool sediment destroy plant and animal life essential to the area's living components, including park visitors.

Kolob Canyon—a grand, yet less-visited side of Zion National Park

When asked, your children may be able to explain this park policy more eloquently. Tired hikers or those pushing strollers can turn around here.

Winding up and around a gang of stout boulders, the trail turns left through brush and leads to the middle pool at 0.8 mile. Its backdrop is a spectacular but perilous cliff edge. Keep all children within an arm's reach before approaching the pool.

Without peering over the edge, ask your youngsters where this water spills. Discuss how erosion deepens the pool's shallow slickrock basin. Remember to mention water erosion and alternate periods of freezing and thawing. Never throw anything over the cliff here or elsewhere; hikers are below.

The 0.3-mile hike to the upper pool threads a steep oak brush hill littered with roots and rocks. Point out that dry-habitat plants such as yucca, cactus, and pinyon or juniper trees grow here, but not along the trail below. There are many faint paths along this section. Prevent further destruction by staying on the main trail.

As the trail tops out, hikers face a red, cavernous canyon wall looming above a sand-bottomed pool. Large boulders rim this north-facing oasis (which is shaded by midafternoon) and serve as perfect perches to contemplate delicate hanging gardens or watch rays of sunlight filtering the mist. Children, however, prefer a more vigorous mode of appreciation, like climbing the rocks. Depending on spring runoff, the waterfall usually continues through May.

To return, retrace the same trail or complete a loop by following one of two other trails. The 1-mile hike to the trailhead footbridge veers right 0.25 mile below the upper pool. To return via the 0.8-mile trail to the grotto picnic area, turn left at the middle pool. Upon reaching the picnic area, the hike back to the parking area is an additional 1.5 miles along the road if a shuttled vehicle is not parked there.

Toilet and water facilities are provided at Zion Lodge.

RIVERSIDE WALK

Location ■	Zion National Park
Type ■	Day hike
Difficulty ■	Easy for children
Hikable ■	Half of trail open year-round. Last half is closed because of falling ice December through March
Distance ■	1 mile, one way; an optional 1.8 miles, one way
Starting Elevation ■	4411 feet
High Point ■	4460 feet
Maps ■	USGS Temple of Sinawava; Zion National Park brochure

www.nps.gov/zion
National park entrance fee
Wheelchair accessible (some assistance required)

See the directions for Emerald Pools, Hike 46. The trailhead for the Riverside Walk is at the end of the Zion Canyon Scenic Drive, at the Sinawava parking area.

This lush entry into the heart of Zion National Park follows an increasingly narrow slot into a canyon 2000 feet deep. Its sandstone walls, flocked by hanging gardens, create a cool corridor, misted by seeps and waterfalls that spill into inviting pools. This partially paved trail along the Virgin River gives hikers of all sizes a shorter, dry-land version of Zion's famous 16-mile, 2-day wade through the river's canyon course.

Tall cottonwoods shade the trailhead for the Riverside Walk. Here a sign advises hikers of the river's condition beyond this portion of the trail. Informative displays describing the formation of this narrow canyon are nearby, on the right. At the hike's beginning the canyon bottom is shared by the Virgin River and a wide strip of vegetation. Explain to your companions that the canyon narrows until there's room enough for only the river and the walkway. Kids will understand how tall the canyon walls are if you compare their height to that of a 200-story building—taller than the highest building in the world!

Initially fascinated by the canyon walls looming overhead, children are soon captivated by the lush plant life at their feet. Called a desert swamp, this collection of algae, cattails, duckweed, and horsetails thrives in the shallow pools on the left at 0.2 mile. Ask youngsters how the seeds of these different water-dependent plants arrived here. Encourage them to trace the source of the water that feeds these pools. They'll discover that underground springs and seeps from the canyon walls supply water to this desert swamp area.

At 0.4 mile a spectacular wall, glistening with water, stops nearly every visitor. In spring and early summer the waterfall here sprays a cooling mist. Children enjoy sending their leaf "boats" through the pipe under the walkway and into the stream. Where will the boats

end up? At the time of this writing, the remaining portion of the trail was being prepared for paving. This stop is a good turnaround point for little ones or those in wheelchairs. In winter months ice falls are common in this area.

Hanging gardens, regardless of the direction you walk, are abundant and within arm's reach of every hiker. Stop to carefully look, but do not touch these rare and fragile plant Edens. Throughout the summer ferns and mosses form the dark green backdrop to the yellow-flowered columbine and monkey flower. The cardinal flower and pink shooting star also find a home in this unique habitat. Observant youngsters may find here the tiny Zion snail—found nowhere else in the world.

The trail continues edging the canyon wall until it stops at the start of the narrows. This is the turnaround point for those who want to keep their feet dry. When weather conditions permit, those 12 years and older who wish to sample walking a river bottom may continue for another 1.8 miles. Be prepared, however; conditions change rapidly and unexpectedly in desert canyons.

Drinking water and toilet facilities are available only at the trailhead.

CANYON OVERLOOK

Location	■ Zion National Park
Type	■ Day hike
Difficulty	■ Easy to moderate for children; caution advised
Hikable	■ March through mid-December
Distance	■ 0.5 mile, one way
Starting Elevation	■ 5124 feet
High Point	■ 5300 feet
Maps	■ Trails Illustrated Zion National Park; USGS Springdale East; Zion National Park brochure

www.nps.gov/zion
National park entrance fee

From the Zion Visitor Center drive 5 miles east through the Zion–Mount Carmel Tunnel (UT-9) to the east portal. Parking is provided in a lot immediately to your right. The trailhead is on the opposite side of the road.

Breathtaking is the word that best describes this self-guided canyon rim walk to a fenced viewpoint of Zion's stunning western features. Early morning allows relatively cool summer walks in this high desert environment, and early-afternoon hikers can take dramatic photographs before the setting sun washes out rock definition. Folks who fear heights or children quick to scamper ahead should not attempt this trail.

In addition to the excellent trail guide available at the trailhead, the following suggestions will help hike leaders give their crew a fun, experiential trek into the high desert's ecosystems.

- Before starting the hike tell youngsters that they will be walking along the edges of cliffs, and must watch where they are stepping.

- At the trailhead remind them to use the handrail because the trail climbs quite steeply here. After 200 feet it levels and follows the rock ledges above Pine Creek.

- A lizard darting from sun to shade may look like it's playing hide-and-go-seek with your youngster. This cold-blooded creature is

The Zion–Mount Carmel Highway switchbacks to a tunnel, as viewed from Canyon Overlook.

actually adjusting its body temperature by moving from sunny to shaded surfaces. Have children place their palm on rocks of different colors and sun exposures to feel where a lizard warms and cools itself.

- Other animals' signs may capture kids' attention at the first rock overhang. Tell them bighorn sheep are often seen feeding on the grasses and shrubs in the area. Also, eagles and mule deer are frequently sighted here. Look for signs of wildlife all around you.

- Rows of tiny holes, the woodpecker's trademark, dimple the large juniper tree on the trail's left side. Kids are intrigued to hear that a woodpecker called a sapsucker drilled the holes to create an insect trap. After insects get stuck in the tree sap that dripped from the holes, the sapsucker returns to feed on both.

- A little farther ahead, also on the left, a much larger animal has scarred a pinyon pine (identified by needles in bundles of two). Stop to feel the teethmarks gouged in the soft inner bark and decide what creature dined on the tree. Could it have been a porcupine or a bear?

- Tell kids to watch for a cavelike place where a line of jewels can be found. Tiny treasures such as maidenhair fern, monkey flower (a yellow-petaled flower with red dots), and mosses bloom in the meager, but moist soil along what's called the seep line of the next rock overhang. Children are fascinated to learn that rainwater percolates through the sandstone before reaching this point. Please respect these natural gems by leaving them untouched.

- After a short switchback encourage kids to look for orange and greenish gray crusts on the rocks. Although these colorful patches, called lichen, look to be lifeless, they actually grow—and are even eaten by certain animals. Scientists now study lichen as an indicator of air pollution. They have found that as pollution increases, the number of lichens decreases. Talk with your group about what sources of pollution would cause the lichens to die off in this natural area noted for its clear air.

- Thriving along the trail are two varieties of cacti and two of yucca. Prickly pear grows as a low-lying cactus plant and as a tall, erect plant. Narrow and broadleaf yucca also share the desert floor. Ask kids to find, but not touch, these desert plants used by both men and animals. What parts of a cactus can be eaten? Native Americans used yucca in many ways. Can your companions think of any?

- At the viewpoint children like pointing out the peephole windows of the Zion–Mount Carmel Tunnel and the baby cars along the highway that zigzags into Zion Canyon.

- They'll need just a bit of imagination to visualize the surrounding cliffs as dunes of drifting sand millions of years ago. Pointing to the cliffs on the right, show your crew the diagonal lines called crossbeds that were made as the winds changed and the dunes shifted.

- Tell kids that West Temple, the highest peak in the view, was once the mud of an ancient sea until it hardened and began rising up about 13 million years ago.

Before heading back on the same trail, stop to listen and feel the forces that continually shape this scene. What are they?

A vault toilet is located at the east end of the parking lot. No water facilities are provided.

49 DUNES EXPLORATION

Location	■ Coral Pink Sand Dunes State Park
Type	■ Day hike or overnight camping
Difficulty	■ Easy for children
Hikable	■ Year-round; snowshoes suggested for snowy winter visits (bring a toboggan!)
Distance	■ 0.1 mile to 0.5 mile, or more, one way
Starting Elevation	■ 6000 feet
High Point	■ 6350 feet
Maps	■ USGS Yellow Jacket Canyon; Coral Pink Sand Dunes State Park brochure

www.nr.state.ut.us/parks/www1/cora.htm
State park fee for campground or day use

 From Kanab drive US 89 north 15 miles to the Hancock turnoff. Turn west (left) and continue about 10 miles to the park entrance.

Hiking becomes a rolling, crawling, even cartwheeling activity at Coral Pink Sand Dunes, a natural playground that brings out the kid in everyone. The very pleasant twenty-two-unit campground with heated restrooms makes an overnight stay an attractive option. It's best to schedule trips to the dunes for early spring or late fall, or for midweek during other times of the year when off-highway-vehicle (OHV) use is less likely.

Near the picnic area in the campground, a 5.5-acre area is barred from OHV use. This lot allows great opportunities to truly experience the dunes. In fact, the crest of the highest dune here is only 0.5 mile away. Kids have endless fun climbing, crawling, and clambering up this peak.

For those unwilling or unable to immerse themselves in navigating sand, a 200-foot boardwalk climbs the play area's first knoll, allowing a view of the dunes. Interpretive signs along the boardwalk and the trail through the picnic area identify desert plants and wildlife signs.

 However, chances are good your dune explorers will discover their own signs of wildlife, especially if they are alert in the early morning. Lacy, 0.5-inch-wide lines are often seen along the dunes. Their creator, a black beetle an inch or longer, will surprise youngsters by not

Sand dunes provide ample opportunity for photography and play.

scampering away from them. The beetle is not harmful, but all admirers are asked not to disturb it. Tracks of tiny feet with a line down
the center could be left by a lizard, or possibly a kangaroo rat. This
desert-dwelling rat uses its long, tufted tail to propel itself, making
up to 10-foot leaps.

Visitors here during the 4 days surrounding the full moon may
happen to see the 3- to 4-inch-wide track of a mountain lion. As with
most cats, a mountain lion's tracks form a single line. The shy animal
leaves no claw marks because it walks with its claws retracted. Using
the moon's light to hunt food, this night feeder knows to find its
prey—kangaroo rats, lizards, and mice—near the campground's outer
limits. Mountain lions are rarely seen, so there's little cause for concern, even during a 3:00 A.M. walk to the "potty."

Jackrabbits, cottontails, and snakes frequently leave their tracks in
the sand. During the spring and fall watch for tracks left by deer during their seasonal migration.

Hikers wanting to explore beyond the fenced-off area are advised to walk the crests of hills. This approach avoids sudden encounters with an OHV surging up a dune.

Toilet and water facilities, thanks to a 1000-foot-deep well, are located at the campground.

50 ALPINE POND TRAIL

Location ■	Cedar Breaks National Monument
Type ■	Day hike
Difficulty ■	Easy to moderate for children
Hikable ■	Mid-June to late September
Distance ■	2 miles, loop
Starting Elevation ■	10,476 feet
High Point ■	10,500 feet
Maps ■	Trails Illustrated Bryce Canyon National Park; USGS Brian Head; Cedar Breaks National Monument brochure

www.nps.gov/cebr

From Cedar City drive east on UT-14 approximately 19 miles. Turn north (left) on UT-148, continuing 3 miles to the Cedar Breaks National Monument Visitor Center. The trailheads for the Alpine Pond can be reached by driving north 3 miles to Chessmen Ridge overlook and parking on the left, or proceeding another 1.2 miles to the parking lot for the Alpine Pond Trail.

Walking this gentle trail through an old-growth forest rekindles everyone's spirit. Whether enthusiastically trekked as a budding naturalist, inspecting pond edges and tree root crevices, or quietly strolled, listening for messages the wind sends through the trees, all hikers will appreciate this trail's distant and close-up views. Steady summer showers can dampen the experience; but they also provide a lively look at the forest's response to rain. Seek shelter in a car or building if lightning threatens.

The twenty-five numbered posts that mark this loop are interpreted in a trail brochure available at the trailhead or visitor center. Rather than reword the explanations and points provided in this excellent pamphlet, the following questions and suggested activities are designed to enhance a child's, and thus a parent's experience. In addition, each provides an opportunity for your crew to gain a better understanding of and appreciation for the environment.

- Because the Chessmen Overlook is a "must-see," starting the trail here is recommended. Signpost 13 begins the loop. The bristle-cone pine near here deserves a hug, but it's so big it would take several pairs of arms to encircle it. Encourage children to calculate this tree's present age, knowing it was growing here in 1776. Do they see any nearby trees that look half this one's age?

- Follow the trail to the right where signpost 14 marks a wildflower meadow. My toddler liked shouting each flower's color, while older children tended to devise clever names that describe the flower's features.

- Between signposts 15 and 16 ask your companions if more trees appear healthy or injured by the bark beetle. Can you find tree seedlings that will replace them? Should the Park Service remove the dead trees? Why? Why not?

- Aspens are featured at signpost 17. After letting kids know that these trees rarely live to be 100 years old, ask them how old this cluster is. Does it look like fir and spruce trees will have taken over when they return here after high school? When they become parents? Grandparents?

- At the lightning-scarred tree, signpost 18, look for signs of insects or woodpeckers.

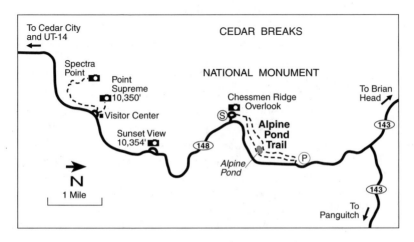

- Encourage kids to compare the initials carved into the aspen at signpost 19 with graffiti seen on city alleys and buildings.

- At signpost 20, repeat the alliterative description "*f*irs are *f*lat and *f*lexible and *s*pruce are *s*quare and *s*piky," to help reinforce tree identification.

- Do stop to listen to the forest at signpost 21. Children like interpreting the calls heard, and some even respect this special quiet long enough for all to appreciate.

- At signpost 23 talk about the trees identified thus far. How does a limber pine give its identity away?

- Between signposts 24 and 25 old, dead, but standing trees creak and moan as hikers walk below them. Do you suppose they're still mourning the fallen trees at your feet? Imagine passing through here without a cleared trail.

- The trail veers right, into the open, to signpost 1, where hikers retrace their steps back into forest to meet the rock apartment at signpost 2. Discuss each of the rock dwellers' lifestyles. Pikas gather piles of grass in the summer and scamper about all winter on ice-gripping furred paws. Marmots lay in the sun and eat grasses throughout the summer then sleep all winter. Chipmunks and squirrels gather food all summer and wake periodically in the winter to eat. If you had to choose between the life of a pika, a marmot, and a squirrel, which would you choose? Why?

- Continue down this needle-padded path to view the alpine pond at signpost 7. Stop to admire such wonders as a water strider, a daddy longleg–like water-walking insect, along the pond's quiet shore. Children who move slowly toward the strider may see the tiny hairs on its legs. These help the strider maintain its position on the water. If a pebble is dropped into the water, the strider will move away from it. If an insect falls to the water, the tiny vibrations may lure the strider to it.

- Follow the trail around the pond's very wet tip to meet signpost 8, where a sign for the Chessmen parking lot directs you to the left.

- Do stop to savor the private view of Cedar Breaks at signpost 9. Expect intense shades of yellow, red, and lavender after a rainstorm.

A short walk completes the loop at Chessmen parking lot.

Toilet and water facilities are provided at the visitor center.

51 CASCADE FALLS

Location ■ East of Cedar City
Type ■ Day hike
Difficulty ■ Moderate for children; caution advised
Hikable ■ June through mid-October
Distance ■ 0.8 mile, one way
Starting Elevation ■ 8900 feet
Ending Elevation ■ 8800 feet
Maps ■ Trails Illustrated Dixie National Forest;
USGS Navajo Lake, Henry Knolls, Straight
Canyon and Strawberry Point

From Cedar City travel 29 miles east on UT-14 to Duck Creek
Campground. Turn south (right) on the road opposite the campground. Follow this gravel road past the visitor center 1.5 miles on
Forest Road 370, turn left at the fork onto Forest Road 54, and continue 1.5 miles to where the road ends in a parking area; the trailhead is on the right. A visit to the ice cave requires veering left at
the first fork on the road from the visitor center.

A combined visit to an ice cave and waterfall, both formed under unusual geologic conditions, makes for a fun outing near Bryce Canyon.

In late June a large chunk of snow greeted us at the entrance to the
ice cave, which is actually a small limestone cavern. This 10-foot-deep,

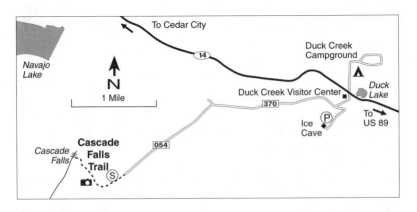

20-foot-wide hollow in the ground formed as water percolated through the area, dissolving the limestone. Under nondrought conditions, the floor of the cavern is usually covered with 2 or more feet of ice. As kids step into this natural freezer, they'll feel the temperature difference. Did they notice moss and columbine edging the cave? What conditions help these plants grow here, but not in the surrounding forest?

From the parking area at the Cascade Waterfall Trail, head right to the viewpoint of Strawberry Point. This pink landscape of cliffs and spires is similar to those seen at Cedar Breaks National Monument and Bryce Canyon National Park. Keeping a safe distance from the perilous cliff edges, the trail descends through stands of bristlecone and ponderosa pine to a fenced viewing platform on the left.

The North Fork of the Virgin River, edged in limy siltstone spires, is presented here. Explain to your companions that they are looking at the Pink Cliffs, the top step in what geologists call the Grand Staircase. If a giant walked up this staircase, she would start at the north rim of the Grand Canyon, where the staircase's oldest rock (which is 225 million years old) is exposed. (If she stepped down into the canyon, she'd rest on the world's oldest rock, 2 billion years old!) Each step up the giant took would bring her to a younger layer until she reached this top layer, a young 60 million years old!

As the trail veers right from the viewpoint, it edges steep, unfenced cliffs. Little ones who tend to wander must be reined in along this final stretch to the waterfall.

A rest bench tucked in the shade of a rock overhang is provided midway. Those who would rather avoid the final steep trail to the waterfall's viewing platform, though staircased and short, can sit here.

Gushing from a crevice in the rock wall, Cascade Falls is a drainage for Navajo Lakes. Geologists believe that quite recently (2000 to 10,000 years ago) lava spilled from fissures in the earth, damming a stream and forming Navajo Lake. As the lake's water seeped through cracks in the limestone, the rock dissolved. Over time, geologic time that is, water continues to dissolve the limestone, creating a wider tube.

A sign here may need some explanation. It warns that because of sudden loss in oxygen level in the area near the waterfalls, climbing into the waterfall cavern can be dangerous. Many youngsters know that water, H_2O, contains oxygen. Tell them this waterfall drains from the bottom of Navajo Lake, where the oxygen level is quite low. As the water tumbles through the confined tube, it takes on the oxygen it needs, sometimes removing all the oxygen from the atmosphere in the small area. Under what conditions do your scientists think the oxygen loss would be greatest?

Point out the lush vegetation formed along the stream that flows in an otherwise stony canyon. Discuss what causes this.

The jewels children see embedded in the boulder just below the stairs near the waterfall will captivate them. They are admiring chunks of quartz crystals surrounded by a pastel array of limestone.

Returning via the same trail, stop in the forested section, where kids can enjoy playing a game finding members of the pine, spruce, and fir families. Tell them spruce tree needles are square and spiky, fir needles are flat and flexible, and pine needles come in packages of two or more. An aspen glen near the beginning of the trail can serve as a lovely stop for a snack or rest.

A vault toilet is installed near the Cascade Waterfall trailhead, and drinking water is available at the visitor center at Duck Creek.

52 BIRDSEYE, PINK LEDGES, AND GOLDEN WALL TRAILS

Location ■	Red Canyon, west of Bryce Canyon National Park
Type ■	Day hike
Difficulty ■	Moderate for children
Hikable ■	May to mid-October
Distance ■	Birdseye Trail, 0.7 mile, one way; Pink Ledges Trail, 0.5 mile, one way; Golden Wall/Castle Bridge Trails, 2.5 miles, loop
Starting Elevation ■	All trails, 7140 feet
High Point ■	7160 feet (Birdseye and Pink Ledges); 7640 feet (Castle Bridge)
Maps ■	Trails Illustrated Paunsaugunt Plateau, Mount Dutton and Bryce Canyon National Park; USGS Bryce Canyon; Red Canyon hiking map

From the junction of UT-63 and UT-12 near the entrance to Bryce Canyon National Park, drive west 13 miles on UT-12, where parking and the Red Canyon Visitor Center are located on the right.

Hoodoos and spires, fancifully shaped in intense shades of red, get a close-up look along Red Canyon's trails. Everyone has fun naming the imagination-teasing formations found along the trails in this Bryce Canyon look-alike. The Red Canyon campground allows families full days to explore this unique hiking destination. If time allows, ask about the 0.5 mile Losee Canyon Trail featuring fifteen small arches and spectacular scenery. This trail is located only 3 miles from Red Canyon's center.

The Birdseye Trail begins at the visitor center, heading west (left) into Red Canyon's vivid pink and scarlet rock formations. If you feel you're being watched here look around. Following your moves is the trail's namesake, a rock, shaped like a bird's head with a small hole for the eye. The sharp-eyed hiker in your group may see the "bird" before it sees you. As your group explores the red rock formations along this 0.7 mile trail does the "bird" ever stop watching? Follow the Birdseye Trail to the Photo Trail, which ends at the highway pull-off.

Pink Ledges Trail begins behind the visitor center, near the pay phones. As the trail veers right, it switchbacks briefly before reaching a trail junction. Passing the first trail, which leads back to the parking lot, the second option edges the canyon's most unusual formations. A less challenging trail parallels this one, which ascends stone stairs to enter a fortress of vermilion rocks known as Ambush Rock. Kids enjoy scrambling up to the "Indian Peephole" here.

The upper trail continues paralleling the lower trail, offering bird's-eye views of the stone sentinels that seem to guard this richly decorated amphitheater. Kids can make up their own titles for the

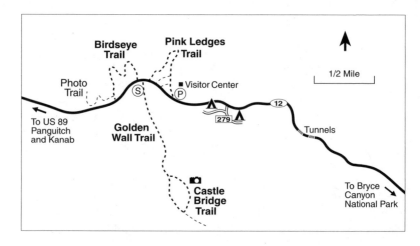

Day-Glo orange goblins gathered at what is named War Paint Hills. From here the trail climbs to a viewpoint of two prominent pinnacles, then follows a rather nebulous route down the short and steep gravelly hill to rejoin the lower trail.

Benches and interpretive signs explaining Native American uses of desert plants border the trail as it heads west along the amphitheater. As the trail enters a level area dotted with pinyon pines, it meets the smooth gravel path back to the visitor center.

The Golden Wall Trail begins west of the visitor center, across the highway from the end of the graveled walkway. Parking is provided here.

Maintaining a very gradual uphill grade, the Golden Wall Trail leads to a panoramic endpoint where an alternative route back on the Castle Bridge Trail begins. On the way, look for a formation that resembles the trail's namesake.

A balanced rock as it appeared near Castle Bridge Trail until 1997

Clusters of juniper, ponderosa pine, and limber pine shade the first portion of the trail. Stop to compare the needles, bark, and odor of these common Southwest trees. Youngsters I met here even tasted the foliage, a practice not recommended by forest rangers or chefs.

Pass the Castle Bridge Trail junction at 0.7 mile and continue to the right on the easier route to the viewpoint. Pink cliffs and canyons make up this scene, which is a good place to explain how it all came to be. Tell your companions to imagine standing knee-deep in the sediment of the lake that blanketed this landscape only 60 million years ago (which is considered young by geologists). Streams dumped loads of sediment into the lake. Millions of years later minerals in the deposit acted as a dye, coloring the rock in shades of red, pink, and yellow. Erosion formed the shapes we see now. Tomorrow's visitor, especially if it's a winter day, will see a slightly different formation. Freezing and thawing fractures the rock, causing the greatest changes to these fragile spires.

The large rock you see near the viewpoint once balanced there on a thin neck. It is believed to be a victim of vandals who knocked it down in 1997. Talk with your companions about why someone might do this. What difference does it make to visitors that the boulder is no longer balanced on a thin rock pedestal? How does the boulder's new position affect mammals, birds, and insects? What would you say to the vandals to prevent them from moving the rock? Remind kids that they are encouraged to report such harmful acts to the environment to forest or national park officials.

Return the same way or continue on the Castle Bridge Trail, switchbacking through hoodoos and statuesque formations. Look for the rocks for which the trail is named. Rejoin the Golden Wall Trail at the 0.7-mile junction and continue down the trailhead.

Toilet and water facilities are available at the visitor center.

53 NAVAJO LOOP AND QUEEN'S GARDEN TO RIM TRAIL

Location ▪	Bryce Canyon National Park
Type ▪	Day hike
Difficulty ▪	Moderate to challenging for children
Hikable ▪	April through November
Distance ▪	2.9 miles, loop
Starting Elevation ▪	8000 feet
Low Point ▪	7479 feet
Maps ▪	Trails Illustrated Paunsaugunt Plateau, Mount Dutton, and Bryce Canyon National Park; USGS Bryce Point; Bryce Canyon National Park brochure

www.nps.gov/brca
National park entrance fee

From the junction of US 89 and UT-12, 7 miles south of Panguitch, drive 13.8 miles west on UT-12. Turn south on UT-63 into Bryce Canyon National Park. From the visitor center proceed 1.1 miles

Intertwined rows of pink and gold spires enchant hikers at Zion National Park.

south to Sunset Point, where the overlook and trailhead are located. Ample parking is provided in the lot west of the view area.

Winding through a pink-and-gold fairyland of delicately shaped spires, this collection of trails combines the best of what many visitors to Bryce simply photograph from the rim. Summer hikers appreciate its shaded rest stops. Wintertime hikers can expect snow and ice accumulations in most areas. Trail guides for Navajo Loop and Queen's Garden trails sell for 50 cents and are available at the trailheads.

While mesmerized by Bryce Amphitheater's intricate forms and brilliant oranges viewed from Sunset Point, tell your companions this scene resulted from uplift and erosion. Sixty million years ago what you see here was the muddy bottom of the many lakes that covered this area. As southwest Utah began rising about 13 million years ago and the sediment hardened into rock, water began its work as a sculptor. Though heavy rains have washed away the rock's soft layers, when water penetrated tiny cracks in the rock it eventually froze. As any young scientist knows, water expands when it freezes. When trapped in rocks it forces the cracks wider, which exposes more soft rock to the erosive powers of freezing and thawing rain.

Though it may seem complete, this geologic masterpiece is continuously being shaped; 1 foot of rim is washed away every 65 years or so. Ask youngsters to scan the amphitheater's edge, looking for hoodoos that are just beginning to form. Do the heads of any stone men look ready to topple off? Late winter or early spring visitors might actually hear the force of erosion as falling rocks are released from their frozen hold.

From the Navajo Loop sign at Sunset Point, follow the trail down two long switchbacks to another sign directing hikers to the right and left. (Watch for a spur to the right leading to a window in the rock where Silent City can be viewed.) The route to the right promises a gradual descent via short, narrowly spaced switchbacks (count them!). A miniature arch lurks along the trail's right side, but do keep your eyes on the path; falls here can be dangerous.

As the switchbacks cease, the trail enters a steep and narrow stone passage where hikers are bathed in an orange light. This section of canyon is known as Wall Street. At this point kids prone to stump their parents with "Why is the sky blue?" questions are apt to ask,

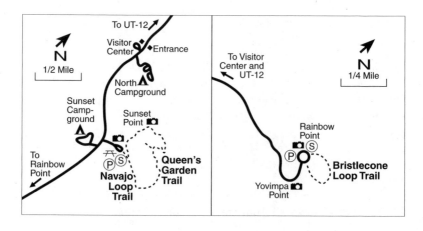

"Why are the rocks orange (or yellow or pink)?" The savvy parent says, "minerals," adding that iron and manganese were deposited along with the sediments, later coloring the rocks their lovely hues.

At 0.7 mile the trail rounds a bend and comes to a four-way junction. This is a good spot to rest on the log bench and drink water from your water bottle. Notice how the hoodoos are bottom-heavy and their tops look delicately shaped. Ask your companions to explain this.

Photo opportunities abound in this area, especially if the photographer gets down low to capture hoodoos and pinnacles edging the horizon, with kids in the foreground.

As the trail begins its up-and-down 0.8-mile route across the amphitheater bottom, follow the signs to the Queen's Garden Trail.

After hiking through open ponderosa pine forests, the trail veers west, ascending to a junction where a short spur on the left leads to Queen Victoria. Reigning over this gathering of hoodoos, she's appropriate to include in a group photograph. Do you think the Queen, who is reportedly unchanged in the last 100 years, shows signs of aging?

After visiting the Queen retrace your steps back to the main trail and follow it to the left through a hole blasted in the rock. Many faint trails ribbon this steep area, but do stay on the main trail to prevent unnecessary erosion.

After passing through the third stone arch, the trail begins its zigzag route up. (Follow the signs for Sunrise Point directing you to the left.) During breath-catching breaks admire the vistas and the trees.

Directly in front of you stands a member of the world's longest-lived species, the bristlecone pine. Gnarled and thick-trunked, these bristlecones are youngsters compared to their 4000-year-old kin living in California and Nevada. Visit what may be Bryce's oldest bristlecone along the Bristlecone Loop Trail at Yovimpa Point. A dead branch on a bristlecone pine tells you dry conditions over a long spell triggered the tree to shut down its channels to that part. While that branch withered and died, the remaining portions were sufficiently fed by water and nutrients. Do these trees look as if they've weathered a drought?

Hot, sweaty hikers are rewarded by cooling breezes as the trail climbs to the canyon rim at Sunrise Point. A level 0.5-mile walk along the rim leads back to the starting point at Sunset Point.

Toilet and water and picnic facilities are available at the Sunset Point parking area.

54 BRISTLECONE LOOP TRAIL

Location ▪	Bryce Canyon National Park
Type ▪	Day hike
Difficulty ▪	Easy for children
Hikable ▪	May through October (in dry years)
Distance ▪	1 mile, loop
Starting Elevation ▪	9000 feet
High Point ▪	9100 feet
Maps ▪	Trails Illustrated Paunsaugunt Plateau, Mount Dutton, and Bryce Canyon National Park; Rainbow Point; Bryce Canyon National Park brochure

www.nps.gov/brca
National park entrance fee

 To access Bryce Canyon National Park, see directions for Hike 53, Navajo Loop and Queen's Garden to Rim Trail. From the visitor center travel 17 miles south to the end of the road at Rainbow and Yovimpa points. Ample parking is provided here.

For a cool perspective on Bryce's spectacular views, walk the Bristlecone Loop. Located in the park's highest terrain, the trail maintains a safe distance from cliff edges as it winds through bristle-cone and spruce–fir forests en route to the park's oldest living tree. Kids are thrilled to jump into the patches of snow that are here even in late June. (Remind everyone to stay on the trail when possible.)

From the parking area walk to the adjacent Rainbow Point kiosk, where the trail is on the right. Before starting the hike encourage youngsters to imagine this dramatic view of pastel pinnacles as it once was, a featureless land with a slow-moving river, now called the Paria, flowing across it. Explain that about 13 million years ago, this area, now part of what's called the Colorado Plateau, began uplift-ing, reaching 1 mile in height in some places. As this land mass rose up, it stretched and fractured, forming smaller plateaus. You are standing on the edge of a plateau called the Paunsaugunt, looking east to the Aquarius Plateau. The Paria River became a fast-moving force that carved its way through the plateaus during the massive land lift. It washed away much of the soft rock leaving behind fins. Fanciful shapes are continuously formed as water penetrates the rock and cracks it during more than 200 freeze-and-thaw cycles a year, despite only 15 inches of rain a year.

Following the loop to the left leads through clusters of white and Douglas fir. Stop to compare their needles and bark. How do their cones differ in appearance? Continue past the Under-the-Rim Trail sign at 0.1 mile, where a bristlecone pine tree mingles with other coniferous, or cone-bearing, trees. Count the needles in each bundle. Another pine with needles in packages is the ponderosa, a distinctive, large tree on the left. Get to know this tree by counting the needles in a bundle and giving it a hug (watch out for sap!). How does it smell?

Within 0.3 mile the trail meets a fenced overlook on the left offering a rare look at the two plateaus. Point out the Kaiparowits Plateau, the soft, gray layer visible in the distance contrasting with the stunning red-orange-hued spires of the Claron Formation, which is part of the Paunsaugunt Plateau. Also, views of Navajo Mountain, just 80 miles away, are good here. Depending on air quality, the sights here extend 200 miles.

Bending to the right, the trail climbs a short hill 0.1 mile to a walled overlook of the Pink Cliffs, the top step in what geologists call the Grand Staircase. Youngsters (and accompanying "oldsters") will understand this label when told to imagine a giant climbing a staircase, starting at the Grand Canyon's north rim, and stepping on six different rock formations to reach this point.

While the Pink Cliffs surrounding Bryce may be the youngest formation (60 million years old) in the staircase, behind you stands the park's oldest tree. Gnarled and warped by the harshest of temperatures, winds, and droughts, this bristlecone is more than 1600 years old. How does this senior show its age? Bristlecones possess the remarkable ability to grow in favorable years and nearly stop growth during years of drought. Feel a cone's stout scale armed with a curved bristlelike prickle, the tree's namesake.

As the trail loops back into the forest, watch for a tree trunk on the right dimpled in orderly rows of sapsucker holes. A woodpecker drilled these holes, returning to them to collect the dripping sap and the insects sticking to it.

The trail completes the loop at the trailhead.

Drinking water and toilet facilities are provided at Rainbow Point.

55 PETRIFIED FOREST NATURE TRAIL

Location	■ Escalante State Park
Type	■ Day hike
Difficulty	■ Moderate for children
Hikable	■ March through November
Distance	■ 1 mile loop, with optional 0.75-mile spur loop
Starting Elevation	■ 6000 feet
High Point	■ 6200 feet
Maps	■ Trails Illustrated Canyons of the Escalante; USGS Wide Hollow and Escalante

www.nr.state.ut.us/parks/www1/esca.htm
State park entrance fee

Located 44 miles east of Bryce Canyon, the park's entrance is 0.75 mile west of Escalante on UT-12.

Museum-quality petrified wood lies scattered along this interpreted trail. Boulder-size to fist-size, each piece displays a rainbow of colors luring little ones and their leaders for a closer look. Views of the surrounding staircased plateau country help orient visitors to the geologic splendor of southern Utah.

The trailhead and day-use parking are located just past the stop sign at the entrance on the right. An Escalante State Park nature guide is available here at the sheltered trail sign, where a map showing the trails is on display.

Via two switchbacks the trail climbs to an open area offering views of Wide Hollow Reservoir and the camping facilities. The trail brochure identifies and explains many plants and geologic formations seen along the way. Each of the following suggestions provides an opportunity for your crew to gain a better understanding of and appreciation for the environment.

- The pygmy forest at signpost 6 may be a good place to point out, in an indirect way, the value of eating and drinking sufficiently. Explain that although these trees are short, they started growing long before mom and dad, grandma and grandpa, even great-

Climbing a petrified log at Escalante State Park

grandparents were born! Because they didn't get enough water and nutrition to grow, they remained small.

- Children can determine a tree's age by measuring its trunk, using their little finger as a ruler. By holding their 1.5- to 2.0-inch-long "pinkie" next to the trunk, they can calculate its diameter. Trees 150 years old are 6 to 10 inches across. Ask them if they can find the oldest tree this way.

- Spring visitors here will see flowering cactus and sego lily, Utah's state flower. The bulb of this plains plant was eaten by the Mormons during their first difficult years. At any time of year kids will see blackened boulders, remnants of a volcano that erupted 50 million years ago.

- At signpost 8 turn right, following the trail to the viewpoint overlooking Escalante. Point out how the many plateaus of the area look like staircases up to the sky. This will help explain the town's name, which means "staircase" in Spanish.

- From here the trail levels off, then descends slightly to colorful examples of petrified wood. Note the logs' colors here and compare them to other displays farther on. When asked the meaning of *petrified*, some kids think it means "really scary" or "scared stiff." Explain that these logs are not frightened, but they certainly are stiff. This hardening occurred millions of years ago when the tree fell and was deeply covered by sand and mud. The logs became petrified as groundwater seeped into the wood fibers and left behind its minerals, which crystallized around the wood grain.

- At signpost 11 those who walk the Sleeping Rainbow Trail, a challenging spur trail, begin their walk as a ramble through a pinyon–juniper forest littered with chunks of petrified wood. After a

0.5-mile steep descent, the trail turns to the left, where a border of multihued petrified wood marks the route up a drainage. A final 0.2-mile climb and you reach a high point of the desert where the trail veers right before it rejoins the main loop at signpost 11. Your conversation here might include why this trail was named Sleeping Rainbow. Is it shaped like a rainbow? Why call it Rainbow? Is it sleeping? How?

■ Displayed at signpost 14 is one the park's finest examples of petrified wood, lying on its side with only half of the trunk exposed. It's fun to count the tree rings to learn how old this tree was.

From here the trail meets signpost 8 and returns to the trailhead. Water and toilet facilities are provided at the campground.

56 CALF CREEK FALLS

Location ■	Between Boulder and Escalante
Type ■	Day hike
Difficulty ■	Moderate for children
Hikable ■	April to November
Distance ■	2.75 miles, one way
Starting Elevation ■	5300 feet
High Point ■	5600 feet
Maps ■	Trails Illustrated Canyons of the Escalante; USGS Calf Creek; BLM Calf Creek Falls trail guide

From Boulder on UT-12 drive 15.1 miles south to the turnoff for Calf Creek Recreation Area. Ample parking is provided adjacent to the picnic area.

The waterfall at the end of this trail splashes 126 feet down a slickrock wall into a sand-bottom pool, creating the ultimate reward desert hikers dream of. En route to the falls ancient rock art and granaries adorn distant canyon walls. For these and more reasons, Calf Creek is popular. Midweek and off-season visits here promise fewer people on the trail, at the creek, and on the picnic grounds.

It's best to plan this hike for early in the day in order to enjoy a sunny swim at this cool destination. Filled water bottles are a must for this sandy hike, while binoculars and cameras make it even better.

Splashing fun at the creek near the picnic grounds may cause your group to linger. The trailhead to an even finer reward is reached 0.1 mile beyond the picnic area on the left. The trail brochure is available at the registration box here.

Though your feet tread sandy terrain much of the walk, your eyes view lush plant life along Calf Creek. In many places beaver ponds have thickened the stream. Because of frequent flash floods in this area's drainages, beavers here dig bankside dens and tunnels. However, flash floods rarely occur in the upper portions of Calf Creek where you will see large beaver lodges. While looking for movement around a lodge, tell children that the beaver's entrance is underwater. They will be surprised to learn it leads to a dry, hollow den.

The entrance to the granary just below the rim at signpost 7 looks to be more challenging than the beaver's entry. Binoculars are useful here. Discuss how the prehistoric farmers stored their crops in these high, dry cabinets and why they chose such remote locations. At signpost 13 look to the canyon's east wall, near the bottom of a cliff, where four large figures, centuries-old Fremont-style pictographs, are painted in red.

The old fence at signpost 11 remains as an explanation for the canyon's name; settlers held their weaned calves behind the fence to keep them from their mothers. Another remnant of pioneer life, though very much alive, is horsetail, which is found near signpost 21. Also called scouring rush, it was used by homesteaders to clean pots and pans.

Beyond signpost 21, poison ivy flourishes on the trail's right side. Encourage careful, distant observation to avoid future close encounters.

The lush area beyond here is a welcome change from the arid

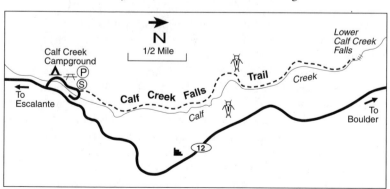

Lower Calf Creek Falls rewards desert hikers with its cool pool.

slickrock. From the trailside bench, stop to listen to the many different bird melodies or watch trout swimming in the creek's clear, sand-
bottom pools.

The sound of splashing water pulls hikers into a cool, misty arena
where the waterfall spills over slickrock. Sand-castle builders may discover black sand under the white on the pool's shore. Explain that
each grain of black sand was once part of a volcanic rock that formed
when volcanoes erupted far north of here long ago. Perhaps your
kids can build their own model of a black sand volcano.

After a cooling visit, retrace your steps to the trailhead.

Water and toilet facilities are available at the picnic area.

57 DEER CREEK LAKE TO CHRISS LAKE LOOP

Location ■	Dixie National Forest
Type ■	Day hike or overnight backpack
Difficulty ■	Moderate for children
Hikable ■	June through September
Distance ■	5.5 miles, round trip
Starting Elevation ■	Deer Creek, 9280 feet; Chriss Lake, 8700 feet
High Point ■	9980 feet
Maps ■	USGS Deer Creek Lake and Lower Bowns Reservoir

From the junction of UT-12 and UT-24, west of Capitol Reef's entrance, drive 26.5 miles south on UT-12. (From Escalante it's 38 miles north.) Turn north at the turnoff to Deer Creek Lake, driving 0.4 mile to the parking area near the horse trailer turnaround. If two vehicles are available, shuttle one to the Chriss Lake trailhead, 1.3 miles south on UT-12, turning north at the turnoff for Chriss Lake.

An unexpected green treasure in southern Utah, this lovely loop winds through flowered meadows and aspen groves, passing lakes for fishing and ponds for pondering. A portion of the Great Western Trail, the Canada to Mexico footpath, is included on this walk up and along Boulder Mountain's broad slopes. Fall hikes here are fondly remembered as sensory immersions in the season's splendor.

The trail begins 30 feet beyond the Forest Service trail information sign in the parking area. A sign reading "Deer Creek Lake 2.7 miles" and "Great Western Trail Access" marks the trailhead, where a registration box is located. The gentle ascent begins here.

Bark art, engravings made by hikers who didn't heed the "leave not a trace" ethic, mar many an aspen along the trail's initial 0.5 mile. However, children's interests awaken when dates and cattle brands from the 1920s and 1930s are pointed out. Ask your companions to search for the earliest year. (I found 1926.) The majority of names they'll read are Hispanic, recordings made by shepherds and cattlemen tending their herds on Boulder Mountain. These historic markings are considered arborglyphs. They reflect a culture and lifestyle

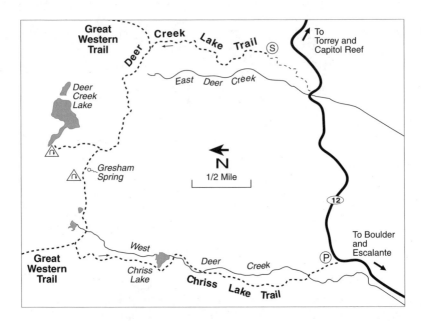

of a brief time in the West. Encourage kids to describe the solitary life of a cattleman who for months at a time wandered these slopes.

Continuing up Utah's highest plateau, you'll hear pikas sounding their alarms to one another as you pass through open meadows. At 1 mile an old jeep road can be seen far to the right, just when the trail veers to the left. Signs posted on a large aspen indicate that this portion of the trail is part of the Great Western Trail.

From the sign the trail follows a path of plant succession in crossing an open meadow, then going into an aspen grove, followed by a fir–aspen forest, and finally a coniferous glen.

After descending a bit into an aspen grove, the trail edges a pond. Avoid the faint paths here. At 2.5 miles a sign indicates Deer Creek Lake is straight ahead, 0.2 mile, and to the left sits Gresham Spring, 0.2 mile, and Chriss Lake, 1.6 miles. Head up to Deer Creek Lake for lunch, camping, or simply a pleasant pause. Retrace your steps to the main trail.

Four tall poles held upright by rock piles mark the route through the tall grasses to Chriss Lake. At the fourth marker watch for a faint trail veering left, which leads into a mixed forest. Gresham Spring seeps out of the ground alongside the trail on the left. Perhaps shepherds favored this water source long ago.

Square-and-rectangle blazes, trail symbols made by cleaving the

A beaver lodge in Deer Creek Lake

tree's bark, mark the route through the forest and to a small green pond on the right. The trail is thin at this point so watch the blazes. (Over the years, bark growth has rounded the shapes.)

During our visit here, we watched two beavers industriously carry twigs into the lodge's below-surface entry. Find an aspen stump with a chiseled, conical shape to encourage children to feel the teeth marks made by this timber harvester. Remind them that beavers' teeth, unlike our own, continue to grow, and the process of gathering food and lodging materials keeps the animals' teeth trim!

Proceeding on this level portion of the Great Western Trail, views of Boulder Mountain's 50,000-acre top can be seen as the trail edges an aspen forest on the left. The trail follows an eroded canal as it meets Chriss Lake at 4.1 miles. Fishing is reportedly good here, so another stop might be necessary.

The final 1.5 miles descend through glorious stands of aspen, interrupted with openings for viewing the staircased landscape of south-central Utah. Someone with a good eye and knowledge of the region will recognize Navajo Mountain in the south, the Henry and La Sal mountains to the east, and in the foreground the Circle Cliffs.

If your hike occurs in mid- to late September, you'll notice distinct blocks of aspen splashing a uniform color across the slope. This occurs because aspen share a common root system. After a fire has cleared a slope, aspens are the recovery trees, sprouting from their underground feeding network. Look around—do you see any lone trees?

By the way, trees don't really change color. The greens, golds, and reds exist in the leaves all year, but are hidden by chlorophyll, the tree's food producer (which is green). As autumn approaches, decreasing sunlight, and hence colder temperatures, causes the chlorophyll to slow its production, which allows the other colors a chance to show off.

No water or toilet facilities are available at either trailhead.

58 FREMONT RIVER WALK

Location	■ Capitol Reef National Park
Type	■ Day hike
Difficulty	■ Easy, then challenging for children
Hikable	■ March through October
Distance	■ 1 mile, one way
Starting Elevation	■ 5250 feet
High Point	■ 6120 feet
Maps	■ Trails Illustrated Fish Lake and North & Central Capitol Reef; Capitol Reef National Park brochure

www.nps.gov/care
National park entrance fee
Wheelchair accessible with assistance first 0.5 mile

 From the visitor center at Capitol Reef National Park, drive 0.7 mile south on the Scenic Drive Road, turning right into the second entrance to the campground. Follow the signs to the amphitheater parking area. The trail is adjacent to the parking area.

Enjoy a stroll along Capitol Reef's riverbank where a green corridor of orchards and pastures sits nestled in a desert world of pink and orange sandstone. Families with very young children generally limit their hike to the trail's first 0.5 mile, where seeing an apple tree loaded with fruit is as thrilling as watching yellowbelly marmots stand up to whistle. Ambitious siblings (and an adult) can complete the hike by climbing the last 0.25 mile to a fabulous view of the area.

The first 0.5 mile of the trail follows a wide, firmly packed (wheelchair-accessible) surface along the Fremont River. Depending on the season of your visit here, the orchards may be in blossom or fruit. Flowering times for the fruit trees (apricots, cherries, peaches, apples, and pears) begin in March and end mid-April. During harvest time, July through September, there's nothing like strolling through an apple orchard (or any unlocked orchard) and sampling its fruit. Your family is free to do this in Capitol Reef. However, if they pick more than their mouths or bellies can hold, a fee is collected. Ask at the visitor center for more information.

Fruita, named by the settlers here during the 1880s, once supplied neighboring towns with horse-drawn wagonloads of fruit. Today the National Park Service manages the orchards, which consist of 2800 trees. The orchard's irrigation trenches intrigue children, fascinated by any form of moving water. Have youngsters find these ditches' water source.

As the trail bends to the riverside, allow children to look for evidence of a beaver. Tall cottonwoods scarred by gnawing are obvious indicators. Looking at smaller trees, they may find

Remains of early farm settlements in the Fremont River Valley

leaves have been torn off, branches nibbled, or the bark stripped in places. Don't expect to find any beaver lodges or dams. Even nature's best dam builder won't compete with the Fremont River's fast current. Instead, these beavers build their dens in the hollows of riverbanks.

Another critter more often heard than seen is the yellowbelly marmot. It whistles to warn other marmots in the colony of your presence. Unlike squirrels, marmots dig burrows in tall grasses or rock piles. If your companions found 4- to 5-inch-wide holes in the meadow, perhaps they were looking at a marmot's front door.

Where cottonwoods shade the trail, stop to listen to their soothing windsong as their leaves ripple in the slightest breeze. Your children's imaginations and listening ability are stimulated when you tell them to listen quietly, just as the meadow's deer, marmots, snakes, and lizards do, for special messages from the wind. Ask them what kind of messages they hear.

At the far end of the meadow, the trail ventures into desert slickrock. Pungent sagebrush flavors the air as the trail approaches the base of a cliff. Some folks turn around here or at the fence opening just before the transition zone between river and desert.

Those who proceed follow a steep, switchbacked ascent to the top of a ridge. But they can do much more than that. They can watch swallows perform for them, swooping and soaring on the updrafts, snatching at insects. Lizards may be doing their push-ups, a courtship display, or sunning themselves to maintain their body temperature. As their hands touch the chocolate brown rock of the Moenkopi Formation, the climbers can imagine how it felt 200 million years ago, when it was the flat, wet land near an ancient sea. Hikers can feel the rock's ripple pattern, knowing it is the sea's gentle current, set in stone.

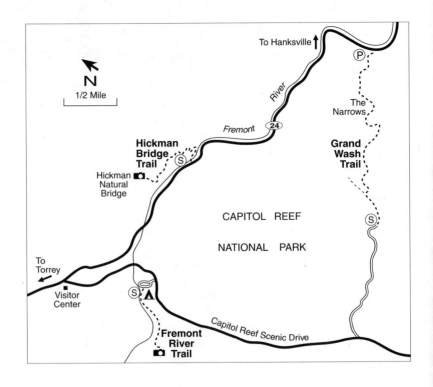

Upon reaching the top of a cliff face where the trail levels, hikers can head to its edge for views of the Fremont River canyon, then carefully follow a series of short switchbacks to a rock cairn.

Taking a drink of water while seated comfortably on a rock, hikers can see why they climbed to this point. Far below, the Fremont River shimmers like a silver snake threading through a lush forest. Surrounded by the many-hued, sculpted rock, the geologist in the group might point out the Moenkopi Formation, the brown bottom layer rising from the valley floor. Above it lays the gray-green Chinle Formation. Most everyone will recognize the scattering of black boulders as lava. The geologist might add that they arrived here 25 million years ago via glacial outwash that transported them from high-plateau volcanoes west of the park. Sheer red-tinted cliffs above the formation are Wingate Sandstone. Once a sand dune, it now forms Capitol Reef's Castle. Navajo Sandstone dominates the views with its magnificent domes.

Then the group might shut their eyes, feeling the desert's pulse as it shifts particles of sand, reshaping the views before them. Turning around to head back, they will realize the landscape has changed just now.

Toilet and water facilities are located at the visitor center and campground.

59 GRAND WASH

Location ■	Capitol Reef National Park
Type ■	Day hike
Difficulty ■	Easy for children
Hikable ■	Year-round
Distance ■	2.25 miles, one way
Starting Elevation ■	5300 feet
Ending Elevation ■	5200 feet
Maps ■	Trails Illustrated Fish Lake and North & South Capitol Reef; Capitol Reef National Park brochure

www.nps.gov/care
National park entrance fee

From the visitor center at Capitol Reef National Park, drive 3.5 miles south on the Scenic Drive Road to the dirt road on the left. Travel 1.75 miles to the road's end, where a parking area is provided adjacent to the trailhead. A shuttle vehicle can be left at a signed pullout 4.5 miles east of the visitor center on UT-24, on the south side of the road.

Grand Wash has sculpted towering sandstone walls along a nearly level path into the Waterpocket Fold. The beautiful but short narrows section awes children, who delight in seeing lizards and toads scurrying into the shadows. The elevation gain here is negligible, allowing families to start their hike at either end or shuttle a vehicle to either trailhead. Flash floods occur in narrow canyons, so do not enter Grand Wash when rain threatens.

At the trailhead, while gathering day packs and distributing water bottles, instill fascination in youngsters by telling them about the area they'll be walking. Explain that although Grand Wash is dry and barren on most days, after heavy rains it carries water through a portion of what is called the Waterpocket Fold. Using a park brochure, point out Waterpocket Fold, a 100-mile-long buckle of rocks enclosed in Capitol Reef and extending south to the Colorado River. Describe the fold as a big wrinkle in the earth's crust that developed more than 65 million years ago when portions of this part of the country began uplifting. Explore ideas for the reasons why this dry creekbed was named Grand Wash.

A hundred yards from the start, observant hikers see tiny, fist-sized arches on the right. Continuing up the wide span between walls, a trail junction on the left at 0.25 mile leads to Cassidy Arch and the Frying Pan Trail. Both are strenuous hikes to the upper cliffs of Capitol Reef.

Where the walls begin to close in at 0.4 mile, rounded rocks litter the wash. Comparing color and texture, decide if these rocks broke from the walls directly above or traveled here during flash floods.

A many-hued display of desert varnish stripes the increasingly narrow Navajo Sandstone walls at 0.8 mile. Tell youngsters this dark paint may take hundreds of years to develop. It forms when very fine particles of clay stick to wet rock surfaces. Those darker, shinier patches of varnish are not necessarily older; they resulted from water containing higher amounts of minerals forming a black film over the clay. Look for a sample of desert varnish reaching shoulder height so youngsters can examine its durable surface.

Shade welcomes hikers at 1 mile as the canyon narrows to only 16 feet in width. Two very short side canyons, both coming in from the right, offer fun exploring. One meets the wash just before the narrows. The other slot enters the canyon just as the narrows appear to T. Venture up this route before following the canyon to the left.

While in these close quarters, ask your companions their estimates of the wall's height, which averages 500 feet.

After the narrows, many hikers turn around and retrace their route back to the trailhead. Others walk the remaining mile to where they either meet a shuttled vehicle or head back to examine Grand Wash from another perspective. The canyon's last mile features Navajo Sandstone walls with occasional views of the park's domes.

The nearest toilet and water facilities are at the trailhead.

60 HICKMAN BRIDGE

Location ▪	Capitol Reef National Park
Type ▪	Day hike
Difficulty ▪	Easy to moderate for children
Hikable ▪	Year-round
Distance ▪	1 mile, one way
Starting Elevation ▪	5320 feet
High Point ▪	5720 feet
Maps ▪	Trails Illustrated Fish Lake and North & South Capitol Reef; Hickman Bridge Trail brochure

www.nps.gov/care
National park entrance fee

From the visitor center at Capitol Reef National Park, drive 2 miles east on UT-24. A parking area is on the left side of the road.

Extraordinary views of Capitol Reef are featured along this short trek to an "awesome" destination. Initially, a steep but short climb is required, but the well-designed trail to Hickman Natural Bridge, the park's premier stone bridge, weaves through a variety of landforms and plant species. This trail is both accessible and enjoyable for all hikers in the group.

This interpreted trail begins at the parking lot's east end, initially paralleling the Fremont River, named after a famous frontier explorer, John C. Fremont. The receptacle for the trail brochure, available for 25 cents, is located 20 yards into the walk. The trail then ascends the canyon via switchbacks and steps carved into the rock.

Spectacular views at each switchback provide opportunities to see how Capitol Reef got its name. Show your companions how the surrounding high cliffs form a travel barrier, just like an ocean reef. Point out how the massive sandstone domes look much like the building where our nation's Congress meets in Washington, D.C. Your spelling star may like knowing that *capitol* spelled with "ol" refers to the building at the U.S. capital, or where a state legislature meets, or the formation here at Capitol Reef National Park.

Look about 30 yards (40 child's strides) to the right of signpost 4 for a ring of black boulders. Explain that nearly 1000 years ago the rocks served as a foundation for a pit house used by the people of the Fremont culture. Built partially underground, these dwellings had a fire pit in the middle and a wooden, aboveground roof. Fremont people, a distinct group who lived in what is now called Utah, were named by archaeologist Noel Morss because so many of their sites were located near the Fremont River.

From signpost 4 to signpost 8 (0.2 mile), black boulders scattered across the white-stoned desert plateau capture everyone's attention, especially when they learn the rocks are remnants of the ice ages. They originated some 25 million to 40 million years ago, when volcanic activity occurred in the Tushar Mountains west of the park. It wasn't until "only" 10,000 to 100,000 years ago, when glaciers formed on this volcanic caprock, that fragments broke off. As the glaciers melted and froze (four times, according to geologists), the chunks of volcanic rock tumbled many miles to reach this point. Perhaps your young geologists can explain how these volcanic rocks became round.

At signpost 8 the trail descends briefly as it enters a canyon wash. Tracks made by chipmunks, lizards, and ringtail cats are often discovered in this dry, sandy terrain. At signpost 9 stop to encourage your children to look for lines across the solid, white domes. Explain that long, long ago (180 million years ago) desert winds blew and helped shape these domes from a vast area of sand.

Look up at the cliff at signpost 12. Called granaries, these storage bins held the Fremont people's corn and beans. Children appreciate the ancient food bins' inaccessibility when they learn that because the bins are sheltered from wind, sun, rain, and other animals, they remain intact almost 1000 years later. Follow the trail out of the canyon wash up to slickrock, where cairns, small piles of rock, mark the route.

As the trail curves right Hickman Natural Bridge fills the view. The cooling shade provided under this 133-foot-wide arch lures the laggers in your group. While they're cooling off on a boulder chair,

Hikers may sample the season's fruit from the orchards within Capitol Reef National Park.

explain to your hikers how this ever-silent natural bridge was once a narrow fin of sandstone. For thousands of years a stream flowed alongside the fin, forming a small alcove, which grew deeper until a rock broke through it. Then raging flood waters poured through, widening the hole and forming the bridge we now see. Use a sandy surface to draw an illustration of this formation. Show the stream bending oxbow fashion with a break along a wall.

A short walk from under the bridge leads to an overlook of the surrounding domes and the Fremont River drainage. This wonderfully still destination lends itself to a "silent experience." Tell your companions that if they remain silent and motionless in this quiet corner of the park, they will hear, and perhaps feel, time, wind, sun, and air shaping the rocks.

The trail loops under Hickman Bridge, then rejoins it to return to the trailhead.

Bring plenty of water for each person. Hats are recommended. The nearest toilet is at the trailhead; nearest water is at the visitor center.

61 RAINBOW BRIDGE NATIONAL MONUMENT

Location ▪	Glen Canyon National Recreation Area, Rainbow Bridge National Monument
Type ▪	Day hike
Difficulty ▪	Easy for children
Hikable ▪	Year-round
Distance ▪	0.4 mile to 0.7 mile, one way
Starting Elevation ▪	3700 feet (depending on lake's water level)
High Point ▪	3800 feet
Maps ▪	Trails Illustrated Glen Canyon & Capitol Reef Area; USGS Rainbow Bridge; Glen Canyon National Recreation Area and Rainbow Bridge National Monument brochures

www.nps.gov/rabr
Boat tour fee

 Located about 50 miles above Glen Canyon Dam in Forbidden Canyon, Rainbow Bridge is accessed via boat tour, rental or private boat from any of the four marinas on Lake Powell. Plan on a minimum 5-hour round-trip visit to Rainbow Bridge on tour boats departing from Wahweap or Bullfrog marinas near Page, Arizona. For information on the area and boat rental, call 1-800-528-6154, or write Glen Canyon National Recreation Area, Box 1507, Page, Arizona 86040.

The world's largest natural bridge, once inaccessible in a maze of smooth-sculpted canyons and cliffs, can now be appreciated after a short walk from a boat. The kid in all of us enjoys the boat ride to Forbidden Canyon passing many of Lake Powell's most whimsically or dramatically shaped rock formations.

En route to the boat launch, use a Glen Canyon National Recreation Area brochure and the state of Utah map to show children where the trail to Rainbow Bridge begins. Explain that the lake and its many water-filled canyons began filling in 1963, when the gates of Glen Canyon Dam confined the Colorado River's muddy water. Talk about the lake's water level fluctuating with the yearly precipitation. As

Rainbow Bridge, the world's largest natural bridge arches, over hikers at Glen Canyon National Recreation Area.

the boat passes tall, flat rock spans, be sure to point out the lake's bathtub ring, adding that the white, flaky lines are actually high-water marks. Barely visible is the highest mark, which occurred in 1983. Where the boat docks, children can see the line of alkali and calcium carbonate along the cliff face.

While walking along the boardwalk from the boat, remind kids that this is a sacred place for the people of five Native American nations. Show respect for this inspiring sight by not throwing rocks, swimming, or diving. Sorry, fishing and pets are not allowed here.

Within 0.2 mile the boardwalk meets the footpath. As it veers left into an alcove, stop to admire the miniature fragile gardens thriving in this moist, cool slickrock oasis. Staying on the trail here is necessary in order to revegetate the many trails made by careless visitors. Do not touch these delicate species because each plant has adapted to grow in a specific place within the alcove over thousands of years. For instance, point out maidenhair fern forming mats along the face wall. Below it you might find the small purple-and-white-flowering alcove columbine. When asked where the water comes from that feeds these ferns and mosses, explain that sandstone is like a sponge. Rainwater seeps through the tiny holes between its sand particles and drips out at overhanging walls, as you see here.

Tell children they're looking at Glen Canyon's namesake. When explorer John Wesley Powell admired one of these gardens, he thought of glens; hence he named the area Glen Canyon.

Rainbow Bridge makes its first, though partial, appearance as the trail leaves the alcove. Hikers, who are free to walk as near as desired to the sandstone span, increase their estimates of its height and width as they get closer. After everyone has compared its height to tall buildings they know of, tell them it reaches 290 feet, the same as a thirty-story building.

Help kids understand how this natural bridge was formed, by drawing in the sand the oxbow path of the slow-moving river that flowed here millions of years ago. This entire region, the Colorado Plateau, began tilting up 60 million years ago. Then, 10 million years ago, another uplift caused the slow-moving rivers to become a force that chiseled into the wall of rock where Rainbow Bridge now stands. Show the water flow taking a direct route through the eroded meander.

Also point out the two rock layers seen at Rainbow Bridge. Tell children its base is called Kayenta Sandstone, which formed from muds and sands laid down millions of years ago. The bridge, composed of Navajo Sandstone, resembles its original form, waves of sand dunes piled atop each other.

The brilliant black-and-red streaks striping the natural bridge are called desert varnish. Your children may have imaginative explanations for its formation, so let them know the varnish's many colors may be the reason Indians believed it was a rainbow turned to stone. Perhaps they will develop their own legend from this idea. Your young geologist may prefer knowing that desert varnish forms as wind-blown clay particles cling to wet surfaces on the rock. The color is provided as bacteria, known to kids as "germs," change the minerals in the clay particles, causing them to harden and stick to the rock.

Before heading back on the same trail, explorative hikers who are not committed to a tour boat's return schedule may want to hike the trail extending beyond the bridge for about 1 mile.

Bring drinking water because none is available beyond the boats. Toilet facilities are provided at the trailhead.

SOUTHEAST

62 GOBLIN VALLEY

Location ■ Goblin Valley State Park
Type ■ Day hike
Difficulty ■ Easy for children
Hikable ■ Year-round
Distance ■ 0.2 mile to 3 miles, round trip
Starting Elevation ■ 4960 feet
High Point ■ 5115 feet
Map ■ USGS Goblin Valley

www.nr.state.ut.us/parks/www1/gobl.htm
State park entrance fee

Access to Goblin Valley State Park is 11 miles west of Green River on UT-24 (exit 147). Drive south 24 miles and turn right (west) on the paved road, continuing 6 miles to the junction with a dirt road. Turn left and drive 7 miles to the park entrance. Follow the park entrance road 1 mile to its end at the Valley of the Goblins observation point.

Goblin Valley's geologic showcase of chocolate brown, mushroom-shaped rocks invites hikers of all ages to discover the park's diverse collections of rock creatures in this trailless terrain.

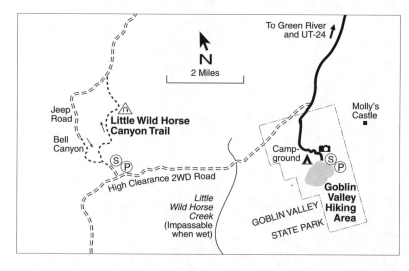

Hikers peek and perch at Goblin Valley State Park.

Information placards provided at the shaded observation deck acquaint visitors with the area's unique geology. Ask your group to visualize a shallow sea blanketing this vast area. The strangely shaped spires they see were once part of the sea's bottom sediment. As the climate here became drier, the sea disappeared, leaving behind the sandy sediment. Over millions of years it developed into a rock layer. In some places the sediment was held together; in other places it washed away, forming ghostly spires and hoodoos. Pretend they are stone ghosts from an ancient era.

Goblins are continually growing and falling. In fact, when your youngster returns here in 5 years he or she may discover the goblins have grown a few inches. The soft ground surrounding them erodes with each rainstorm, causing the goblins to appear to grow taller, even though their tops stay at the same height. During your hike look for the goblins most likely to grow during the next rainstorm—those standing in loose rock. Perhaps you'll find one that's recently fallen or others starting to form along the amphitheater's edge.

From the observation point hikes head in every direction, often changing course several times before returning. Frisbees are fun to toss between the spires and hoodoos in the valley below. Many groups play hide-and-go-seek in this natural playground.

However, some explorers see in the distance (0.4 mile to 0.8 mile

east) three greenish gray rock formations of Curtis Sandstone as separate destinations they'd like to aim for. Near the middle green-gray
rock, eager hikers discover kid-size caves to curl into. Beyond the formation on the right is a vast array of goblins, as well as access to viewpoints of the Henry Mountains, the San Rafael Swell, Temple
Mountain, and Molly's Castle. And those who hike to the left encounter a gallery of goblins sure to tease anyone's imagination. In several
places staircased rocks lead to the uppermost ridge of this valley, where
hikers enjoy standing in silhouette-like versions of the goblins below.

Despite a yearly visitation of 60,000 rock scramblers here, rain-
storms effectively wash away their footprints. If trails were created or
mountain bikes and recreational vehicles allowed, a continuous track
would form where serious erosion would take place with each rainfall. Ask your companions why plants are not growing here.

Plan a visit to Goblin Valley during a moonlit summer night, when
goblins cavort with their zany shadows. Only those registered to
camp here are allowed in the Valley of the Goblins after 10:00 P.M.

Limited water is available for those who pay the per vehicle entrance fee to the park. A vault toilet is located near the observation
point.

63 LITTLE WILD HORSE CANYON

Location ■	Southwest of Green River, near Goblin Valley State Park
Type ■	Day hike
Difficulty ■	Moderate; not for children carried in a backpack
Hikable ■	March through October
Distance ■	1 mile to 2 miles, one way
Starting Elevation ■	5000 feet
High Point ■	5650 feet
Map ■	USGS Little Wild Horse Mesa

 See directions for Hike 62, Goblin Valley. Where the road forks just
before the park entrance, turn right. A sign for Muddy Creek and
Wild Horse Canyon directs travelers. Drive 5.5 miles along this
sandy road. (Caution is advised at 2.3 miles, where a broad, sandy

A little hiker explores Little Wild Horse Canyon.

wash can be difficult to cross during or after rains.) Turn right and
park in the parking area marked with an information kiosk and vault
toilet. Walk 0.3 mile to the large cottonwoods. Motorized vehicles
are restricted from the wilderness study area beyond here. The trail
begins to the left of the trees and is often obscure. Encourage your
crew to use the toilet before venturing into this narrow rock corridor.

This lively walk follows a slender, sinuous slot between canyon
walls in what many hikers consider Utah's best narrows. Because the
trail is not maintained or signed, an adventurous spirit and flexible
physique help in exploring what a 10-year-old Wild Horse hiker
called an "earth artery." Do not venture into this canyon if rain
threatens. Be prepared to hoist youngsters and yourself up and over
slickrock and boulder barricades.

The trail begins in a dry, flat canyon bed with a finger of the San
Rafael Reef, Little Wild Horse Canyon, on the right. Within 0.3 mile
a dry pour-off requires either lizardlike shimmying up the wall or
turning around and retracing your steps, following the canyon wall
on the left (heading south). Where it meets the canyon floor, follow
this route up and around the pour-off along a faint path that leads
back down to the canyon bed, about 0.1 mile farther. Mark with a
pile of rocks where the trail drops down so you'll know where to ascend on the return hike. Keep an eye open here for the first side
canyon entering on the right; that's Little Wild Horse Canyon.

Following the canyon bed as it veers slightly left accesses Bell Canyon, with narrows not quite as confining as Little Wild Horse's.

About 0.4 mile up Little Wild Horse, the canyon walls close in. Feel the finely sculpted sandstone that gets continuous polishing with each flash flood. Have children look for evidence of heavy rains from the high country funneling through here. Pine cone bits deposited in the gravel and scrapings on the wall suggest the torrential flows that frequent southern Utah's dry canyons in the late summer and fall. During some flash floods the water level in these slots has reached 12 feet! You'll need to hoist your hikers up to your shoulders in order to find proof of high water flows.

Three sets of narrows are encountered in this 2-mile walk. The first, though short, contains the narrowest passages. Children have fun measuring the canyon width using their arms as rulers. They also like looking up at the sky through the narrowest of slots. On clear days the smidgen of sky they see appears dark blue, almost black. Likewise, when the daytime sky is viewed through a very long, narrow tube, stars can be seen because of the small amount of sunlight entering the tiny viewing space.

Soon the walk enters an amphitheater-like opening. The second set of narrows begins here. After winding through 100 yards of smoothly sculpted sandstone, you need to shinny up a rock blockage.

Just past here another rock straddles the canyon walls, passable by crawling under it. This can be a turnaround point at 1 mile.

Beyond the rock obstacles the canyon walls loom high, up to 400 feet in places, creating a cool retreat even in the middle of a hot summer day. The third set of narrows tucked in this towering canyon is the longest, nearly 1 mile, with 3- to 6-foot-wide slots. Characterized by water pockets and holes that Swiss-cheese the walkway, this area is a good place to investigate what nature has deposited in the

reachable rock pockets. At the end of this section, where a boulder pileup precedes the canyon opening, turn around and head back.

For those who want to make a loop hike, continue walking another 1.5 miles to a jeep road, turning left and following it 1.25 miles to the head of Bell Canyon, which returns to the trailhead.

At any point along the walk, stop to feel the silence surrounding you. Observe the life here: cottonwood seedlings creeping from tiny fissures of massive rock walls, lizards defying gravity as they scamper up sandstone overhangs, blackbirds' wings flapping, a pebble tumbling, your heart beating.

Nearest water facilities are at Goblin Valley State Park.

64 HORSESHOE CANYON

Location ■	Canyonlands National Park, near Green River
Type ■	Day hike
Difficulty ■	Moderate to challenging for children, better suited for older children
Hikable ■	March through November; accessible year-round
Distance ■	3.4 miles, one way
Starting Elevation ■	5400 feet
Ending Elevation ■	4800 feet
Map ■	USGS Sugarloaf Butte

www.nps.gov/cany

From I-70 drive 11 miles west of Green River to UT-24 (exit 147) and proceed 24 miles south, turning east at the junction with a dirt road (about 0.75 mile south of Goblin Valley sign). (After heavy rains two-wheel-drive vehicles may have difficulties using this road.) Drive 25 miles to the next junction and turn left at the signed junction; then travel 5 miles to the next junction and turn right, proceeding 2 miles to the parking area.

Ghostly figures adorned in unusual headdresses and belts come

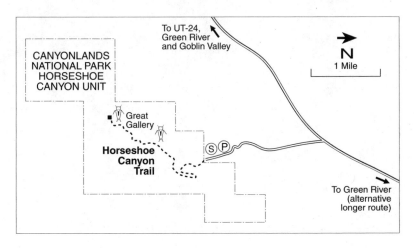

alive in the imaginations of hikers viewing the Great Gallery, the ancient rock art destination in Horseshoe Canyon. The petroglyphs and pictographs of Horseshoe Canyon are considered "... some of the finest rock painting in the world" by Polly Schaafsma, a leading authority in the field, making this hike well remembered by everyone who completes it. Bring binoculars for better viewing of the rock art.

This hike is not recommended for young children or anyone unprepared for walking in sandy, sometimes steep terrain. In addition, visitors must have an interest in ancient rock art otherwise their boredom leads to innocent vandalism of the resource. Parental supervision here includes preventing any collecting or carrying out of rocks, weeds, tadpoles, or other found items. This is a national park.

Before starting the hike, dab a drop of insect repellent around ears,

The Great Gallery of Horseshoe Canyon

necks, and other vulnerable spots to discourage annoying no-see-ums, especially mid-May to early June.

Begin the hike from the parking area, where the trail leads to the right. Within the first 0.4 mile, views of the canyon below can be seen. As the trail traverses slabs of slickrock, you'll notice grooves carved in the rock at your feet. These were made by trucks and jeeps used in gas and oil exploration in the 1940s. Although walking this steep, narrow path is challenging, imagine trying to drive it. Vehicles are no longer allowed in this portion of Canyonlands National Park, which accounts for the barricade at 0.9 mile.

Descending the sandy switchbacks leads to the canyon bottom at 1.4 miles. Follow it to the right, planning a rest stop in the cotton- woods just a bit farther. During this stop explain to children that they'll be seeing unique and very old "Barrier Style" art created by Archaic Indians who lived nearly 3000 years ago. Encourage children to imagine visiting this silent, dry canyon as an artist. Does the canyon have a special feeling to it? As an artist, what would they want to draw here? Remind them not to touch the extremely fragile rock art; acids from skin oils deteriorate the rock. The park service has recently installed barricades to protect the sights for future generations. Please stay behind them.

Alert children to be on the lookout for each of the four rock art displays. The first, called High Gallery, is on the left, less than 0.5 mile from where the trail meets the canyon floor. Horseshoe Shelter, the second group, is 0.4 mile up-canyon and across on the right. When archaeologists studied this site several years ago, materials from three different cultures and ages—Mesa Verde, Fremont, and Archaic—were found. Ask children why they think this canyon might have been a popular place for prehistoric people. What features does it offer that aren't present elsewhere along the drive here?

The third display is 0.8 mile farther on the right in a large, deep overhang. Closer looks require a short walk up the slope. Vandalism, however, has marred its special effect. Discuss why altering or removing prehistoric artifacts is considered a federal crime. What could be done to prevent further destruction of ancient remnants?

The Great Gallery is another 1 mile on the right. Your group may want to admire the display from the canyon floor, then walk closer to inspect each drawing. The group on the far left is called the Holy Ghost and Attendants. Note that it appears to be three-dimensional, which is rare in rock art. Ask if these beings appear human. Why not? What makes the drawing seem supernatural? Why were the drawings made? Questions like these and their imagined answers can go in many directions. Whatever is decided, everyone should leave with an increased appreciation of this sacred site.

Return via the same trail.

Ranger-led hikes to the Great Gallery are offered on weekend mornings in the spring and summer. A ranger must accompany groups of 20 or more. Call the Hans Flat Ranger Station at 435-259-2652 (8:00 A.M. to 4:30 P.M. daily) for more information.

The National Park Service recommends that each adult drink at least a gallon of water per day in this desert environment. Carry at least a gallon of water per person. Toilet facilities are located at the trailhead. Camping is no longer allowed in Horseshoe Canyon. It is acceptable to camp in the parking area at the top.

65 CANYON RIM TO DEAD HORSE POINT

Location ■	Dead Horse Point State Park
Type ■	Day hike
Difficulty ■	Easy to moderate for children
Hikable ■	Year-round
Distance ■	1.5 mile, one way
Starting Elevation ■	5906 feet
High Point ■	5950 feet
Map ■	Dead Horse Point State Park brochure

www.nr.state.ut.us/parks/www11/dead.htm
State park entrance fee

 From Moab drive 11 miles north on US 191 to UT-313. Turn west (left) and proceed 14 miles to the turnoff for Dead Horse Point State Park. Turn left and drive 6 miles to the visitor center and campground.

Nonstop spectacular views of the canyons carved by the Colorado River accompany hikers on this path to an unforgettable overlook. The foot trail keeps a safe distance from precipitous canyon edges, allowing the whole family's participation. A vehicle shuttled to the parking area at the Neck, located 0.5 mile before the overlook at Dead Horse Point, makes possible a one-way hike.

Walking the 0.25-mile interpreted Nature Trail near the visitor center offers an ideal introduction to the plants and geology seen along the rim. Encourage kids to become acquainted with a few of the desert species identified on the nature trail. They'll enjoy recognizing them along the rim walk.

From the Nature Trail join the trail to Dead Horse Point behind the visitor center and toilet facilities. A small sign with the word "Point" marks the trail.

Beginning on slickrock and following the rim's contours, the trail winds through high desert terrain, an apparently lifeless land at first glance. Kids who stop for hands-and-knees inspections (watch out for cacti, scorpions, and snakes!) of desert life under a slab of stone, or beneath a low-lying branch, or between the stems of Mormon tea are surprised at their findings. They may want to keep an accounting of their discoveries, which might include mule deer pellets, lizard tracks, harvester ants hauling huge seeds, a pinyon jay's feather, a tuft of rabbit fur, and human litter. Other than trash, be sure to leave all natural items in their original location.

At 0.5 mile a 0.25-mile spur trail veers left from the main trail to an overlook that features views of the Colorado River and Dead Horse Point. (Caution: This and other overlooks in the park are not fenced!) This junction can serve as a turnaround point.

Solar evaporation ponds, sparkling like brilliant turquoise jewels set in the bronze river valley below, are seen along most of the walk. Potash, which is used in almost every garden fertilizer, is the end result of these man-made pools. Potash is mined near Moab. Could this kind of evaporation process work in other parts of the country? Why not?

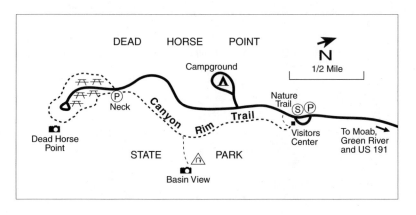

The view from Dead Horse Point

At 1 mile the trail curves to the right, briefly paralleling the road to the point. Look for the impassable fence made of entwined juniper tree trunks. Put in place by park personnel, this barrier mimics the one early cowboys used to contain the mustangs they corralled. In the late 1800s cowboys drove wild horses onto this unique neck of rock. Here they roped and broke the horses, then sold them to buyers nationwide. The park gets its name from a legend that tells of a group of wild horses that were left to roam free. Although the fence was left open, for an unknown reason they stayed at this promontory and died of thirst. Your companions may have their own explanations for the horses' reluctance to leave.

The final 0.5-mile walk leads to the overlook area. The point rises 2000 feet above the Colorado River. The Colorado River's largest tributary, Green River, joins it 40 river miles downstream from here. Remember, much of this area is unfenced, so watch those little ones who tend to wander.

Ambitious hikers may continue the walk another 2 miles on the other side of the promontory, back to the visitor center.

During the summer months ranger-led walks and evening programs for the whole family are scheduled. Junior Ranger programs for kids are offered here as well.

Toilet and water facilities are located at the visitor center.

66 MESA ARCH TRAIL

Location ■	Canyonlands National Park, Island in the Sky District
Type ■	Day hike
Difficulty ■	Easy for children
Hikable ■	Year-round
Distance ■	0.5 mile, loop
Starting Elevation ■	6050 feet
High Point ■	6080 feet
Maps ■	Trails Illustrated Arches/Island in the Sky; USGS Canyonlands National Park; Canyonlands National Park brochure

www.nps.gov/cany
National park entrance fee

From Moab head north on US 191 for 11 miles to UT-313 and turn left. Drive 24 miles to the visitor center on the right. Mesa Arch trailhead is on the left, about 6 miles past the visitor center.

"Wow" and "Be careful," probably the most commonly used words at Mesa Arch, sum up the attraction this short trail has for children. Met halfway on the loop, Mesa Arch frames a stunning portrait of Utah's grand expanse of red canyon country rimmed by white-capped La Sal mountains.

This easy walk begins from the parking area, where it circles left from the trail sign. A trail brochure is available here. Remind all hikers to stay on the trail because cryptobiotic soil crust (previously termed cryptogamic soil), the black, lumpy soil that forms in patches throughout the West's deserts, holds the region's sandy soil in place. Tiny rootlets and fibers contained in cryptobiotic crust bind together sand particles, preventing wind and rain erosion. Explain that once stepped on, this fragile crust breaks down and it requires 100 years or more to rebuild itself. Allow children to examine, without harming, a patch of cryptobiotic crust. They will notice that plant life grows where this living layer blankets the ground. From this observation they will understand its function as a soil builder for desert plants.

The trail brochure identifies a variety of plants common to the high desert. Pinyon pine, probably the trademark tree of the Southwest's deserts, can be identified by its short needles growing in groups of two. Children are surprised to find out that what may look to be a small, young tree with a trunk 3 to 5 inches wide is actually a tree twice as old as Mom and Dad (50 to 100 years old). Tree age measuring should take place only at trees located along the trail or accessible via stepping only on rocks.

Equally common to the desert terrain here are prickly-pear cacti, which flower April to June. In early summer, cacti sprout their "tuna," the red-purple fruit eaten by many creatures, people included. Children who peer close to the plant can see this desert dweller's air-conditioning unit. Its spines absorb and reflect light, cooling the cactus flesh almost 20 degrees. Also, the bristly hairs at the base of each spine trap air next to the stem, insulating the plant

from heat. Caution! Feeling the effectiveness of a cactus' cooling system is not advised.

As the trail circles to the right and climbs slightly, a grand view of red-rock canyons capped by an equally exquisite mountain range commands everyone's attention. In fact, Mesa Arch is initially overshadowed by this natural spectacle. As eyes drift to the lower portion of the view, the white Navajo Sandstone of the arch frames the picture. From this first view, the trail turns left and then winds down and across slickrock to the base of the arch and an unguarded viewpoint.

Arch-exploring little ones may want to search for a route to the

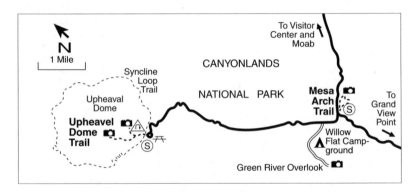

Mesa Arch frames superb views of Utah's canyon country and the La Sal Mountains.

top of this easily accessible, but completely unsafe, rock span over a 500-foot drop. This is where "Be careful!" gets its use. Climbing to the arch's top is against park regulations!

After the initial awe wears off, children are intrigued to learn that arches such as the one in front of them are forming right now. Explain that an arch was once a span of rock consisting of a layer of soft sandstone topped by a harder, more resistant rock layer. In most cases, the soft area erodes much faster than the harder rock layer, creating an arch until the upper layer finally collapses.

Geology in the making can be pointed out at this very viewpoint, which is void of cryptobiotic crust. Ask children why this is so. Discuss what will happen over the years to the nearby nooks of sand (that toddlers love to play in). Will the sand wash away with wind and rainfall? What could be done so that cryptobiotic soil could form here?

The return trail continues the loop back to the trailhead.

Toilet facilities are located at the visitor center, 6 miles north. (The nearest toilet is at Willow Flat Campground.) No water facilities are available here.

67 UPHEAVAL DOME TRAIL

Location	▪ Canyonlands National Park, Island in the Sky District
Type	▪ Day hike
Difficulty	▪ Easy to moderate for children
Hikable	▪ Year-round
Distance	▪ To first viewpoint, 0.5 mile, one way; to second viewpoint, 0.8 mile, one way
Starting Elevation	▪ 5600 feet
High Point	▪ 5800 feet
Maps	▪ Trails Illustrated Arches/Island in the Sky; Canyonlands National Park brochure

www.nps.gov/cany
National park entrance fee

Follow the driving directions for Hike 66, Mesa Arch Trail, to the Island in the Sky Visitor Center at Canyonlands National Park. Proceed past the visitor center approximately 6 miles to a paved road on the right leading to Upheaval Dome. Turn and follow the road approximately 5 miles to its end at the picnic grounds and trailhead.

Young canyon hikers scamper the slickrock to the viewpoint of Upheaval Dome, Canyonlands' most spectacular and debated geologic formation. Ideal for groups of children new to hiking and those eager to explore, the Crater View Trail offers two destinations. The short walk up a slickrock trail leads to an unguarded viewpoint of the crater. The slightly longer trek requires cairn-following skills and leads to another equally grand view of the formation.

The trail begins at the picnic area, where a brochure describing Upheaval Dome's structure is provided. Before the hike begins tell your companions to watch for clues that something special has happened here. Remind them that everywhere in the region, they've seen rocks arranged in layers, newer rock stacked on top of older rock.

The Colorado River cuts an exciting corridor through Canyonlands National Park.

But here they will find rocks tilted or colored differently than the surrounding formations, indicating that a major geologic event has occurred.

Within the first 50 feet, observant hikers will notice a round, hollow rock on the left side of the trail. They may also see white, dark red, yellow, and pink chunks of sandstone and shale seemingly littering the area. Point out that these out-of-place rocks were set here millions of years ago when layers of rock were pushed up into a dome, the remains of which they will see at the first viewpoint.

Rocks edge both sides of the trail as it traverses slickrock and winds through rock crevices. In addition to marking the trail, the rocks are intended to prevent little and big feet from wandering onto fragile cryptobiotic crust. This dark, lumpy surface is a complex living soil unique to arid regions. It contains a web of microscopic lichens, mosses, fungi, and bacteria that hold the sandy land in place.

Without cryptobiotic crust few plants could establish themselves in this harsh environment.

CAUTION

At 0.15 mile the sign for the overlook points to the right, and it is 60 yards from there to the unfenced viewpoint. Groups with young children should use extreme caution if they proceed in that direction.

"Wow" and "cool" are the words most kids use upon seeing Upheaval Dome, a mile-wide crater filled with multicolored spires and boulders. The round, smooth structure the name implies no longer remains. Encourage children to look at the dome's center for a white-and-black pinnacle, which is composed of White Rim Sandstone. They probably saw this rock layer from one of several viewpoints here at Canyonlands' Island in the Sky District. Explain that the crater, which looks like the remains of a rock explosion, contains a mixture of young and ancient rocks.

Scientists haven't agreed on how this unique geologic sight occurred. Most kids like the Ground Zero theory, in which 60 million years ago a meteorite struck just above this point, vaporizing nearly everything in sight (including dinosaurs and trees) and scattering rocks near and far. Erosion then stripped away much of the core, leaving the 0.75-mile-deep crater we see today.

The Salt Dome theory, the other leading explanation, describes an enormous salt layer, which evaporated from ancient seas, forming beneath hundreds of feet of rock. Under pressure, the salt layer became bendable and moved upward, pushing up the overlying rock. Erosion then took over, exposing the tilted, deformed layers.

Depending on your children's imaginations and/or geologic knowledge, they may have their own theories to explain Upheaval Dome. Encourage their hypotheses.

Those who continue to the next viewpoint follow cairns, piles of rocks, marking the route over slickrock. Man-made steps chipped into the smooth rock mark the way up a short section, followed by a walk down a slight depression, veering slightly left. (For steep ascents, some kids and their parents have fun gearing into their own four-wheel-drive mode.)

The second overlook is well fenced, offering another spectacular view. Here children see where Upheaval Creek, which flows only during flash floods, carries sediment out of the crater and into the Green River. Encourage them to see that as Upheaval Dome continues to erode, its sediments are forming yet another site that will someday be part of another geologic event.

Toilet facilities are available at the picnic area. No water facilities are available here.

68 DELICATE ARCH TRAIL

Location ■	Arches National Park
Type ■	Day hike
Difficulty ■	Moderate to challenging for children
Hikable ■	Year-round, depending on snow
Distance ■	1.5 miles, one way
Starting Elevation ■	4349 feet
High Point ■	4829 feet
Maps ■	Trails Illustrated Arches/Island in Sky; USGS Arches National Park; Arches National Park brochure

www.nps.gov/arch
National park entrance fee

From Moab drive north 5 miles on US 191 to the Arches National Park turnoff on the right. Proceed 12 miles from the visitor center to the Wolfe Ranch and Delicate Arch Road. Turn right and proceed 1.3 miles to the trailhead. Parking is provided here.

Canyon-country vistas and slickrock climbing are but two of the attractions along the hike to Utah's premier geologic formation—Delicate Arch. The trail begins at the remains of a pioneer's ranch before it crosses a bridge and winds up on elegant Entrada Sandstone. All hikers need hats, long-sleeved shirts, sunscreen, and water bottles on this shade-free trail.

The first 100 yards from the parking lot lead to what was John Wesley Wolfe's ranch, an 1898 homesteader's feat. Its weathered corral and tattered log cabin straddling a sandy plot may not match children's (and many adults') notion of a cattle ranch, but close examination of these remnants teases imaginations.

Look at the chinking between the cabin's logs. Observant youngsters may find the little fingerprints of Wolfe's two grandchildren in the mud plaster. Some children notice juniper bark insulating the roof frame. At the root cellar encourage hikers to imagine pumpkins and potatoes, bags of flour and sugar, cans of lard, and jars of salt stored here. Talk about what needs to be done to start a garden again on this ranch. (Build irrigation channels from Salt Wash, clear the land, gather seeds, plant them, collect wood to build a fence.)

Star trails above Delicate Arch, as captured by an all-night "shot in the dark"

A walk across the bridge lures most children across Salt Wash at 0.1 mile. Look for petroglyphs on the cliff on the left, just beyond the crossing. Ute Indians who camped here made the petroglyphs. Centuries later Ute people traded with Wolfe for his meat and vegetables. Ask hikers what messages they think the rock art is telling them. Also explain that native people began living and hunting here nearly 1000 years before Wolfe arrived. The bridge can serve as a turnaround point for very little hikers.

As the trail winds along the valley floor for 0.5 mile, caution children about leaving the pathway. Their footsteps may harm patches of cryptobiotic crust, formerly called cryptogamic soil. This dark, crumbly formation clinging to sandy soil consists of microscopic plant life with minute rootlets that bind the soil together. Tell children that cryptobiotic crust is alive, that it contains thousands of tiny plants that hold particles of sand together. A single footstep can destroy hundreds of years of growth in the layer. Show that the desert's trees, shrubs, and cacti grow in areas blanketed by the dark, lumpy surface.

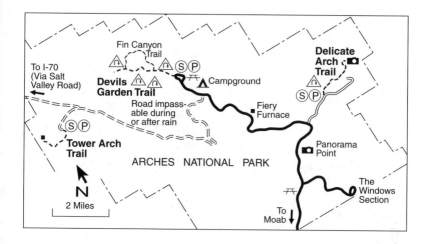

Explore ideas of what cryptobiotic crust does to help plant life. What
might happen if park visitors did not stay on the trail?

Cairns, piles of rocks used as trail markers, lead the way across the
Entrada Sandstone beginning at 0.6 mile. The climb begins here and
continues for 0.5 mile. Lug-soled hiking shoes or sturdy sports shoes
help when climbing on slickrock.

While crossing flat slabs of sandstone, watch for potholes, which I
heard one young hiker call "baby bathtubs in the rock." Explain that
over millions of years, sand grains cemented together to form sandstone. Depressions or potholes formed in places where it was laid
down unevenly. As rainwater—which contains a weak acid—collects
in the depression, it dissolves the cementing material. (Contrary to
popular belief, windblown sand has little erosional effect on sandstone.)

Although some potholes appear barren, those with a thin layer of
mud contain a finely tuned community of tiny shrimp, insect larvae,
and algae adapted to long waits between rain. Take a moment for
your hikers to lie upon the slickrock to look at, but not touch the
contents of a pothole. After a rainstorm many potholes are teeming
with minuscule life forms.

The trail's final 0.3-mile portion is a teaser. As it rises above the
Entrada Sandstone and crosses sandy soil, the trail gives no clue to
where it's headed. However, as it contours up a rock cliff on the right,
a dramatic view of Delicate Arch fills the sky.

For a child-friendly explanation on arch formation, see the description in Hike 70, Tower Arch Trail. Ask children to think of ways

they could measure the arch's height and width without the use of a measuring tape or ruler. Encourage them to estimate the length of their stride for use in measuring. Your advanced math student may know how to use the ratio of his height to his shadow's to calculate the height of the arch. Many people are surprised to learn the arch is 45 feet tall at its highest point. What makes it look so big?

 Caution children against running or walking under the arch, a very steep area. Also keep visits near the arch short, as photographers from around the world come here for a people-free photo of the arch. By the way, photographically the best time at Delicate Arch is evening. Early mornings, however, draw far fewer visitors.

Return via the same trail.

Vault toilets are available at the trailhead. Bring plenty of water.

69 DEVILS GARDEN TRAIL

Location ■	Arches National Park
Type ■	Day hike
Difficulty ■	Easy to Landscape Arch, moderate beyond
Hikable ■	Year-round, except after heavy snowfall
Distance ■	0.4 mile to 2.5 miles, one way
Starting Elevation ■	5200 feet
High Point ■	5300 feet
Maps ■	Trails Illustrated Arches/Island in the Sky; USGS Arches National Park; Arches National Park brochure; Devils Garden trail guide

www.nps.gov/arch
National park entrance fee

From Moab drive 5 miles north on US 191 to the Arches National Park entrance. Proceed 18.3 miles on the main road to its end at the Devils Garden trailhead parking area.

This end-of-the-road destination is a best-in-the-park hike. Eight arches, including one of the world's longest, lie within distances that delight both beginning and seasoned hikers. Water is unavailable beyond the trailhead and shade is scarce, so bring loaded water bottles and wear a wide-brimmed hat. Be prepared to monitor roving little ones at the overlooks, which are not fenced.

The trail guide available at the visitor center and trailhead shows the distance and walking time to each of the trail's arches. Do read the guide's cautions regarding safe visits to this fragile area.

Beginning on a wide, gravel path, the trail to Landscape Arch includes a spur to Tunnel and Pine Tree arches. Only 0.1 mile from the trailhead, where the trail threads a pair of thin sandstone slabs, hikers are introduced to the famous fins of Arches National Park. For a child-friendly explanation on how these fins were formed, refer to the last few paragraphs in Hike 70, Tower Arch Trail.

Turning right at the first side trail leads to a choice. Take the right fork for a view of Tunnel Arch sitting high on a sandstone slope to the left. Encourage youngsters to look for a smaller arch left of Tunnel Arch.

Go left to have a more intimate look at Pine Tree Arch. Ask children, "Does the arch appear to be aging?" Explain that the flakes of rock they see resulted from water freezing and expanding in rock cracks, then thawing, gradually breaking off thin layers of stone. Look for the arch's namesake. Pinyon pine trees growing near the arch produce a cone that bears a nut many of us have tasted and pinyon jays depend on. Late-summer and fall visitors may see the blue-gray robin-size bird searching the pinyon pine's open cones for seeds.

Back on the main trail and turning right to Landscape Arch, observant hikers may notice a splash of color on many fins. Close examination shows the orange to greenish patch to be lichen. Explain to kids that these crusts, a combination of two very small plants that are dependent on each other for survival, are actually alive. The plants in lichen have no leaves, stem, or flowers yet make a mild acid that breaks down rocks over a long period of time. Discuss how lichen is important to desert landscapes.

Just before reaching Landscape Arch, a trail to the right leads through Fin Canyon, a primitive trail and an alternative return route for those continuing their hike to Double O Arch. However, everyone's interest is directed to one of the world's longest spans of rock, stretched across the sky to your left. Children's estimates of the arch's width will vary as they follow the short spur trail off the main route. Ask the football fan in your group to guess the length in yards. (The arch measures 102 yards, or little more than a football field's length.)

In September 1991, a large chunk of rock fell from Landscape

Arch. More recently, in 1996 a few smaller rock pieces fell. The chunks' remains are piled under the arch. Ask your companions why the broken-off rock is sharp and lighter colored, while the arch rock appears smooth and darker in color. The best photos are taken here in the morning.

Many groups return from here on the main trail. Those who continue the hike follow cairns 0.3 mile up a slot between two sandstone walls. Here Wall Arch appears as a large hole on the right. Looking through the wall, what do you see?

Another 0.2 mile farther, on the left, is the trail for Navajo and Partition arches. This junction for the easy 0.3-mile spur hike can serve as another turnaround point.

Beyond this junction cairns mark the route over sand and slickrock. The trail continues west 0.8 mile to where it overlooks a sea of fins called Fin Canyon. A desert banquet of Mormon tea, thin-bladed yucca, cactus, and blackbrush flanks the edges of the trail. Your hike leader can tell if rain has fallen recently by examining a cactus. Parched, wrinkled flesh between the spines indicates a long dry period.

Just before arriving at Double O Arch, a trail on the right heads north 2.1 miles through Fin Canyon back to Landscape Arch.

CAUTION Beginning or unprepared hikers are warned not to continue on this primitive trail. Many hikers head back from Double O Arch, where the main trail ends. On the horizon to the north, find the dark

Hats provide needed shade for happy hikers of all ages.

layer of rock called Book Cliffs. Dark Angel, a rock pinnacle 0.5 mile to the west, serves as the final destination for this trail.

Water and toilet facilities are available at the trailhead. Water is not available in the winter.

70 TOWER ARCH TRAIL

Location ■	Arches National Park
Type ■	Day hike
Difficulty ■	Moderate for children
Hikable ■	Year-round; check road conditions
Distance ■	1.2 miles or more, one way
Starting Elevation ■	5450 feet
High Point ■	5560 feet
Maps ■	Trails Illustrated Arches/Island in the Sky; Arches National Park brochure

www.nps.gov/arch
National park entrance fee

From the visitor center at Arches, follow the main park road 17 miles, turning west on the two-wheel-drive high-clearance dirt road just past Skyline Arch. (This road can be impassible during or after storms.) Proceed 8 miles on this road through the Salt Valley, past the signed 4-wheel-drive road to a signed road on the left (south). Follow it for 1 mile to a parking area at the end of the road.

Venturing into the Klondike Bluffs area of Arches means entering an intricate but colorful upthrust of fins, pinnacles, and weirdly shaped sandstone formations. Kids have fun naming the character or creature they see eroded in the spires surrounding the area. They are impressed by the panoramic view of Arches and the surrounding region from the trail's high point. Anticipate a quiet hike, as this rather primitive and remote trail receives less foot traffic than others in the park.

From the parking area the trail veers left, following cairns up a steep, rocky ridge. Along the way thick ropes of juniper tree roots lay twisted among the rocks. Trace a root to its above-ground tree. Does it appear to be young or old? Cairns, the only visible clue to the route above the ledge, lead to a high point at 0.1 mile, where everyone stops to scope out the views. Looking east to the Fiery Furnace in

Tower Arch frames views of the Colorado Plateau's intriguing rock formations.

Arches, kids with imagination see its fins of red rock as flames flashing from a giant basin. Orient them to the east where the La Sal Mountains fill the view, and to the north where the long, dark ridge in the distance is the Book Cliffs.

As the trail crests another ridge at 0.3 mile, the Marching Men, a towering crowd of human-shaped rocks, looms on the right. Like soldiers they stand as sentries to your gradual descent into a large wash between rock walls. Ask your youngsters what they might call the similar, but smaller, formation on the left.

As the trail descends to its low point at 0.9 mile, the rock landscape reaches its high point. Fins and pinnacles, both stubby and slender, take on imagination-teasing shapes in this rock labyrinth.

After crossing the wash, a steep sandy ridge leads to a sign directing hikers to the northwest. Here a sea of fins becomes a navigational game, with cairns the only guideposts to Tower Arch. The unpeopled nature of this geologic gem makes exploring here especially treasured, but do keep at least an eye on every potential wanderer.

Knowing how sandstone fins form might add to your companions' appreciation. Children readily remember the rock's name from feeling its sandy surface. Letting them know sandstone began forming from the shallow seas of the dinosaur era, about 160 million years ago, might give geologic time some meaning. Tell them that this layer eventually collapsed into Salt Valley, the wide area they drove through on a gravel road just before the trailhead. As it flexed around the edge of Salt Valley, fractures formed. Use one of your hands clasped over your other fist to demonstrate the bending. Your knuckles are the fractures. The gaps widened as weathering—in the form of water dissolving the chemical bonds between the sand, and water freezing in narrow slots—eroded sand and larger bits away. Spread your fingers to illustrate the widening gap between fins.

After a short walk alongside a fin, you arrive at Tower Arch. Although a sign marks it, it's best to walk directly under the arch to experience the slice of sky and stone overhead. Tell children this arch was probably once a fin, much like its surrounding rock kin. The same forces that shaped the fins made the arch. However, the missing area was most likely a softer, easier-to-erode type of sandstone. Look around you. Do any fins look to be potential arches?

It is possible to explore this amazing network of fins and pinnacles for hours and days. When your group decides it's time to return, follow the same trail back.

Along the return hike, whiptail lizards may dart across youngsters' path, inviting them to a hide-and-go-seek game. Tell children that lizards are cold-blooded desert creatures without sweat glands. By moving from sun to shade they're actually maintaining their temperature balance. Stop to watch their pattern of movement from covered niches to sun-warmed rocks. In what ways are humans like lizards?

Some children like to capture a lizard by the tail to test its special escape technique—dropping its tail. When this defense works, however, the desert reptile also loses its fat reserve. Discuss the tailless lizard's fate when food is not available. Knowing this, children will know it's not fair to test an animal's defense system.

Remind kids to keep the hide-and-go-seek game limited to the trail, as delicate cryptobiotic crust (previously termed cryptogamic soil) blankets much of the sandy terrain. Its dark, microscopic roots hold the otherwise loose soil and sand in place. It takes hundreds of years for this complex of lichens, mosses, fungi, and bacteria to form. So "don't bust the crust" by stepping on it. Find areas where cryptobiotic crust thrives and compare it with sandy surfaces that have had plenty of foot traffic.

Toilet and trash facilities are provided at the trailhead. Water is available at the visitor center, 26 miles away, or at Devils Garden picnic area or trailhead, 9.5 miles away (except in winter).

71 NEGRO BILL CANYON

Location ■	Northeast of Moab
Type ■	Day hike or overnight backpack
Difficulty ■	Moderate for children
Hikable ■	March through November
Distance ■	1.6 miles, one way
Starting Elevation ■	4000 feet
High Point ■	4300 feet
Maps ■	Trails Illustrated Arches/Island in the Sky; USGS Moab and Rill Creek; Moab Area Hiking Trails brochure

From Moab travel north on US 191 for 3 miles to UT-128, turning east (right) just before crossing the Colorado River. Follow the river road 3.1 miles to the dirt drive on the south (right) side of the road. Parking is provided at the trailhead.

Happy hikers with wet feet are the probable outcome of this desert canyon exploration to the refreshingly shady oasis at Morning Glory Arch. Winding through lush vegetation or over slickrock terrain, the trail crosses the stream frequently, offering fun maneuvers and tempting pauses. During the summer, plan this hike for early in the day. Groups with hikers of varying abilities find enjoyable destinations at several points along the trail.

Shortly beyond the trailhead the trail drops from the cliff side to creekside. A variety of trees and shrubs, representing both desert and riparian zones, shade the walk. Encourage children to find plants common to the desert, such as cacti and yucca, as well as leafy bushes or flowers growing along streams. As the trail edges slickrock (at 0.5 mile), point out the hanging gardens clinging to moist rock. Explain that water seeps through the sandstone, supplying moisture to the mosses, ferns, and flowers of these desert gardens. Ask your kids, "Are the plants along the seep line the same as those growing along the creek? What conditions are similar? Different?"

At 0.2 mile the foot trail meets an old jeep road at the first creek crossing. Sign in at the trail registration box near here. The road follows the east side of the creek and serves as the trail for another 0.5 mile. Several campsites dot this stretch.

A campsite offering grand views of the canyon and several pools for splashing in is located at 0.7 mile, where a canyon drainage enters on the right. This is a good turnaround point.

Creek crossings increase in number and difficulty as the trail continues up and out of the canyon bottom. On hot days deep pools alongside the trail are inviting. However, swims should be limited because body oils, and particularly sunscreen lotion, harm the delicate habitats of animals dependent on these water sources. Your children will appreciate this when they spot the brownish green crawfish that thrive in the stream's larger pools.

At 1 mile the trail climbs above the stream and traverses the desert for another 0.2 mile, where it forks into the second canyon on your right. Follow the trail to the right and cross the stream. Continue 0.4 mile; looming ahead is a dark canyon wall where Morning Glory Arch spans 243 feet. Nestled against a cliff and over a spring and small

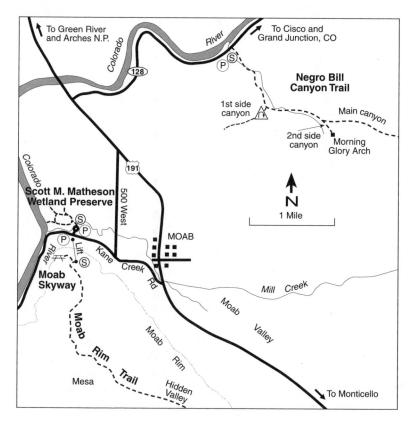

pool, this sixth-largest rock span in the United States is hard to distinguish until you are right under it.

Hanging gardens and the creek's gurgle under the rock surface here intrigue visitors. While hike leaders relax in this cool oasis, those with ample energy like exploring the area in search of the spot where the stream resurfaces. Caution eager explorers about the poison ivy growing here. Its big, bold leaves, which look different from other desert-dwelling plants, are protected from the sun's drying rays by fine hairs and a waxy surface. Still, anyone, even a budding young botanist, is vulnerable to poison ivy's revenge.

Many hikers like knowing this trail is named for a trapper, William Granstaff, who raised his cows along this stream in the late 1800s.

The nearest toilet facilities are located in the BLM campgrounds adjacent to the Colorado River along UT-128.

72 MOAB SKYWAY

Location ■	Moab
Type ■	Day hike or evening hike
Difficulty ■	Easy for children
Hikable ■	Year-round
Distance ■	0.25 mile to 2.0 miles, round trip
Starting Elevation ■	4900 feet
High Point ■	5000 feet
Map ■	Site brochure

www.moab-utah.com/skyway
Lift fee
Wheelchair accessible

From Main Street in Moab, turn west onto Kane Creek Boulevard (at McDonald's). Follow the road 0.75 mile to a fork in the road. Take the left fork for 0.5 mile where an ample parking lot for the Skyway is on the left.

Climbing nearly 1000 feet in 12 minutes is a feat everyone appreciates—especially if it involves riding a chairlift above spectacular red rock formations etched with prehistoric images. The destination allows those in wheelchairs or in seasoned hiking boots access to the kind of terrain featured in bicycling and jeeping magazines.

If possible, time your Skyway trip around the sun. Summer riders enjoy shade during the ride up after 3:00 P.M.; in autumn it's 1:00 P.M. (Note that the lift may be temporarily closed before and during storms.) Evening riders should expect great temperature differences during their trip; check with the lift attendant about recommended jackets.

During the ride up, most passengers become owl-like, turning their heads in all directions to take in the sights. Relax, there's even more to see at the top. Those who watch the rocks below catch glimpses of life here long before bicycle wheels were invented. On the right, between towers 2 and 3, watch for petroglyphs. There's a star shape and a squiggly line in the flat face of a boulder varnished black. Ask your chair companions what the line might represent (most probably the Colorado River). Watch for other rock images and a miniature natural arch.

At the top, a wheelchair-accessible boardwalk leads to a viewpoint, picnic tables, and several foot trails. A wonderland of landscapes begins here. Despite the rugged appearance of this desert terrain, stay on the trails whenever possible. The plants and soils here have adapted to the arid conditions, but not the impact of hiking boots.

Hikers looking east see Moab Valley edged by the Book Cliffs and the Windows of Arches National Park. Shimmering green in its red rock surroundings sits the Scott M. Matheson Wetlands Preserve. This crow's eye view gives your kids a chance to see how the 875-acre preserve is truly an "oasis in the desert." This is also an opportunity for them (and you!) to see what 875 acres looks like.

Colorado Vista Overlook trail is a short path leading to views of

Scenic viewpoints surround hikers atop the Moab Skyway.

the Colorado River canyon. Red rock spires and walls fill both land-scapes and skyscapes viewed from Panorama Point. The views at your feet are also worth noting because the cliffrose, saltbrush, rice grass, and rabbitbrush were all important sources of food, medicine, and tools to the people who left their markings on the rocks below. Return via the chairlift.

Hikers with ambition may choose a 5-mile return hike via the Moab Rim Trail and Hidden Valley Trail. The Rim trail begins just south of the Skyway's top terminal and continues 3 miles before meeting the Hidden Valley Trail. Hikers should be well prepared for this trek because it requires an elevation gain of 700 feet followed by steep switchbacks. For more information on this hike and others, visit the Moab Visitor Center at Center and Main Streets.

If you missed seeing the petroglyphs from the chairlift, you will walk past a cluster of them at the base of the hill. Look for the etchings on the boulder below the ticket booth. As with all ancient artifacts, touching, rubbing, tracing, or chalking rock images causes them to slowly disappear.

Restroom facilities are available at the upper and lower terminals, with bottled water and soda sold at the upper terminal.

73 SCOTT M. MATHESON WETLANDS PRESERVE

Location ■ Moab
Type ■ Day hike
Difficulty ■ Easy
Hikable ■ Year-round
Distance ■ 1 mile, round trip
Starting Elevation ■ 4900 feet
High Point ■ 4900 feet
Map ■ Preserve brochure

www.utahnature.org
Wheelchair accessible

Follow directions for the Moab Skyway, Hike 72, continuing 0.1 mile past it to the parking area on the right for the preserve.

An exotic green world nestled in a sea of red rock, the Scott M.

Wildlife tracks in the mud are among the attractions at Scott M. Matheson Wetlands Preserve.

Matheson Wetlands Preserve soothes, delights, and intrigues its visitors. The wheelchair-accessible 1-mile loop trail features spurs to wildlife viewing spots and an undeveloped path to the banks of the Colorado River. Water defines this desert wetland, attracting a wide variety of birds and mammals. Water also shifts the habitats within the preserve, creating an environment that changes dramatically from season to season and day to day. Repeat visits here promise a new understanding and appreciation of this natural sponge for the Colorado River.

Before stepping into the preserve, remind your companions that quiet hikers are the ones who see a red-winged blackbird perched on a cattail or hear a beaver slap its tail on the water. Also, "edge of light hikers," those who visit early or late in the day, are more likely to see wildlife. The cool shadows of the preserve welcome everyone on hot summer days.

The trail from the parking lot to an information kiosk leads through a dense stand of tamarisk, a nonnative tree with enduring and invasive properties. A self-guided tour map and brochures describing the wildlife, ecology, and management of this preserve are available here. (During our October visit, the "Mammals, Amphibians, Reptiles, and Fish" brochure helped us identify scat on the trail as that of a coyote's.) From the kiosk follow the path to the right.

Your kids will appreciate the unique qualities of this lush wetland when they look up and see an arid land of rocks in all directions. Most of the wetland's water comes from the La Sal Mountains, visible to your tallest hikers. The Colorado River occasionally floods this preserve, an event that is now understood as necessary for the health of the soil and many plants.

A spur trail at the first bench changes to a boardwalk that ends at the bird-viewing blind. Approach it quietly. Several openings in the bilevel blind allow all viewers, from toddlers to teens, to listen and look at the activity of the bulrush marsh. Count the different species your group sees. Try imitating a bird's call. Nearly 200 different bird species have been identified at this preserve.

Head back on the boardwalk and follow the gravel path under a willow tree that arches over the trail. Russian olive trees border the trail. Stop to feel the bark of both trees. Use caution here because some kids like to test the sharpness of the olive tree's spikes. Talk with your companions about the animals and insects that might use these trees. The rough bark of the willow provides many tiny habitats for insects. Deer eat the willow tree twigs. Birds line their nests with the willow's downy seed tufts. (Fall visitors enjoy holding these soft bundles.) Bees visit the tree's flowers. What animals might eat the fruit of the thorny olive tree?

The aroma of a cattail marsh fills the air at the next stop. Tell your kids that bacteria, better known as "germs," release this wetland odor as they eat tiny bits of plants that are rotting in the water. Right now millions of microscopic life forms in this marsh are changing plant material into food for very small insects, snails, and worms. They are starting the wetland's web of life. Ask what other animals belong to the web of life here.

Those who follow the footpath to the Colorado River notice wire fencing around large cottonwood trunks. Talk about why these trees are being protected from beavers. At the river's shore look for the wildlife tracks in the mud. Follow the trail back to the kiosk.

To protect its natural qualities, dogs, bicycling, and picnicking are not permitted anywhere in the preserve, which is open from dawn to dusk. For information on naturalist-led walks held on Saturday mornings at 8:00 A.M., call the preserve at 435-259-4629.

No water or toilet facilities are provided.

74 WARNER LAKE TO OOWAH LAKE

Location ▪	Manti–La Sal National Forest, Moab
Type ▪	Day hike
Difficulty ▪	Easy to moderate for children
Hikable ▪	June through October
Distance ▪	Warner Lake, 1 mile, loop; Warner Lake to Oowah Lake, 1.7 miles, one way
Starting Elevation ▪	9370 feet
Ending Elevation ▪	8700 feet at Oowah trailhead
Map ▪	None

From Moab drive south to the turnoff for La Sal Mountain Loop Road. Follow this scenic byway 24 miles to the road for Warner Lake Campground. Turn right, driving 5 miles. The trailhead is at the end of the road, where parking is provided and the lake is visible.

Shuttle to Oowah Lake: Return on the dirt road from the Warner Lake Campground to the La Sal Mountain Loop Road. Turn left and proceed 1.5 miles to Oowah Lake Road at Mill Creek. Make another left turn and drive 2.5 miles to the trailhead on the left. The lake and primitive camping sites are located 0.5 mile farther up the road. Parking is provided in a small area near the trailhead.

Aspen shade and cool mountain air provide a welcome retreat from the hot desert around Moab, and this pair of trails offers hikers of all abilities a chance to appreciate it. The loop trail winds through aspen forests adjacent to Warner Lake. The other trail follows a downhill slope through aspens to Oowah Lake. Plan to fish at Warner Lake, where I saw a 10-year-old proudly walk away with four trout on her stringer.

The trailhead at Warner Lake is the beginning for both hikes. The sign here, with Haystack Mountain (11,642 feet) framed behind it, indicates Oowah Lake is 1.75 miles and Burro Pass is 3.5 miles. Follow the trail past Warner Lake, where after passing through a gate, it enters an aspen forest. After 0.1 mile into the forest, the trail forks and the sign directs Oowah Lake hikers to the right onto a closed road.

Loop hikers stay on this wide path throughout their hike, while those heading to Oowah Lake head left after 0.3 mile. Those following the loop trail near Warner Lake will see carvings made in the bark marring many an aspen along their walk. Although most hikers are now abiding by the "leave not a trace" ethic, they'll find it interesting to see old carvings, generally made in this area by shepherds and hunters. They are also known as "arboglyphs." The clues I use to find their names, and in some cases their ranch brand, are cursive letters, thick and blackened over the years. At 0.5 mile, near the remains of a cabin on the left, look for a horse-head silhouette and cattle brand emblazoned on an aspen.

A gentle climb leads to a view of the Abajo Mountains and the canyon country west of Moab. As the trail crosses a fence and veers right, it joins the entry road into the campground. For perhaps the most interesting aspen art, look to the right just before the campground entrance where one unfortunate aspen appears to be a bear's scratching post.

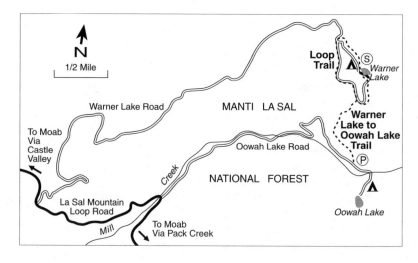

The loop completes itself at the campground.

Oowah Lake hikers walk 0.3 mile on the closed road, as described previously, to a faint trail on the left. It's easy to miss if the sign is down, as it was during my visit. Shepherds and cattlemen of 30 and 40 years ago carved interesting autographs on these trees as well.

At 0.5 mile the descent gets serious, with rocks adding to the challenge of this narrow trail. Views of Haystack Mountain and the desert plateaus northwest of Moab are framed by aspens along this walk. Evidence of the mountain's drainage system can be heard, but not seen. However, a small spring spills out on the trail's left side at 0.75 mile. Notice the different plant life around the water source.

The trail levels, then veers left until it descends to meet the road to the campground. Parking for shuttled vehicles is along this narrow road.

Toilet facilities are provided at Warner and Oowah Lake.

CAVE SPRING

Location ■	Canyonlands National Park, Needles District
Type ■	Day hike
Difficulty ■	Easy with moderate climbs
Hikable ■	Year-round, except after snowfalls
Distance ■	0.6 mile, loop
Starting Elevation ■	5000 feet
High Point ■	5025 feet
Map ■	Trails Illustrated Needles/Island in the Sky Trail Guide, available at the trailhead or purchased at the visitor center

www.nps.gov/cany
Park entrance fee

From Moab drive 40 miles south on US 191, turning right on UT- 211 on the west side of the road. (From Monticello drive 22 miles north on US 191). Take UT-211 approximately 35 miles to the Needles visitor center. From here drive 0.6 mile on the paved road, turning onto the first road on the left. Drive 0.7 mile to the next dirt road and continue 1.1 mile to the parking area and trailhead.

Potholes of all sizes, each an oasis of animal and insect life, dimple the sandstone of Canyonlands.

An authentic cowboy camp, ancient pictographs, ladders to climb, and cairns to follow are among the attractions of this short loop trail. Grand views of the colorful spires of the Needles district highlight the hike as do the shady retreats under rock overhangs.

The trail begins in a tall stand of sage and rabbitbrush, leading directly to the cowboy camp. A wooden fence prevents hikers from wandering through the camp, but the table, stove, and cattle-grazing paraphernalia left by the cowboys are easy to see. Ask your companions why tin cans surround the table legs. (To prevent rodents from crawling on top.) This camp was used as recently as 1975 when the last of the cattle were removed from the park.

At the camp, point out the smoke-charred ceiling and the nearby streaks of desert varnish. How do they differ in appearance? Desert varnish takes thousands of years to form. It is usually made of dust, clay particles, and minerals. Tiny living creatures called microorganisms actually form desert varnish by using and changing the minerals, causing them to stick to the rock surface. Streaks of black desert varnish are often seen where water cascades over the cliffs.

Signs of a much earlier life here are visible near the seep located just past the cowboy camp. Stand still and away from the pictographs to prevent dust from settling on the rock images. Groups of Ancestral Puebloans probably lived here more than 1000 years ago. The seep may have been an important water source, and evidence suggests that the flat area behind where you are standing was used for farming. Perhaps water once flowed over the cliff edge now stained by desert varnish.

The trail passes under rock overhangs trimmed with maidenhair ferns. Notice the coolness of the air here compared to the sun-drenched portions of the trail. In fact, the temperature of rock or sand in direct sunlight compared with the air temperature 6 feet above it is often 25 to 50 degrees. Encourage your hikers to feel the difference using the palm of their hand.

Two wooden ladders provide an easy route up and over the rock formations. Spectacular views of the Needles greet hikers at the top. Cairns, or piles of rock, serve as guides across the sandstone rock. Pay attention to the cairns, or finding your way back to the parking lot may not be easy.

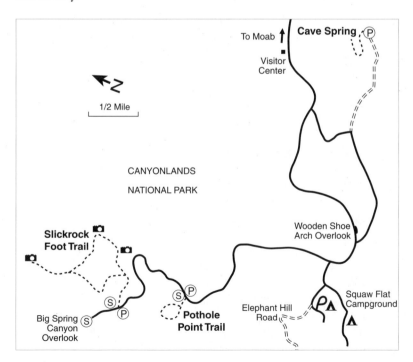

Potholes, or dimple-like depressions in the rock, dot this landscape. If rain has fallen recently you may see potholes filled with water—an attraction thirsty hikers find hard to resist. Avoid disturbing these tiny oases, wet or dry, because they are home to many tiny creatures. Learn more about potholes as discussed in Hike 76, Pothole Point.

The final portion of the trail edges an overhang. Look for tiny dimples in the dust here. These little pits are made by antlions—the larvae of a dragonfly-like insect that eats ants when they slide down the steep sides of their traps. Carefully drop a few grains of sand into the pit. If it's occupied, you may see the antlion grab at the sand—prey the eyeless creature hoped to sting, paralyze, and eat. By late summer and early fall, antlions leave their pits as adults. They do not eat; they simply mate and die before leaving their eggs on the sand for next year's brood of antlions.

Nearest water and toilet facilities are at the Needles Visitor Center and at Squaw Flat Campground.

76 POTHOLE POINT

Location ■	Canyonlands National Park, Needles District
Type ■	Day hike
Difficulty ■	Easy
Hikable ■	Almost all year
Distance ■	0.6 mile, loop
Starting Elevation ■	5000 feet
High Point ■	5010 feet
Maps ■	Trails Illustrated Arches/Islands in the Sky; trail guide available at trailhead

www.nps.gov/cany

See Hike 75, Cave Spring, for directions to the Needles District at Canyonlands National Park. From the visitor center here, follow the paved road 5.8 miles to the sign on the left for Pothole Point Trail. Parking is provided at the trailhead.

Considered desert gems, potholes jewel this easy trail. Along the way hikers feast on grand views of the Needles and retreat into cool caves under rock ledges. Cairns mark the way over slickrock, providing route-finding fun for everyone.

At the trailhead where stands of narrow leaf yucca, rabbitbrush, pinyon, and sage flock the landscape tell your kids they are walking through a storehouse of food, medicine, clothing, and shelter supplies. The Ancestral Pueblo who lived here 1000 years ago used each of these plants in many ways. For instance, yucca provided the fibers they wove to make sandals. From its roots they made soap. They ate fruit produced by the yucca and used the plant's needle-like tips as tools. Encourage your hikers to name ways in which they could use or eat the surrounding vegetation. Help them recognize the nuts of the pinyon tree's cones as a source of food—even today.

Patches of cryptobiotic soil blanket the region near the trailhead. "Don't bust the crust" is one way of reminding hikers to stay off this living soil. This lumpy, often black crust acts like a sponge and stores water. Cryptobiotic soil acts like an intricate, sticky web, holding rock and soil particles in place. Once damaged by footprints or traffic, some patches of cryptobiotic soil never recover. While in canyon country, stay on the slickrock or in sandy washes whenever possible. Do stop and feel this "tough stuff" along the trail.

Follow the cairns to rock formations on the trail's left side that look like a "land of stemless mushrooms," a name coined by my 9-year-old companions. Plenty of rock overhangs here make for fun forts and shady hideouts. A spire with a bulbous top and narrow neck on the right side of the trail is useful for showing how each rock layer weathers differently. A short side trail on the left leads to a 360-degree view of the area's spires and formations.

Potholes dimple the slickrock. These oases are more than occasional water holes for animals. A close-up investigation of a water-filled pothole reveals such tiny creatures as worms, snails, shrimp, and tadpoles. But please keep hands and feet out of potholes because oils and lotion on human skin pollute these temporary waterholes.

When dry, these miniature reservoirs hold the eggs of animals and insects that survive extreme weather conditions—temperatures near 140 degrees in the summer and below freezing in the winter. The organisms that breed in potholes have adapted to the extreme conditions in different ways. Some tadpoles and winged insects, such as mosquitoes, live where water doesn't dry out and then travel to temporary pools, like potholes, to mate and lay eggs. Other organisms like snails and mites have a waterproof shell or exoskeleton that prevents them from drying out when no water is in the pothole. Certain shrimp eggs, worms, and tadpoles have an even more fascinating way of adapting to dry conditions: water molecules in their body change into sugar molecules that can tolerate the drought. In fact, after a flight on the outside of a spacecraft, brine shrimp hatched from this sugar molecule state.

If your hike here occurs shortly after a rainstorm, stop to watch a pothole. You may see an organism hatch out and begin its 10-day life span. On the return, explore with your group what pothole organisms probably do during their short, active life. Follow the cairns back to the trailhead.

The nearest toilet and water facilities are at Squaw Flat Campground.

77 SLICKROCK FOOT TRAIL

Location ▪	Canyonlands National Park, Needles District
Type ▪	Day hike
Difficulty ▪	Moderate for children
Hikable ▪	March though October
Distance ▪	2.4 miles, loop
Starting Elevation ▪	4950 feet
High Point ▪	4970 feet
Maps ▪	Trails Illustrated Needles/Island in the Sky; trail guide available at trailhead or purchased at the visitor center

www.nps.gov/cany

 From the Needles District Visitor Center at Canyonlands National Park, follow the paved road 6.7 miles southwest to the parking area for the Slickrock Foot Trail.

Octogenarian park volunteer Larry Requa had 8-year-olds in mind when he designed this loop trail. For most kids, following the trail's cairns across the pothole-pocked plateau becomes a game some parents can't keep pace with. However, everyone gathers at each of the trail's four viewpoints to point out canyon country's prominent features

Six Shooter Peak as seen from the road to the Needles District

etched across the sweeping horizon. Caution is needed at these over-looks because there are no fences.

The trail begins at the bottom of a shallow slope before it climbs gradually, veering left and then weaving between boulders and slickrock slabs. Observation skills are important throughout this hike because cairns mark the counterclockwise route. Rarely does a foot-print remain to mark the way to go.

However, some children race in all directions, chasing a lizard as it darts across the slickrock. The cold-blooded reptile is not playing a game. It is regulating its body temperature by moving from sun-warmed rock or sand to cooler, shaded areas. On hot summer days lizards are more likely to be seen in the morning than at midday, when it is too hot for even a lizard to go hiking. Springtime hikers may notice a lizard doing "push-ups." This exercise is actually a courtship display used by males to attract females. Upon seeing this behavior, stop to find the female viewing the show.

At 0.3 mile the first viewpoint faces east where profiles of the La Sal Mountains, North Six Shooter Peak, and Needles Overlook fill the horizon. Encourage youngsters to estimate the distances to each of the features. They might be surprised to learn that the mountains are only 40 miles away, while the Needles Overlook is less than 10.

Observant hikers are thrilled to find a mini-arch, only 10 inches high, peeking over the trail's right edge shortly after the first viewpoint. However, their interest may be diverted to the numerous potholes that dimple this area.

When filled with rainwater for a long enough period of time, these desert waterpockets come alive with desert shrimp, algae, and young amphibians. Their life cycle—eating each other, breeding, and laying eggs in the sediment—consists of a few frantic days. During dry spells the eggs in these tiny desert lakes remain dormant. Whether they are in their wet or dry state, observe closely, but do not put hands or feet into these enticing pools. To learn more about potholes, see Hike 76: Pothole Point.

Access to the second viewpoint requires caution, as a step over a deep crevasse leads to a rock peninsula surrounded by steep drop-offs. Before doubling back 50 yards to join the trail, help your children find the chasm 15 miles northeast where the Colorado River flows.

While following the route to the next viewpoint, remind those with big or little feet not to step on patches of dark, lumpy crusts bonded to sand or sandy soil. Known as cryptobiotic crust (previously termed cryptogamic soil), these areas are loaded with bacteria, lichens, mosses, and fungi. These microflora send out minute threadlike filaments and rootlets that bind granules of sand together. Eventually plant life takes root in these areas. However, when a careless hiker steps on cryptobiotic crust, its fragile structure breaks down and it takes years to begin rebuilding. Children will understand the significance of cryptobiotic crust when shown a 3-inch-tall section that took hundreds of years to develop to its present stage. They'll remember your suggestion "Don't bust the crust."

En route to viewpoints 3 or 4, some hikers lose sight of the cairns, finding themselves rimmed on a high point or forced to make a monkeylike leap to higher ground. If you find yourself in such a predicament, head back, retracing your steps until you've found the last cairn.

At viewpoints 3 and 4, Little Spring Canyon and its confluence with Big Spring Canyon dominate the foreground, with silhouettes of the Needles and the Abajo Mountains on the horizon.

The loop rejoins the trail's short neck before returning to the trailhead. Return the trail guide at the register.

The nearest toilet or water facilities are at Squaw Flat Campground.

78 EDGE OF THE CEDARS INDIAN RUIN TRAIL

Location ■	Edge of the Cedars State Park Museum
Type ■	Day hike
Difficulty ■	Easy for children
Hikable ■	Year-round
Distance ■	0.2 mile or more, one way
Starting Elevation ■	6200 feet
High Point ■	6200 feet
Maps ■	Trails Illustrated Manti–La Sal National Forest; USGS Blanding

www.nr.state.ut.us/parks/www1/edge.htm
State park admission fee to the museum
Wheelchair accessible

From US 191 just north of Blanding, turn west on 200 North, drive to 300 West, and then turn right. Turn left at 400 North and proceed three blocks to the Edge of the Cedars Museum and the parking lot on the right.

Climbing into a kiva just as young boys did a thousand years ago is among the experiences children sample at Edge of the Cedars State Park Museum. The museum displays a diverse collection of prehistoric pottery, contemporary Ute and Navajo relics, and artifacts of the Anglo settlers in southeastern Utah. A barrier-free concrete trail from the museum leads directly to an Ancestral Pueblo village. A special attraction is the sculptures by Joe Pachak, inspired from rock art themes, including a new solstice marker on the hillside behind the ruin.

The museum is a natural, child-friendly first stop for this visit. The colorful macaw feather sash and displays of dresses worn by pioneer women especially intrigue kids. The concrete path leaves from the museum's second floor.

The ancient village you'll see outside the museum consists of a rock dwelling sitting on a ridge of mounds. In 1972 an excavation crew from Weber State College in Utah completed stabilization work on the only exposed dwelling site. The other living and storage quarters that housed families from A.D. 850 to 1220 remain buried under the grassy mounds. Children and many adults are surprised to learn that before the digging work begins, archaeologists spend months researching and mapping the area in order to safely remove rubble and rebuild tumbled walls. Each shovel of dirt requires careful sifting for remnants of a culture we are just now learning about.

After a visit to the Navajo hogan just outside the museum, children will race along the walkway to the area's main excavated site. In doing so they will pass several unexcavated sites. Called Complex 4, several storage, living, and ceremonial rooms are contained here. Next to the excavated Complex 4 site is an unexcavated Great Kiva, which points to important connections to other Ancestral Pueblo sites. Advise children that walls built over a thousand years ago are quite fragile and should not be climbed on. However, a quite sturdy wooden ladder extending from a rooftop entry hole invites everyone to enter the kiva.

When your crew is seated on the earth floor or stone bench circling the underground room, tell them children spent many a day and night here listening to clan stories and learning their people's traditions. Explain this dark, often cold, smoky, and crowded room served as classroom, courthouse, and church for the collection of

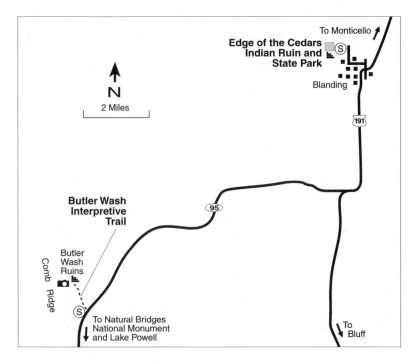

A toddler rests on an entry into a stabilized prehistoric home. Remember not to lean on or enter ruins, except where specifically permitted.

small families living here. There was no written language, so learning required listening, telling, and retelling. How does this way differ from learning in school now? Many archaeologists believe men were the primary teachers in the kiva while women taught the girls living skills in areas above the kiva.

Before leaving the kiva notice where the fire pit and ventilator shaft were. The sipapu, a fist-size hole in the ground, is opposite the fire pit. Tell children it is believed that to the Ancestral Puebloan the sipapu represented the place of entry from the underworld through which the first people and animals came into this world. Explain that just as a crucifix is found in most Christian churches, so too is a sipapu found in a kiva. The rectangular hole near the sipapu is believed to be a foot-drum.

Much of the kiva and dwelling have been repaired by archaeologists, so encourage youngsters to find examples of modern and original plaster between the rocks.

Outside the kiva look for two other circles, the largest being the Great Kiva. Plans to excavate the dirt that has filled this underground room are scheduled for future archaeologists. Anyone who has seen other great kivas knows them to usually be much larger. This one, though considered small, has a subterranean entrance, a characteristic of a great kiva. Little ones love to peer into the southeast corner room where the tunnel-like entry is located.

As your group of budding archaeologists walks the path, they will notice other unexcavated mounds and depressions, which indicate room blocks and kivas. As they survey the mounds tell them they are doing the initial survey work of an archaeologist.

After visiting the few dwelling and storage sites, many children may think the Ancestral Pueblo people were tiny. Reassure them that the early Puebloans, whose lives were spent primarily outdoors, were usually about 5 feet tall. Their small stature is believed to be a result of the small amounts of protein in their diet.

Children may also wonder how they farmed this dry area. Stop at the park's vegetable garden to learn how Puebloan people grew corn and probably other crops long ago.

During the drive back talk about how the archaeologists studying the past provide us with answers for today's problems. Discuss how an archaeologist is continually learning new techniques to safely excavate ancient remnants and that in most places in the Southwest items remain well preserved in the ground. Why would this be so?

Toilet and water facilities are located at the museum.

79 BUTLER WASH INTERPRETIVE TRAIL

Location ▪	West of Blanding
Type ▪	Day hike
Difficulty ▪	Easy to moderate for children
Hikable ▪	Mid-April through November
Distance ▪	1 mile, loop
Starting Elevation ▪	5200 feet
High Point ▪	5300 feet
Maps ▪	Trails Illustrated Manti–La Sal National Forest, Grand Gulch Plateau; USGS Hotel Rock

Drive 3 miles south from Blanding on US 191 to UT-95 and turn west. Continue 10 miles to the sign for Butler Wash, where a paved road on the right leads to the parking area and trailhead.

A sandstone alcove shades an ancient home in Butler Wash.

Slickrock scramblers of every size follow cairns through the high desert to this exclusive viewpoint of an early Puebloan dwelling complex.

Beginning at the parking lot, the trail traverses slickrock and sandy terrain, with views of Comb Ridge profiling the horizon to the west. This 90-mile-long ridge of Navajo Sandstone extends south to near Arizona's Monument Valley. The ancient dwellings you will see are tucked in an alcove located at the base of Comb Ridge.

Keep an eye on the cairns, lest you lose the trail and end up walking across cryptobiotic crust. Appearing like a black, lumpy surface on an otherwise sandy soil, this living crust is what holds the soil in place.

Explain that millions of microscopic filaments, along with lichens and mosses, are contained in a square inch of cryptobiotic crust. Sticky sheaths surround these living cells forming webs that hold loose particles of sand together. When rain falls these living bacteria swell to hold the water. A 2-inch-high section of this crust represents at least 200 years of development, which can be destroyed by a single footstep. Watch for areas where plants are flourishing. Point out that cryptobiotic crust surrounds them. Ask your companions to look for the oldest and the least developed examples. Discuss what happens to the area when cryptobiotic crust is destroyed. Remember, one misplaced step turns crust to dust!

Another common, life-giving feature of the high desert is Utah juniper. This tree requires a lot of water. It has adapted to the desert's dry conditions by being able to shut off water flow to one or more branches, keeping enough for the rest of the tree to survive. Do you see any trees that have adapted in this way?

As the trail reaches the crest of a small ridge, follow it to the right along the top edge of a huge depression. Slickrock, which is true to its name when there's snow, covers the remaining portion of the hike to the overlook. Cairns cemented together provide long-lasting trail markers to the viewpoint.

A fence surrounds the sandstone platform overlooking the ruins. Talk about how many people may have occupied these dwellings. Find the four kivas, deciding which one is Kayenta, or square-shaped, in style. Discuss what makes this a good home site. How did the Anasazi get into their dwellings? Where did they grow their crops? Binoculars are useful here.

Return by following the cairns.

No water facilities are available here. A vault toilet is located near the parking lot.

80 SIXTEEN HOUSE RUIN

Location	Bluff
Type	Day hike
Difficulty	Easy to moderate for children
Hikable	Almost year-round
Distance	2 miles, round trip
Starting Elevation	4320 feet
High Point	4400 feet
Maps	USGS; Bluff, Recapture Pocket

From Bluff drive north to the intersection at the Cow Canyon Trading Post. Turn right on UT-163, which parallels the San Juan River. Continue 3.5 miles, passing St. Christopher's Mission on the left, to the dirt road on the right. This turnoff is 200 yards east of milepost 44. Follow this road 0.5 mile as it descends to the river bottom. Parking is available at the trailhead.

Crossing the San Juan River via a swinging footbridge is an exciting way to start and end any hike. The destination, a sandstone amphitheater rimmed in ancient dwellings, provides an intriguing look at life here 1000 years ago. The hike to Sixteen House Ruin, also known as Echo Mesa Ruin, enters the Navajo Reservation. Please respect property rights by staying on the road until reaching the bottom of the alcove containing the dwellings.

Steep stairs lead to the top of the footbridge. At this high point scan the long cliff across the river looking for the alcove. In the shade of a rock overhang is the string of cliff dwellings. Few kids fear crossing on the swinging bridge until more exuberant walkers swing the walkway. Encourage kids to count their footsteps over the river, then calculate the distance of the bridge (500 feet).

After crossing the river follow the road 0.25 mile, turning left at the fork. A sign for the "trail to 16 House Ruin" is visible amongst the Russian olive and tamarisk trees of the river bottom. Follow the road around privately owned fields, turning right on the two-tire-track road that parallels the base of the cliff. Within 0.25 mile a row of stone walls rimming a shady alcove in the cliff above is visible from the road. Scramble to the top, cautioning hikers not to follow too closely behind one another in the loose rock. Also, please do not hold onto or sit on the ancient walls in the alcove.

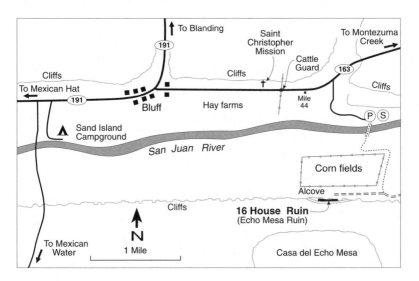

Hands shadow the past at Sixteen House Ruin.

Encourage your companions to count the rooms. Imagine how many people lived here and why they chose this alcove. Explain that the Ancestral Puebloans spent most of their time hunting and preparing foods outside of these dwellings. In many cases the rooms were used for storage and sometimes sleeping. Orient your kids to help them realize that the site is facing north. This is unusual because most cliff dwellings face southeast to receive the morning sun. It would be very cold here in the winter. Also, there are no black soot marks from fires on the ceiling. Was this site used only in summer? Why or why not?

Notice the handprints decorating the wall behind the dwellings. Look for signatures on the wall from Bluff residents of 1890. Why do we not do that now?

Toeholds and handholds have been pecked in the rock just below a dwelling. Nimble explorers may want to use these ancient ladders to climb into a room. Along the rock shelf just below the dwellings watch for four smooth ridges about 4 inches long. They were probably used for sharpening stone tools.

Pink flowering columbine greets visitors here beginning in late

March through October. Feel the rock surrounding the plants. Notice its cool dampness. Besides a desert cave, where else might this plant grow? How may the Ancestral Pueblo have used the moisture from the rock where the columbine now grows?

The tiny seep of water where the columbine grows is what formed this cave over tens of thousands of years. Water dissolved the cliff from underneath where the sandstone contacts the clay stone. The water you see here comes from snow and rain trapped in the sand dunes above and beyond the cliff.

Return is via the same route. At the bridge let your kids know that Navajo children living near here once used this bridge to attend school at Saint Christopher's Mission, located across the river and down the road. Before the bridge was built in 1957 they often had to ford the river, sometimes staying a week or more in Bluff waiting for the river to recede after a flood. Ask your kids what they would learn about the river by crossing it daily during the school year.

The nearest toilet or water facilities are in Bluff.

81 SIPAPU NATURAL BRIDGE TO KACHINA NATURAL BRIDGE

Location ▪	Natural Bridges National Monument
Type ▪	Day hike
Difficulty ▪	Moderate to challenging for children
Hikable ▪	March through November
Distance ▪	4 miles, one way; 5.6 miles, loop
Starting Elevation ▪	6200 feet
Low Point ▪	5700 feet
Maps ▪	Trails Illustrated Manti–La Sal Forest; USGS Moss Back Butte and Kane Gulch; Natural Bridges National Monument brochure

www.nps.gov/nabr
National monument admission fee

From Blanding drive 4 miles south on US 191, turning west (right) on UT-95. Travel 31 miles to UT-275. Turn right and proceed 4 miles to the visitor center. Continue 0.5 mile to Bridge View Drive.

Horse Collar can be viewed from a short trail at Bridges National Monument.

Bear right and proceed 1.75 miles to the parking area for the Sipapu Trail. (Sipapu Overlook is passed along the way.) A shuttled car parked at the Kachina Bridge Overlook allows a one-way hike.

Two stone bridges, one spanning a lush desert oasis, the other arched over a once-inhabited canyon bottom, provide a natural attraction for new and seasoned desert hikers. The unmaintained trail follows a level route along White and Armstrong canyons. However, the short but steep climb in and out of the canyon is not recommended for young, inexperienced hikers. Families with little ones enjoy walking the 0.3-mile trail to the Horse Collar Site Overlook before meeting their older offspring at the Kachina Bridge Overlook.

Before leaving the visitor center, take a few moments to walk the signed nature trail. Kids will like recognizing and naming plants along their canyon trek. Also, a visit to the photovoltaic display across from the visitor center can be an interesting side trip. A brochure explaining how the solar energy resource functions is available at the visitor center.

The trail immediately descends from the parking lot, following a stone staircase, and then edges the canyon wall. Two metal stairways allow a descent to the next level. White-throated swifts soar the skies above this canyon and make their homes in cliffs. Look up to find their nests made of saliva-glued twigs and mud, tucked into rock crevices.

As the trail veers from the canyon wall, turn right at the sign for Sipapu Bridge. Steps allow for a safe descent down this steep grade. Near the base of the last ladder dropping into White Canyon, poison ivy thrives, but at a distance from the trail. Trees shade the trail as it crosses the creek where a trail register is located.

Before heading down-canyon, do look up to appreciate the area's largest natural bridge, Sipapu. Encourage your companions to imagine this canyon millions of years ago, when the three bridges spanning it were sandstone walls. A snakelike stream began winding through the canyon, occasionally scouring the base of each wall with a great force of water and sand. Raging flood waters eventually broke through the thinned walls, helping to create what we see here. Guess

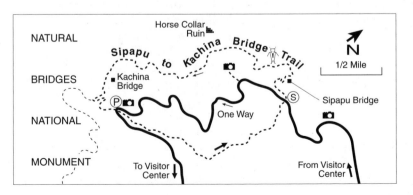

Sipapu's height. Find out your children's theories on why it was named after the Hopi word meaning "place of emergence."

From Sipapu continue walking downstream, watching for plants seen at the nature trail, as well as animal tracks in the mud along the creek. Within 3 miles beyond Sipapu Bridge, increasingly deeper slickrock pools, home to thousands of tadpoles in May and June, may distract youngsters from Kachina Bridge's youthful elegance. Ask how this rock span differs from Sipapu. Note differences in rock color, signs of erosion or shaping, and size. Unlike its older sister, Sipapu, which spans the canyon above stream flow, Kachina still experiences the eroding effects of flash floods. Look to see how its "feet" sit where stream waters occasionally flow.

Once under the cool span of rock, you will want to take day packs off to enjoy a lunch, and later explore the area for Puebloan dwellings and rock art. If your visit to Natural Bridges occurs during spring or summer, you'll notice that most of the ancient dwellings here, found on the right, are in the shade, even at midday. Winter hikers see the sites drenched in sunlight. Ask your companions why this occurs. Did the Ancestral Puebloans build their homes here on purpose? Look for other possible passive solar-heated home sites.

Clues to why the bridge was named after kachinas, or dancers representing supernatural beings, can be found along the abutments of the dwellings. Remember that these petroglyphs, as well as the home sites, are irreplaceable. Even touching rock art or sitting on dwelling walls is considered "innocent vandalism," a process that Park Service and BLM personnel have learned causes more destruction than malicious destruction. Please do not touch or disturb them. Leave everything in its place.

The trail from Kachina Bridge turns left, following Armstrong Canyon for 0.3 mile before meeting, on the left, the trail up the canyon wall to the parking area for Kachina Bridge Overlook. Once again, handrails and strategically placed rocks and cairns add to the safety of this 0.75-mile ascent. Just before reaching the top, watch for a miniarch, only 6 inches high, tucked alongside the slickrock on the trail's left side.

Upon reaching the parking area, cross the road to meet the 1.7-mile trail through a pinyon-juniper forest and return to the Sipapu Bridge parking lot. Those hikers with shuttled vehicles waiting for them end their hike here.

Toilet and limited water facilities are available at the visitor center.

82 KANE GULCH

Location ■ Grand Gulch Primitive Area
Type ■ Day hike or overnight backpack
Difficulty ■ Moderate to challenging for children
Hikable ■ April to November
Distance ■ 5.5 miles, one way
Starting Elevation ■ 6400 feet
Ending Elevation ■ 5800 feet
Maps ■ Trails Illustrated Grand Gulch Plateau; USGS Kane Gulch; BLM Grand Gulch Primitive Area

www.ut.blm.gov/recsite/grand.html/
Use fee for day hikes.
Registration required for overnights spent in Grand Gulch Primitive Area. For information on fees and registration call the Monticello Field Office at 435-587-1532.

From Blanding travel south 4 miles on US 191. Turn right (west) on UT-95 and travel 29 miles to UT-261. Turn left (south) and proceed about 4 miles to the Kane Gulch Ranger Station on the left. Park here. Registration and trail information are available here. There is no public drinking water. Ranger presence at the station is periodic, but the station is staffed from middle March to early November.

A treasure land of Ancestral Pueblo sites, rock art, and artifacts awaits hikers who enter Grand Gulch via its most easily accessed route. Given the proper respect this visit deserves, young and old feel honored to hold a prehistoric corncob, to examine a tiny patch of woven yucca, to imagine the original function of pottery pieces scattered about. This introduction to the region's finest freestanding archaeological site is best experienced as an overnight, allowing another day or more to investigate additional sites farther down-canyon.

The trailhead for Kane Gulch is directly across the highway from the ranger station. After a short, grassy area the trail enters a cottonwood-choked canyon, crossing the creekbed many times.

Just when your eyes have become accustomed to seeing the rock and sand of slickrock country, a stand of aspens appears on the trail's left side at 1 mile. Look for blue spruce and columbines to complete this mountain scene. Remnants of a glacier that left seedlings here 10,000 years ago, these aspens have repeatedly sprouted from the same roots. Ask your companions how many generations of aspens, which live approximately 100 years, have grown here?

Past the aspen stand, a gang of boulders begins the slickrock formation that predominates in the canyon. Depending on rainfall, pools here can be brimming with water, and in spring, even swimming with tadpoles. Stop to examine these slippery creatures, looking for the beginnings of legs protruding from their round bellies. Visitors in July and August will hear the adult, frog version of the little black wigglers.

Cairns mark the route around car-size boulders, although in most cases it's a matter of following the creek drainage.

As the trail enters deeper into the canyon, the sandstone walls, striped with desert varnish, loom higher. The descending melody of canyon wrens provides fitting accompaniment to the stair-stepped walk down to the creek bottom. Watch for a spring near the trail at 3 miles.

Before approaching the area where sites are found, discuss with hikers the privilege they have in walking into a home of the ancestors of today's Pueblo people. Remind them that walls, artifacts, even mounds of dirt near dwellings are extremely fragile and can never be replaced. They'll see a lot of potsherds, bits of ancient pottery—but none of these pieces, no matter how small or numerous, should be

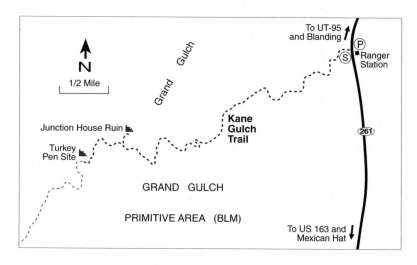

Stick and mud walls formed what may been a turkey pen, one of several prehistoric sites in Kane Gulch.

removed. The collection they'll see represents a tiny fraction of what has remained after thousands of hikers who entered here took "just one." They may understand this issue better if the question is posed, "How would you feel if every time a family visited your home someone took 'just one part' from your Lego collection?"

Where Kane Gulch joins Grand Gulch at 5 miles, the first site, Junction House Site, is to the right, a few hundred yards above the canyon floor. At first it appears inaccessible, but its lower parts can be safely viewed after a short walk up. Caution, however, is advised because only a few of the ruins have been stabilized. Regardless of a site's apparent stability, never sit on its walls or walk through the structure.

This extensive site, despite its many rooms, housed no more than one extended family. However, the site was used for a long time, perhaps as long as the pre-Puebloan occupation (A.D. 900 to 1300). Under the site's overhang look for two openings in the ground leading to kivas, underground ceremonial rooms. Young observers here may also see ghost walls—the light stripes that mark where walls once stood. The site's back wall bears the scratching "J. Wetherill 1920," made by the son of Richard Wetherill, the pioneer explorer of Southwest ruins. Because of its age and context, this "graffiti" is part of the historic heritage of Grand Gulch and must not be touched or altered.

Rock art of intrigue and beauty adorns many sandstone surfaces in this area. Despite their indestructible appearance, petroglyphs and pictographs are extremely fragile. Please do not touch them; acids from skin oils deteriorate these irreplaceable treasures.

You may not locate the spring that feeds this oasis because it is intermittent, but its greening effect on the surrounding land is obvious. (Do not, however, use this water for drinking or cooking.)

Retrace your steps to the entrance of Kane Gulch and hike down another 0.7 mile to Turkey Pen Site. This small, square structure distinguishes itself from the nearby sites by its stick-and-mud ("wattle and daub") walls. No one is sure if it was used to house turkeys, but when Richard Wetherill first wrote about the site, he stated it contained "at least seven feet of turkey droppings."

Near the ruins are impressive collections of potsherds, corncobs, and animal bones. Worked rocks used for grinding corn or sharpening tools are fascinating to youngsters. Ask them to guess what each was used for.

Each discovery brings with it loads of questions, some of which only archaeologists, Native Americans, and imaginative children can answer.

The hike from here can continue down Grand Gulch into other side canyons or return to the trailhead. Do carry a map and at least 2 quarts of water per person. Toilet facilities are located at the Kane Gulch Ranger Station. Do not expect to rewater at the ranger station; water is very limited.

83   HOVENWEEP HIKES

Location	■ Hovenweep National Monument, southeast Utah
Type	■ Day hike
Difficulty	■ Easy to moderate for children
Hikable	■ Year-round, except after heavy rains or snow
Distance	■ Tower Point Loop, 0.5 mile; Square Tower Loop, 1.5 to 2.0 miles
Starting Elevation	■ 5240 feet
High Point	■ 5240 feet
Map	■ Hovenweep National Monument trail guide

www.nps.gov/hove/home.htm
National Monument entrance fee

Straddling the southern Utah–Colorado border, Hovenweep is accessed 35 miles south of Monticello on US 191. Turn east on UT-262 and bear right, passing Hatch Trading Post, for 10 miles to a left turn and 6 miles more to the entrance of Square Tower Unit, where the ranger station is located.

Hovenweep's two short loop trails tour a high desert canyon where an Ancestral Pueblo community thrived for seven centuries. The uniquely shaped towers and dwellings here represent the last 100 years of Puebloan occupation and the world's only collection of pre-Columbian round, square, and D-shaped towers. Interpretive signs along the trail help visitors of all ages discover how the Pueblo people used plants to sustain them in this seemingly lifeless landscape.

Hovenweep's sites are very fragile; they have only been stabilized, and not reconstructed. Equal care should be given to staying on the trails, thereby preventing damage to the surrounding cryptobiotic soil crust, a dark, lumpy layer of microorganisms that hold the soil in place. Self-guided trail brochures are available at the ranger station.

Tower Point Loop

Both Tower Point and Square Tower trails begin south of the ranger station near Hovenweep Castle. A new visitor center, to be completed by 2002, will be located east of here. Though Tower Point Loop is recommended for young children, the canyon rim trail poses a threat to both little wanderers and those watching them!

Hovenweep Castle, the first site on this trail, triggers plenty of questions for kids to ponder. Why does this large multifamily dwelling have just one ground-level door? Which sections of the wall appear original (not repaired by archaeologists)? Through which window did the setting sun shine on the first day of summer? Of winter?

From Hovenweep Castle, walk about 100 feet to the right to see the check dam, rebuilt by archaeologists in 1974. Has the structure recently served its purpose of retaining water and the silty soil it carried? Explore ideas about how the water and remaining silt may have been used.

Turn left and walk easterly in the direction of Sleeping Ute Mountain 0.25 mile along the canyon rim to the Tower Point site. From this location encourage kids to find Hovenweep's round, square, and D-shaped towers. Also ask them to imagine how this tower may have been used and how many people lived here. (Archaeologists believe Puebloans lived in extended families of eight to twelve people.) Look for the tower's peepholes and imagine what Pueblo children might have seen through them.

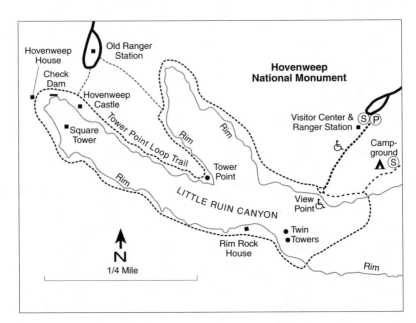

Remnants of an ancient culture—squash stem, twine, corncob, and potsherds—lay gathered for hikers to admire.

As you walk back to the ranger station, look for small rooms, called granaries, tucked under the canyon rim. Tell children that the Puebloans were farmers who stored their harvest of beans, corn, squashes, and plant seeds in the cabinet-like alcoves. At the next large structure on the canyon rim, Hovenweep House, turn left, walking counterclockwise.

Square Tower Loop

The 1.5- to 2-hour walk along the Square Tower Loop offers visitors a more complete look at Hovenweep's towers, vegetation, and geology. Find out about the guided walks to both the petroglyph panel at Tower Point and to Square Tower. These hikes are timed to occur during the shady hours of midmorning and midafternoon.

Beginning at Hovenweep Castle, turn right, passing the check dam (see above description) and stopping at Hovenweep House. Point out that each of its stones is square-shaped, pecked that way by masons over 700 years ago. Ask your group to estimate how long it might take them to shape a stone for Hovenweep House. And how would they do it? Some archaeologists say this site was a Tri-Wall structure that had some unknown ceremonial purpose. Have children notice the fallen walls lying in patterns surrounding the remaining standing walls. Explore their ideas on how one of Hovenweep's largest structures was used.

Moonrise over Hovenweep Castle

While following the trail around the head of the canyon, look below where Square Tower rests on a boulder. Square Tower may have had many purposes. Were messages relayed from here to another tower? Was it used for food storage, ceremonials, or as a solar calendar? Notice the dense green vegetation near the tower, which indicates a spring, the source of life for this community. Imaginations may need stretching when told that as many as 300 people relied on this trickle as their source of water. Some of these thirsty folks lived in the cliff dwelling tucked under the canyon rim on your left.

Rim Rock House, the rectangular structure next on the canyon rim, is perforated with small peepholes slanted at unusual angles. Discuss with your companions how these holes may have been used: for ventilation, viewing, suspending ropes from?

Twin Towers, next on the canyon rim tour, is actually two differently shaped and built apartment houses containing a total of sixteen rooms. How many rooms can your hikers count? Twin Towers, the trail's halfway point, is a good turnaround point for those not wanting to descend into Little Ruin Canyon. Those who continue into the canyon will notice how the grasses and shrubs are taller and thicker here. Why is this? Notice how the towers appear grander from this canyon bottom perspective.

Climbing up out of the canyon brings you to Stronghold House and Tower, perched atop a boulder. Stronghold House is actually the top level of a pueblo, once entered by climbing a short ladder or using handholds and toeholds pecked into the rock. To the right of Stronghold House is Stronghold Tower, which has also lost its foundation—a log that once bridged the creek and supported the tower. Imagine what may have happened to the rock walls after the log collapsed and fell into the canyon.

The last dwelling on this loop is the Unit-Type House, named by early archaeologists who believed that sites with only one room and one kiva were inhabited by only one family or clan. Explain to children that this is an earlier dwelling built 200 years before the others in the canyon. In what ways does it differ from the other sites? Notice the kiva's fine masonry. Of special interest to many visitors here is the east-facing wall near the kiva. At sunrise on the summer and winter solstices, the sun shines a beam at exact points on the walls. Talk to the ranger to learn more about this aspect of astroarchaeology.

Across the canyon from Unit-Type House, look for a boulder surrounded by rock rubble, remnants of the walls from a home or tower. Eroded Boulder House sits below the overhang of a large boulder still remaining as the occupants' roof and walls.

The trail edges the head of the canyon before turning south towards Tower Point. Kids will naturally assume this tower was used for surveillance, though archaeologists have no proof the people living here had enemies. Reminding your budding archaeologists that these Puebloans were farmers may slant their ideas on the tower's purpose.

Hikers may complete the Square Tower Loop by following the trail along the canyon rim to Tower Point, then heading west to the trailhead. Those preferring a half-mile shorter hike should follow the trail around the head of the canyon and take the first trail on the right back to the ranger station.

Toilets, facilities, and information on additional hikes in Hovenweep's area are provided at the ranger station.

APPENDIX

WHEELCHAIR-ACCESSIBLE TRAIL LIST

Name	Park/ Nearest City	Length/ Surface	Phone
Jordan River Physically Disabled Park	Salt Lake City	1.5 miles/paved, wheelchair course	801-533-4496
Red Butte Garden and Arboretum	Salt Lake City	4.0 mile/paved loop, some with assistance	801-581-4747
City Creek	Salt Lake City	up to 5.7 miles one way/paved	801-596-5065
Little Cottonwood Trail*	Salt Lake City	0.3 mile/ "soil-cement"	801-466-6411
Silver Lake	Salt Lake City	1 mile/boardwalk	801-466-6411
Snowbird Barrier-Free Trail	Salt Lake City Snowbird Ski Area	0.5 mile one way/ asphalt paved	801-742-2222, ext. 4147 or 4090
Union-Pacific Grade (Big Fill Walk)	Golden Spike National Historic Site	0.25 mile/paved (wheelchairs provided)	435-471-2209
Ogden Nature Center	Ogden	0.25 mile/wood chips	801-621-7595
North Arm of the Pineview Reservoir*	Ogden	0.5-mile loop/ packed, crushed rock	801-625-5112
Perception Park, trails, fishing ramp, and campground	Ogden	0.5 mile/asphalt	801-629-8600
Cascade Springs	Heber City	0.25 mile/asphalt and boardwalk	801-377-5780

* May require assistance.
† Several other viewpoints are accessible to visitors in wheelchairs at Bryce Canyon National Park. Handicapped parking and ramps are provided at many sites.

Name	Park/ Nearest City	Length/ Surface	Phone
Payson Reservoir Trail and fishing ramp	Provo	0.7 mile/paved	801-798-3571
Utah Lake State Park, fishing ramp	Provo	20 feet/paved	801-375-0731
Tribble Fork Reservoir, ramp	Pleasant Grove	50 feet/paved	801-342-5240
Current Creek Reservoir, fishing ramp	Heber City	0.4 mile/boardwalk	801-342-5200
Haws Point	Strawberry Reservoir	0.4 mile/concrete	801-342-5200
Strawberry River Discovery Trail	Strawberry Reservoir	1500 feet/boardwalk	801-342-5200
Yellow Pine Accessible Interpretive Trail	Mountain Home	0.5-mile loop	435-789-1181
Mirror Lake	Kansas	100 yards/boardwalk	435-783-4388
Flaming Gorge Dam Tour	Flaming Gorge National Recreation Area	0.5 mile/paved	435-784-3445
Red Canyon Overlook Trail	Flaming Gorge National Recreation Area	0.25 mile/paved	435-784-3445
Dinosaur Quarry Visitor Center	Dinosaur National Monument	100 yards/paved (accessibility brochure available)	435-781-8807
Parade of Rock Art Trail (open year-round)	Fremont Indian State Park	300 yards/paved (wheelchair available for visitor use)	435-527-4631
Lakeshore Trail*	Fish Lake, Loa	2.4 miles/gravel	435-836-2811
Fremont River Walk*	Capitol Reef National Park	0.5 mile/paved	435-425-3791
Petroglyph Panel	Capitol Reef National Park	0.25 mile/boardwalk	435-425-3791
Bristlecone Pine Trail*	Cedar City	0.5 mile loop/ packed dirt	435-865-3200

Name	Park/ Nearest City	Length/ Surface	Phone
Rim Trail between Sunset and Sunrise Points	Bryce Canyon National Park	0.5 mile/paved	435-834-5322
Portions of Bristlecone Loop Trail*	Bryce Canyon National Park†	0.1-mile loop/gravel	435-834-5322
Emerald Pools*	Zion National Park	0.5 mile/paved	435-772-3256
Gateway to the Narrows	Zion National Park	0.4 mile/paved	435-772-3256
Virgin River Parkway	St. George	2.5 miles/paved	801-634-5850
Point Supreme (three other viewpoints in the park are wheelchair accessible)	Cedar Breaks National Monument	0.25 mile/paved	801-586-9451
Lake Powell boat ramps and courtesy docks (Glen Canyon Dam tour in Page, AZ, is wheelchair accessible)	Glen Canyon National Recreation Area	variable	877-435-6206
Sand Dune Boardwalk	Coral Pink Sand Dunes	0.25 mile/boardwalk	435-648-2800
Observation Point, Valley of the Goblins	Goblin Valley State Park	paved	435-564-3633
Portions of Canyon Rim Nature Trail*	Dead Horse State Park	0.4 mile/paved and slickrock	435-259-2614
Big Bend Fishing Dock	Moab	100 yards/concrete	435-259-7164
Edge of the Cedars Ruin Trail* and Museum	Edge of the Cedars State Park Museum, Blanding	100 feet or more/ paved, boardwalk	435-678-2238
Sipapu, Kachina, Owachomo Bridge Overlooks*	Rainbow Bridge National Monument	500 yards each/ paved	877-453-6206
Grand View Point Overlook*	Canyonlands National Park	200 feet/paved	435-259-7164, ext. 5
Buck Canyon Overlook	Canyonlands National Park	100 feet/paved	801-259-5164 435-259-7164, ext. 5

INDEX

ABOUT THE AUTHOR
AND PHOTOGRAPHER

Maureen Keilty is a freelance writer, naturalist, and occasional teacher. Inspired by the natural beauty surrounding her home in southwest Colorado, Maureen's work as a freelance writer has appeared in *Family Fun*, the *Denver Post*, *Inside/Outside*, and many other regional and national magazines.

Books and nature tend to be a family project. Maureen's photographer husband, **Dan Peha**, provides the illustrations for most of her articles and photographed all the images for this book and *Best Hikes with Children in Colorado*™ (The Mountaineers, 1998), also written by Maureen. Both books became best sellers in their respective states as did their coffee table book, *Durango*, which she and Dan wrote, illustrated, and published. Maureen and Dan's son, Niko, now nine years old, also helped "child test" all the trails for both *Best Hikes with Children*™ books.

Maureen, Dan, and Niko live in Durango, Colorado, the perfect niche between the San Juan Mountains and Utah's canyon country.

The author and photographer, in an effort to preserve Utah's natural treasures, are pledging at least ten percent of royalties earned from the sale of this book to organizations such as the Southern Utah Wilderness Alliance, the Utah Wilderness Association, and the Utah chapter of the Sierra Club.

THE MOUNTAINEERS, founded in 1906, is a nonprofit outdoor activity and conservation club, whose mission is "to explore, study, preserve, and enjoy the natural beauty of the outdoors. . . . " Based in Seattle, Washington, the club is now the third-largest such organization in the United States, with 15,000 members and five branches throughout Washington state.

The Mountaineers sponsors both classes and year-round outdoor activities in the Pacific Northwest, which include hiking, mountain climbing, ski-touring, snowshoeing, bicycling, camping, kayaking and canoeing, nature study, sailing, and adventure travel. The club's conservation division supports environmental causes through educational activities, sponsoring legislation, and presenting informational programs. All club activities are led by skilled, experienced volunteers, who are dedicated to promoting safe and responsible enjoyment and preservation of the outdoors.

If you would like to participate in these organized outdoor activities or the club's programs, consider a membership in The Mountaineers. For information and an application, write or call The Mountaineers, Club Headquarters, 300 Third Avenue West, Seattle, WA 98119; 206-284-6310.

The Mountaineers Books, an active, nonprofit publishing program of the club, produces guidebooks, instructional texts, historical works, natural history guides, and works on environmental conservation. All books produced by The Mountaineers Books fulfill the club's mission.

Send or call for our catalog of more than 450 outdoor titles:

The Mountaineers Books
1001 SW Klickitat Way, Suite 201
Seattle, WA 98134
800-553-4453
mbooks@mountaineers.org
www.mountaineersbooks.org

Other titles you may enjoy from The Mountaineers Books:

BEST HIKES WITH CHILDREN™ Series:
Fully-detailed "where-to" and "how-to" guides to day hikes and overnighters for families. Includes tips on hiking with kids, safety, and fostering a wilderness ethic.
- **BEST HIKES WITH CHILDREN™ IN ARIZONA,** *Lawrence Letham*
- **BEST HIKES WITH CHILDREN™ IN COLORADO, 2nd Edition,** *Maureen Keilty*
- **BEST HIKES WITH CHILDREN™ IN NEW MEXICO, 2nd Edition,** *Bob Julyan*

ANIMAL TRACKS OF THE SOUTHWEST, *Chris Stall*
The handy pocket-sized guide helps you identify the desert, mountain, and trail animals of the Southwest region with life-size drawings of the animal's characteristic footprints.

BICYCLING WITH CHILDREN: A Complete How-To Guide, *Trudy E. Bell*
Everything a parent needs to know about bikes and kids—from toddler to teen. The first ever guide on the subject answers real questions from real parents.

KIDS IN THE WILD: A Family Guide to Outdoor Recreation, *Cindy Ross & Todd Gladfelter*
This guide offers practical, solid advice on hiking and camping with children. Includes suggestions on the best outdoor activities for families, from backpacking and camping to boating, biking, and skiing.

A FIELD GUIDE TO THE GRAND CANYON, 2nd Edition, *Stephen R. Whitney*
Whether you're an active explorer or an armchair naturalist, you'll be certain to enjoy this colorful guide. It illustrates the area's plants and animals, and offers fascinating in-depth information on the natural history and geology of this dramatic region.